Chiang Kai-shek's Politics of Shame

HARVARD EAST ASIAN MONOGRAPHS 442

Chiang Kai-shek's Politics of Shame

Leadership, Legacy, and National Identity in China

Grace C. Huang

Published by the Harvard University Asia Center
Distributed by Harvard University Press
Cambridge (Massachusetts) and London 2021

The Harvard University Asia Center publishes a monograph series and, in coordination with the Fairbank Center for Chinese Studies, the Korea Institute, the Reischauer Institute of Japanese Studies, and other facilities and institutes, administers research projects designed to further scholarly understanding of China, Japan, Korea, Vietnam, and other Asian countries. The Center also sponsors projects addressing multidisciplinary, transnational, and regional issues in Asia.

The Harvard University Asia Center and the author gratefully acknowledge a generous grant in support of the publication of this work from the Chiang Ching-kuo Foundation for International Scholarly Affairs.

Library of Congress Cataloging-in-Publication Data

Names: Huang, Grace C, author.
Title: Chiang Kai-shek's politics of shame : leadership, legacy, and national identity in China / Grace C Huang.
Description: Cambridge, Massachusetts: Published by the Harvard University Asia Center, 2021. | Includes bibliographical references and index. |
Identifiers: LCCN 2021009313 (print) | LCCN 2021009314 (ebook) | ISBN 9780674260139 (hardcover) | ISBN 9780674260146 (paperback) | ISBN 9781684176328 (pdf)
Subjects: LCSH: Chiang, Kai-shek, 1887-1975. | Presidents—China—Biography. | Presidents—Taiwan—Biography. | China—History—Republic, 1912-1949. | Taiwan—History—1945- | Nationalism—China. | National characteristics, Chinese.
Classification: LCC DS777.488.C5 H83 2021 (print) | LCC DS777.488.C5 (ebook) | DDC 951.04/2092 [B]—dc23
LC record available at https://lccn.loc.gov/2021009313
LC ebook record available at https://lccn.loc.gov/2021009314

Index by Amy Murphy

⊗ Printed on acid-free paper

Last figure below indicates year of this printing
30 29 28 27 26 25 24 23 22 21

Dedicated with love to my parents,
Liang H. and Jane Huang

Contents

Part II. Structure

Maps and Figures

Maps

Figures

Acknowledgments

Seeds for this project germinated in graduate classes at the University of Chicago with the professors who eventually became my thesis committee members. With Bill Sewell as my advisor, I approached research with a sense of play and wonder as we confronted intellectual puzzles in specific paragraphs and bridged gaps in what needed to be done in manageable, concrete steps. Prasenjit Duara introduced me to Republican China through a social historian's perspective; as I deliberated with him, I felt that I was not speaking to one person but to a global community of scholars. Conversations with Susanne Rudolph, which often involved her husband, Lloyd, were wide-ranging yet pinpointed what was essential. I fondly recall visiting their home in Vermont, where we energetically discussed Chiang Kai-shek by candlelight because the electricity had gone out. Lisa Wedeen was the fourth member of my committee, and I am grateful to her sensitivity to word choices and metaphors, which she exhibited exuberantly in the lines between my sentences and in the margins of my chapters.

I spent copious amounts of time looking up Chinese words in a dictionary while reading archival materials at Academia Historica in Taiwan. Yet a phrase's meaning often eluded me, and my need to understand often outweighed my respect for archival decorum. In a traditional classroom seating arrangement, I constantly tapped the shoulders of researchers around me and peppered them with questions. During lunch hours, I would ask questions about the historical period to help me make sense of what I was reading. I am so thankful to those researchers from Taiwan, Japan, and China who had the misfortune of sitting near me, and the following deserve my special gratitude: Wu Jinping, Wu Jing, Toyoko Yoshida, Liu Wei-kai, Alicia Wen-ting Chen, and Ma Yun. I had the good fortune to be a visiting scholar at the Institute of Political Science at Academia Sinica and want to particularly thank Cheng Hsiao-shi, who included me in the intellectual life of the campus and introduced me to the gastronomical and hiking pleasures of Taiwan. I worked briefly as a research assistant to Jay Taylor, who was then working on a biography of Chiang Kai-shek, and I was grateful for the opportunity to help him interview Chiang's secretary, some military officials and family members, and veterans of the Sino-Japanese War, which infused an emotional dimension into the abstract concepts I encountered in my archival materials, like loyalty, nationalism, and humiliation. Finally, I was fortunate to live with my extended family in Taipei during my time there. Although my conversations with my grandfather were limited, as our common language was Taiwanese, his thoughtfulness and love showed through every day, and my aunt, Judy Lin, was like a second mother to me.

I express my appreciation for the generous support for this preliminary work that I received from the Division of the Social Sciences and Center for East Asian Studies at the University of Chicago, the Taiwan Ministry of Education, a Chiang Ching-kuo Doctoral Fellowship, and a US Department of Education Fulbright-Hays Doctoral Dissertation Research Abroad Grant.

The journey of transforming the dissertation that resulted from that research into this book introduced me to new intellectual companions. I treasure the time I spent with Emily Hill and Jeremy Taylor to organize an international conference on Chiang Kai-shek in Kingston, Canada, in 2009, which allowed me to meet many of the authors I reference in this book. I am grateful to Hsiao-ting Lin and Lisa Nguyen for their warm hospitality in hosting a summer workshop at the Hoover Institution at Stanford University in 2013 that allowed me to view the Chiang Kai-shek diaries. Over the years, I have been able to try out draft versions of the chapters and garner invaluable feedback at various conferences of the American Political Science Association and Association for Asian Studies. Finally, I express my deep gratitude for the generous feedback on various chapters of this book provided by colleagues, including Paul Cohen, Yuan-kang Wang, Ke-wen Wang, Sinan Chu, Jennifer Dixon, and Derek King.

I especially extend a sincere thanks to my home institution, St. Lawrence University, for its unwavering and unstinting support for the completion of this book through conference travel, sabbaticals, and multiple scholarship grants over the years. I am lucky to work with departmental and university colleagues whose dedication to the liberal arts enterprise is matched only by their generosity and kindness. I am particularly grateful to Alan Draper, whose sage advice saved me from unnecessary complications, and to Shelley McConnell for her astute observation that I should write so that more than six experts in the world could understand me. Finally, I thank the several talented undergraduate research assistants who reviewed various drafts of chapters and provided a patient soundboard as I talked through different ideas: Josephine Brown, Cassandra DiMarino, Katie McBurney, Sarah Moore, Tatenda Pasipanyoda, and Kyle McDonald.

I am grateful to Bob Graham for his expert and kind shepherding of the manuscript through the publication process, to the two anonymous reviewers who affirmed my vision for this project and provided concrete suggestions to improve the manuscript, and to Laura Poole for her meticulous copyediting work. Parts of my manuscript also benefited from editing suggestions by Richard Gunde and questions from Emily Andrew.

Writing this book was like raising an invisible child, and in this dimension of the writing process, I cannot begin to express my thanks to several people who helped me nurture this child to maturity and make its way in the world. Jeanne Barker Nunn has read every word of this book and many more that have been left out. Her frank and compassionate feedback over numerous drafts has immeasurably improved the manuscript and made revising a joy and a respite from other responsibilities. Alyssa Gabbay was there from the beginning, first as a silent graduate student who sat countless hours diagonally from me on the fifth floor of the University of Chicago's Regenstein Library. This quiet camaraderie eventually blossomed into a friendship that I treasure to this day, and I thank Alyssa for buoying my spirits without fail, believing in this book, and providing feedback that combined loving humor with finding the perfect word. In my final year of dissertation writing, I met my future husband. From the beginning, Cristian Armendariz Picon has unhesitatingly transcended traditional gender roles to help make a book and family possible. From becoming an adept diaper changer to solving our two-body problem by resigning his tenured position at another institution, Cristian unfailingly secured whatever time I needed to complete the best book I could.

Finally, I dedicate this book to my parents. My father instilled in me a sense of curiosity and delight about words, whether in English or Mandarin, and my mother reminded me to attend to the life outside of the mind, which often revolved around delicious food. They were true partners in their support for me. When my parents once accompanied me to visit the Harvard-Yenching Library, my father volunteered to photocopy hundreds of pages of a key chronology of Chiang. When I expressed concern over the tediousness of this job, my mother immediately insisted, "Don't worry, your dad loves to photocopy!" My parents helped prepare me to undertake this journey by periodically reminding me not to take myself too seriously. Their everyday lives continue to exemplify how to enjoy the little things that make the big things possible.

List of Abbreviations

CCP   Chinese Communist Party
INC   Indian National Congress
JZZDSG   *Jiang Zhongzheng zongtong dang'an: shilüe gaoben*
PRC   People's Republic of China
ROC   Republic of China (initially 1912–49 in China and then
         1949–present in Taiwan)
SG   *Jianggong shilüe gaoben*

INTRODUCTION

My parents were born in Taiwan to families who lived there for generations. In 1949, Chiang Kai-shek (1887–1975), after being defeated by Mao Zedong (1893–1976) in the Chinese civil war (1945–49), fled to Taiwan with his army and the remnants of the Kuomintang (Nationalist Party) leadership. These newcomers altered the course of my family's trajectory, as they did for many Taiwanese and Chinese families. My father, then a primary school student, witnessed Kuomintang troops shoot Taiwanese civilians sitting in the back of a pickup truck in a dead-end alley. A few years later, his own father fled to a friend's house to escape capture by Kuomintang troops, but his mother, who was less fortunate, was briefly imprisoned. As a young adult, my father immigrated to the United States because he was convinced that as a native Taiwanese, he could never make a good life under Chiang's rule.

Although I was born in Wisconsin and only briefly visited Taiwan twice while growing up, my family's Taiwanese heritage formed a significant part of my identity. When my high school French teacher declared that I was Chinese American, I felt a surprising resentment about being identified with my ancestral country's Chinese overlords. Thus, when I was undergoing language training as a graduate student in Taiwan during the 2000 historic election that transferred power from the Kuomintang to the Democratic Progressive Party (Minjindang), I was bewildered when I observed my uncle and paternal grandfather, the one who had earlier fled the Kuomintang, give time, money, and enthusiastic praise to Chiang Kai-shek's party. This was just the beginning of a growing sense that Chiang's continuing legacy represented a significant challenge to my understanding of leadership and raised questions that merited my attention as a scholar.

When I returned to the University of Chicago and began investigating the scholarship on Chiang Kai-shek, I found much of the analysis about his leadership confusing and sometimes contradictory. On one hand, Chiang's story appeared to be one of relative success. The China that Chiang ruled from 1928 to 1949 had suffered almost a century of humiliations, beginning with the unequal treaties imposed by Western imperial powers in the mid-nineteenth century and further exacerbated by its defeat by Japan in 1895. Moreover, by the 1920s, China was not politically, territorially, or even culturally united. In the period known as the Warlord Era (1916–28), Chiang rose through the ranks to become the leader of the National Revolutionary Army after the death of Sun Yat-sen (1866–1925), the founder of the Kuomintang. He completed his legendary Northern Expedition (1926–28), uniting most of China under the Kuomintang government in Nanjing. In 1936, Chiang emerged from the Xi'an Incident (during which he was kidnapped by a subordinate in an attempt to influence his policies) as the undisputed leader of China to face and ultimately defeat Japanese imperialism. As Lloyd Eastman argues in his seminal study, by the end of the Nanjing decade in 1937, Chiang had become one of the Kuomintang regime's "principal sources of strength" and gained the "trust and respect of much of the nation."[1] And, indeed, of much of the world: that year, *Time* magazine declared Chiang and his wife, Madame Chiang (Song Meiling) (1898–2003), the International Man and Wife of the Year on its cover.[2] By 1942, the signatories of the Declaration of the United Nations regarded China as one of the four great powers of World War II (1939–45), along with the United Kingdom, the United States, and the Soviet Union.

On the other hand, in 1949 Chiang lost the Chinese civil war to Mao, and this defeat appears to have cast a long shadow on Chiang's previous two decades of leadership. The titles of most of the scholarly studies about Chiang have tended to reflect this perspective on his leadership, including Eastman's *The Abortive Revolution*, Brian Crozier's *The Man Who Lost China*, Pichon Li's *The Kuomintang Debacle of 1949*, Wen Xie's *Huoguo yangmin de Jiang Jieshi* (Chiang Kai-shek: The Man Who

Brought Calamities on the Nation), and more recently, Jonathan Fenby's *Chiang Kai-shek: China's Generalissimo and the Nation He Lost.*[3] Analyses of Chiang through this lens of defeat tended to produce conflicting evaluations of his leadership because any of his successes and strengths had to be explained within the overall outcome of failure. Eastman, for instance, trying to account for Chiang's acknowledged popularity despite his documented aloofness, attitude of superiority, and moralistic sermons, is ultimately reduced to arguing that Chiang's talents were more suited to the old China than the new situation he faced.[4] Following his 1949 defeat, Chiang—unlike Mao, who has become the iconic revolutionary leader for many in the West—has been largely forgotten outside of China and Taiwan, and when remembered at all, is often viewed as a reactionary or a failure.

Despite his accomplishments, scholarly literature has tended to describe Chiang as deeply flawed, a leader who, in Jonathan Spence's words, had "a limited vision of what constituted good government, a marked inability to manage an economy of China's scale," who was "stubborn and inflexible, prodigal with his troops' lives, and tolerant of fearful abuses in China's rural areas."[5] In one example of his apparent cruelty and incompetence, in the midst of the Second Sino-Japanese War (1937–45), Chiang decided to break the Huang River dikes to halt the advance of enemy troops, but he failed to provide advance notice to those who lived in its path. As a result, hundreds of thousands of citizens died and property damage was devastating, while there was little effect toward slowing the Japanese advance.[6] Indeed, even scholarly accounts that take a closer look at his achievements seem to suggest that most of them were merely superficial and short-lived. Although the Northern Expedition ended the Warlord Era, for instance, the resulting unity soon fell apart, and Chiang continued to battle warlords and the communists for the next two decades.

Chiang has also been dismissed by many scholars as outdated and reactionary because of his frequent appeals to Confucian values. Perhaps most notably, he drew on Confucianism to launch the New Life Movement in 1934, which was meant to rejuvenate the citizenry and direct energy toward nation building. The scholarly consensus has been that the movement was a dismal disaster because it neither encouraged mass participation nor institutionalized any of its directives.[7] In this view, Chiang deployed irrelevant, obsolete ideas, in contrast to his mentor,

Sun Yat-sen, and nemesis, Mao, both of whom tapped into Western ideas about modernization and governance and appeared more in tune with the ideas coming out of the May Fourth Movement, which had inspired the first significant expression of Chinese nationalism and repudiation of traditional Confucian values.[8]

Nonetheless, a shift in the conventional view of Chiang began to occur following the 1989 Tiananmen Square protests that ushered in a crisis of legitimacy for the Chinese Communist Party (CCP) leadership. Unlike Mao, who sought to erase Chiang from public memory so as to cement his own legitimacy, the post-Tiananmen Chinese government was willing to partially rehabilitate Chiang as a flawed but patriotic nationalist. In doing so, the government appropriated Chiang to bolster its own legitimacy by harnessing nationalism as the new CCP ideology.[9] Whereas Chiang had long been blamed in the West for having lost China to communism, the collapse of the Soviet Union and reunification of Germany offered new opportunities to revisit this earlier era from a fresh perspective. Even though the resulting literature has generated a deeper appreciation of the difficult context in which Chiang operated, it too seems unable to move beyond an ambivalent analysis of his leadership.[10] Ultimately, the resulting revisionist political agenda and scholarship appears only to have sidestepped the seeming discordance between Chiang's ascension and successes as a national leader and the conventional view of him as a defeated failure.

I was sufficiently intrigued by my initial encounter with these tensions in the analysis of Chiang's leadership to revisit Taiwan a year later. There, I examined some archival documents that had recently been made available known as the *shilüe gaoben*—an extraordinary collection of Chiang's diaries, speeches, and telegrams that make up the raw, uncensored materials from which Chinese historians traditionally created a leader's official history.[11] I quickly realized that the release of Chiang's *shilüe* in the late 1990s, coinciding with Taiwan's transition to democracy, would enable me to conduct a more thorough examination of his leadership during a crucial and perilous period of China's modern history.

These previously unavailable and often deeply personal primary source materials revealed several notable patterns in how Chiang conducted his daily routines and responded to events. In particular, I discovered that he frequently used the Chinese word *chi* 恥, even as a daily entry heading in his diary. *Chi* is a moral Confucian concept that can be translated as either "shame" or "humiliation" and is understood in the context of a hierarchical relational dyad, such as ruler and minister.[12] According to Confucian philosophy, the feeling of shame provides a practitioner with the fortitude to avoid repeating the same mistake, and the experience of humiliation produces the motivation to avenge the humiliation so as to recover one's standing in the Confucian community.[13] According to the *shilüe*, both sentiments pervaded Chiang's thinking and leadership. In his position as a superior in relation to the Chinese people, Chiang often tried to shame them to change their disgraceful behavior while not crossing the line into humiliating them. Because Chiang perceived China's position as inferior with respect to Japan, he often judged Japan's actions toward China as humiliating and therefore attempted to mobilize his countrymen to avenge those humiliations. As this book shows, Chiang also incorporated Western ideas into his wielding of *chi* as a political tool and in the process put his own stamp on those ideas.

Despite the scholarly literature's criticism of Chiang's uses of Confucianism, I eventually became convinced that telling the story of his deployment of *chi* to face Japan's incursion into China and encourage unity among his people could offer a more faithful and rich depiction of his creative efforts as a leader. Even from a position of weakness, as this book illustrates, Chiang was able to use potent cultural tools to inspire his country, persuade posterity of the rightness of his actions, and ultimately shape China's modern national identity in ways that continue to have repercussions today. This articulation of his uses of *chi* addresses an important gap in the literature on China's national humiliation narrative, which has oddly overlooked political leaders as significant contributors to that narrative.[14]

The Exercise of Leadership

After discovering the treasure trove of data available in the *shilüe*, I sought a theoretical framework that would help me employ its riches to reassess Chiang's leadership. Yet the available literature on political leadership seemed to offer little that could help me move beyond analyzing the dynamics of leadership in dichotomous terms—as either transformational or transactional, charismatic or routinized, revolutionary or reformist—that tended to stress a leader's agency at one end and the structural features of leadership at the other. I was coming to believe that such value-laden dichotomies often mischaracterized leaders' complex contributions and tended to locate Chiang on their less exciting and effective side.[15]

Scholars have perhaps found this binary framework of leadership useful because analyses of politics tend to focus on outcomes, such as winning or losing a battle or an election. Accordingly, analyses might focus on political leaders' capacity to act willfully and how their actions shape outcomes.[16] By emphasizing a leader's exercise of agency, or the first part of the dichotomy, such judgments measure the effectiveness of political leaders by how they shape the fortunes of their countries and remake history.[17] However, this perspective tends to overlook that leaders' contributions are often magnified or undermined by actions of their subordinates, advisers, military officers, rivals, and citizens and that the political context in which leaders operate can often influence their ability to achieve results in ways that do not reflect their efforts. Leaders of rich countries, for instance, are likely to appear more powerful and more agentic than leaders of poor countries.

If the agency of leaders has been insufficiently theorized, so too have structuralist analyses of a leader's efforts, exemplified by the second part of the dichotomy. Such studies posit that the main determinants of political outcomes depend on social, political, and economic institutions and relations among actors within these institutional contexts.[18] Despite its welcome recognition of complex variables, this perspective tends to lose sight of the actual creative efforts of leaders. Instead, it focuses on the alignment of structures that either provides opportunities for leaders to exercise their agency to effect enormous outcomes, such as unifying a state or pulling off a social revolution, or severely constrains their ability to achieve a successful outcome.[19]

To avoid these shortcomings, this book builds on Mustafa Emirbayer and Anne Mische's process-driven definition of agency, which views agency as a person's capacity to reactivate past experiences, imagine future goals and projects, and consider the contingencies of the moment to make day-to-day decisions.[20] Moreover, recognizing that analyses of leaders' efforts must also consider the influence of their followers, this book, building on Stephen Skowronek, examines how leaders draw on warrants to justify and legitimate their actions to various audiences.[21] Leaders construct such warrants, this book argues, based on shared understandings of cultural stories, histories, and symbols.[22]

By thinking of a leader's exercise of agency as the construction of warrants over time and of structures as cultural tools and resources, this book attempts to integrate agency and structure without privileging one over the other.[23] Challenging the common notion (perhaps most famously expressed by Max Weber) that leaders derive their authority from having certain exceptional personal qualities, it offers an alternative source of authority that puts the leader–follower relationship front and center: a leader creates viable ideological warrants over time to weave a compelling story about where the group came from and where it is going.[24]

In Chiang's case, the ideological warrants often included Confucian cultural resources such as *chi* despite the fact that China's leaders had begun discarding parts of the Confucian system in the last decade of the Qing dynasty (1644–1912). Chiang recognized that Confucianism nevertheless continued to strongly influence people's thinking in China even into the new republic (1912–49), and he sincerely believed it still held potential answers to China's problems. As this book will show, Chiang's warrants to justify his actions were often riddled with contradictions as he adapted *chi* and other Confucian concepts to various audiences and changing circumstances, but they reflected the creative efforts of a leader who, like his country, struggled to persevere in the face of seemingly endless defeats. In the process, Chiang contributed to a significant alternative narrative regarding nationalism, nation building, and modernization that until now has been largely ignored in the scholarship about this important Chinese leader.

How This Book Unfolds

Part I of this book examines the numerous ways Chiang mobilized *chi* to unite China and break free from imperial influence. The first chapter introduces the *shilüe* as the primary vehicle through which Chiang (with the help of his secretaries) attempted to construct a collective story in which *chi* was a central theme. Arguing that it is inadequate to view the *shilüe* as a mere day-to-day recording of Chiang's words and actions, this book takes seriously the *shilüe's* traditional purpose of upholding Confucian political morality in its analysis of Chiang's exercise of leadership.

Chapters 2 and 3 investigate two specific events during which Chiang's deployment of *chi* as humiliation came to the fore—the Jinan (1928) and Mukden (1931) Incidents—and track his construction of a collective story over those historical moments. Although the Chinese public and subsequent scholars have roundly criticized Chiang's handling of the Mukden Incident (the more well-known of the two events), these chapters articulate an overlooked path that Chiang tried to take in his efforts to mobilize nationalism, confront imperialism, and consolidate sovereignty under his authority.[25] Whereas scholars have largely neglected Chiang's use of Confucianism in the Jinan and Mukden Incidents, they have generally dismissed his most systematic use of it to rejuvenate Chinese society through the New Life Movement (1934). Chapter 4 reexamines Chiang's use of *chi* in light of his overall construction of a collective story in 1934 to reveal that his approach to modernity was more multifaceted and consequential than has been acknowledged so far. Together, the four chapters of Part I uncover how Chiang creatively deployed *chi* as he sought to legitimate his leadership while attempting to unify and strengthen China.

Part II broadens the scope of this study by comparing Chiang's use of *chi* with that of other leaders to consider how the global, domestic, and leadership contexts might have further facilitated or undermined Chiang's deployment of the cultural resource. Chapter 5 compares Chiang's use of *chi* cross-temporally to that of two other Chinese leaders who also gained national stature during the Republican period. The first is Yuan Shikai (1859–1916), who ruled between 1912 and 1916, and the second is Mao, who opposed Chiang's leadership in the 1930s and 1940s and succeeded him in 1949. By comparing these leaders' respective uses of *chi*, the chapter moves beyond the conventional analysis of Mao as revolutionary and Chiang and Yuan as reactionary by exploring how differing circumstances and dramatic changes in the structural context shaped the three leaders' agency in using *chi* to create a credible collective story.

Chapter 6 steps out of the Chinese context to compare Chiang cross-culturally with another Asian leader, Mohandas K. Gandhi (known as Mahatma, 1869–1948). Although I considered other Asian leaders, such as

Indonesia's Sukarno (1901–70) and India's Jawaharlal Nehru (1889–1964), because they were also motivated to confront imperialism, I chose Gandhi because he is both well known in the West and often held up as an icon of transformative and charismatic leadership. Moreover, just as Chiang adapted *chi* to face the Japanese incursion into China, Gandhi drew on an analogous theme of stoicism in his use of *satyagraha* (truth struggle) to challenge British imperial injustice. Through this comparison, the chapter illuminates the generic yet understudied tools that leaders of weak states can wield when confronting strong states and moves beyond dichotomous analyses of leadership to explore the kinds of obstacles and opportunities such leaders face in constructing a national story, identity, and legacy.

The concluding chapter argues that Chiang's creation of a shame and humiliation narrative became a cultural resource for future Chinese leaders from Mao to Xi Jinping (b. 1953). In tracking their attempts to draw on or ignore Chiang's *chi* narrative after 1949, it becomes clear that Chiang's legacy affected these leaders' efforts to adapt the Chinese national narrative in pursuit of their political agendas. Because Chiang later became leader of Taiwan between 1949 and 1975, the chapter also examines his adaptation of *chi* there and what legacy (if any) that narrative left in Taiwan.

• • •

In exploring Chiang's use of *chi* over time and comparing it with that of other leaders, this book invites the reader to take Robert Frost's road "less traveled by." Instead of embarking on the road that examines why leaders win or lose in history, this book investigates the construction of collective stories as an important aspect of leadership that should be neither ignored nor dismissed, especially in the case of leaders who were defeated in history, considered irredeemably flawed, or appeared to rely on outdated tradition (and Chiang was all three). As the book will show, such leaders' contributions to the collective stories and identities of their nations can sometimes have ramifications that last beyond the influence of those who prevailed over them or appeared to have stronger moral leadership. As such, this book brings the analyses of leaders back from the fantastical realms of the larger-than-life saint or the small-minded, incompetent scoundrel into the more mundane yet realistic human realm where leaders can create potent collective narratives as both agent and object of history.

PART I

Agency

CHAPTER I

Drafting Chiang's Narrative
in the Shilüe

Column after column, page after page, volume after volume, secretaries faithfully captured Chiang Kai-shek's movements and words in the black brushwork of Chinese calligraphy. Whatever he uttered seemed to have been recorded, and the man produced many words; he was prone to speeches that lasted for three hours or longer, and he kept a diary for six decades. Based on these and other sources, his trusted secretaries compiled several chronologies related to his life and leadership of the country, including *Difficulties and Self-Encouragement (Kunmianji), Holidays (Youji), Learning (Xueji), Reflections on Overcoming Difficulties (Xingkeji), Family and Friends Draft Chronology (Aiji chugao)*, and *Supplementary Writings on Reviving the Country (Fuxing zhuibi)*. The most comprehensive of these chronologies and the primary source for this book, *Mr. Chiang's Draft Manuscript (Jianggong shilüe gaoben*; referred to in the text as *shilüe*) consists primarily of quotations from Chiang's diaries, telegrams, speeches, and reports. Altogether, the *shilüe* comprises more than three hundred hand-sewn volumes spanning the years 1927 to 1949, all of which ultimately traveled to Taiwan with Chiang and his government after losing the civil war to Mao Zedong.[1]

These chronologies, which contain highly personal and confidential materials, were never meant for public consumption in that form. Instead, they provided the raw materials from which future historians, following Chinese tradition, would produce the official historical record and legacy of Chiang's leadership. As part of Taiwan's democratization in the 1990s, however, Kuomintang officials broke from tradition and began granting public access to this sea of primary historical documents, which led to the publication of several notable biographies of Chiang Kai-shek, new scholarly examinations of key events during his leadership, and several conferences organized to reassess Chiang and his times, especially from a post–Cold War lens.[2]

Nevertheless, the unique nature of the *shilüe* as a source for understanding Chiang's leadership has remained largely unexplored and thus underappreciated.[3] As we shall see, the documents are neither a diluted version of Chiang's diaries that reveal his "true" thinking nor a simple chronological record in which to consider his thoughts and actions.[4] Instead, they offer a window into a largely unstudied but significant aspect of Chiang's agency and exercise of leadership: narrative creation. By providing background information and articulating how the *shilüe* can be read, this chapter sets the stage for drawing on the document to track Chiang's formulation of a national narrative that would legitimate his authority, mobilize himself and others to achieve his political agenda, and shape a lasting legacy.

Purpose

Secretaries modeled Chiang's *shilüe* after a genre in Chinese historiography called the veritable records (*shilu*), which were the authorized official accounts of each emperor's reign. Once the veritable records were completed for a dynastic reign, they formed the basis of a standard history (*zhengshi*), the official historical record of the dynasty. A key difference between traditional Chinese historiography and the modern Western model is that the former aims to uphold Confucian political morality. According to the example set by a chronicle Confucius purportedly compiled, the *Spring and Autumn Annals* (722–481 BCE), the duty of the Chinese historian—like that of the leader—was to promote good and suppress evil. As such, the purpose of the *shilüe*, which was explicitly modeled after the *Spring and Autumn Annals*, was to establish Chiang's record and legacy by serving as a resource and didactic guide for posterity.[5]

Perhaps because the format of the veritable records was somewhat constricting for the new era, Chiang and his secretaries based the chronology on another genre in Chinese historiography that allowed greater flexibility. *Shilüe* refers to a category in Chinese historical writing that can summarize an event, a person's life, or even a dynastic reign by providing details in some areas and skimming over others.[6] By choosing the *shilüe* format, Chiang and his secretaries could compile a chronology that was neither slavish to Chinese historiography nor rejecting of modern and foreign influences.[7]

Regarding the latter, Chiang and his secretaries adapted the veritable records format to take into account the rise of nationalism and mass politics that had begun in the 1910s during the New Culture Movement and saw its most poignant expression during the May 4, 1919, student protest against the Treaty of Versailles. This movement helped vernacularize the Chinese language (*baihua*) so that ordinary citizens could read what originally was in the sole purview of the elite.[8] By including vernacular materials in the *shilüe*, Chiang and his secretaries understood that the modern leader needed to connect with ordinary people, and by extension with future generations of Chinese citizens, by imbuing them with a sense of patriotism and national pride.

The secretaries began officially compiling Chiang's *shilüe* following the outbreak of the Sino-Japanese War in 1937. The high priority that Chiang placed on producing his official record can be inferred from the importance of the office with which he entrusted it, the Office of Personal Attendants (Shicong shi), and from his preservation of more than two decades of his writings and speeches that were now at their disposal.[9] Because the office operated like the emperor's imperial seal in that its stamp of approval was needed for all vital appointments and military movements, the secretaries in this office were clearly trusted officials to be granted access to such confidential materials.[10] Despite the exigencies of war, several of the secretaries in 1940 became tasked with "organiz[ing], compil[ing], and safeguard[ing] Chiang Kai-shek's speeches, reports, correspondence, diaries, and day-to-day notes on events from the Northern Expedition until the present"—that is, to compile the *shilüe* and other chronologies regarding Chiang's leadership on which the later official chronological biography would be based.[11] This eventual official narrative, *A Lengthy First Draft of the Major Events of President Chiang* (*Zongtong Jianggong dashi changbian chugao*), was published in 1978, and due to Taiwan's democratization, the confidential *shilüe* were also photo-reproduced and published between 2003 and 2013.

People

Chiang put his personal writings into the hands of an unbroken line of head secretaries throughout his career, including Mao Sicheng (serv. 1925–34), Chen Bulei (serv. 1934–46), Zhou Hongtao (serv. 1946–58), and Qin Xiaoyi (serv. 1958–75). Under the supervision of second chief secretary Chen Bulei and secretary Tao Xisheng, three undersecretaries (hereafter referred to as secretaries) were responsible for compiling the *shilüe*.[12] Each secretary inscribed his name on the cover of the volume on which he was working and handwrote the manuscript, compiling all the volumes for a single year. Each volume typically covered a month, although some covered half a month and others two months. For the volumes discussed in the following chapters, Sun Yi organized them for 1927, 1930, and 1933; Wang Yugao for 1928, 1931, and 1932; and Yuan Huichang for 1929, 1934, and 1935.[13] Because these secretaries were performing the work of historians, one might note that in the Chinese context, a secretary or *mishu* generally takes on a wider range of activities than most secretaries in the Western context, who often occupy a more constrained role of an administrative assistant.[14]

A comparison of the three secretaries' handiwork reveals notable variations in their portrayal of Chiang in the *shilüe*. Of the three, Sun did the most abysmal job. The volumes he compiled show little attempt at coherence and usually contained only about half as many pages as those by Wang and Yuan. He regularly excluded details from the diaries included in the other secretaries' volumes, such as what time Chiang got up in the morning and what books he read, and at times he barely seemed to bother with excerpting transcriptions from Chiang's speeches. On a few occasions, however, Sun latched onto a speech and wrote it down in full. In one case, to accommodate a speech, Sun expanded his *shilüe* volume to around 250 pages, more than double the average size.[15] His seemingly lackadaisical approach is also evident in the insertions and deletions of text and in the margins of his pages, where he often squeezed in not just one or two forgotten characters, as sometimes seen in the other secretaries' work, but as many as a hundred words written in small characters (fig. 1.1).[16] In an August 1958 note pasted on a page of Sun's 1927 *shilüe*, Qin Xiaoyi recorded that he had corrected seventy-one

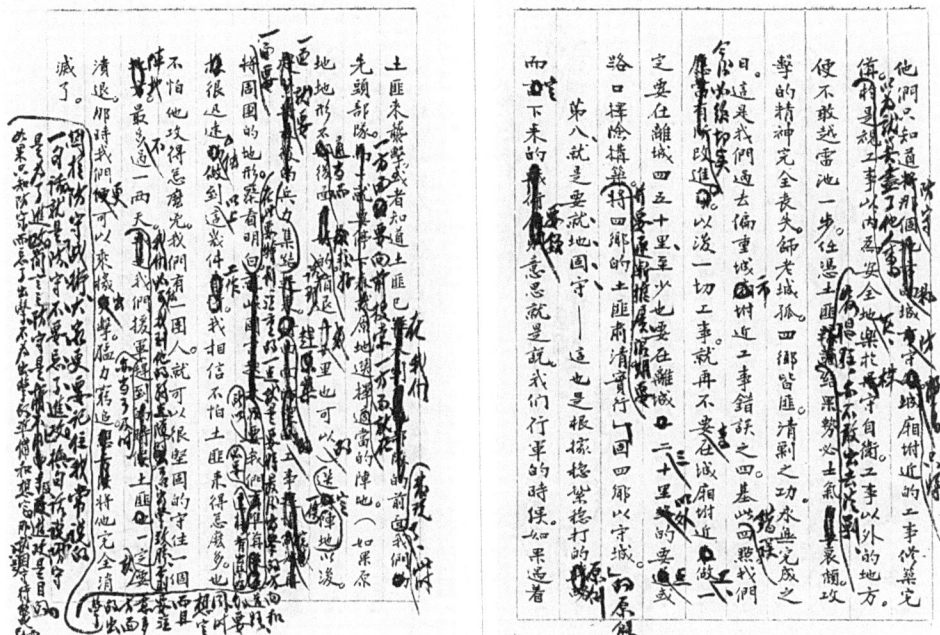

FIGURE I.I: Sun Yi's compilation of the *shilüe* chronology. October 2, 1933, *JZZDSG*, 2005, 23/146–47. Courtesy of Academia Historica, Taipei, Taiwan.

mistakes, six of which he considered extremely important.[17] In reading Sun's handiwork, one envisions a clock-watcher, ready to flee work at the appropriate second.

By contrast, Yuan was meticulous. Later editorial revisions by him or by subsequent secretaries were rare. When he did make a mistake, he would manually cut out a portion of a column with the mistake and paste in the correction.[18] Yet the narrative content of Yuan's *shilüe* is somewhat lacking. For instance, when Chiang began entering quotations from the Bible on a daily basis in his "avenging humiliation" column (a section in his diary entry) in 1934, Yuan doggedly included these in the *shilüe* even though they did little to advance the reader's understanding of Chiang's leadership. Yuan also appeared to lack a clear rationale for selecting excerpts from speeches, thereby providing readers of the *shilüe* little sense of the critical themes in Chiang's thought as they developed over time. Finally, Yuan tended to select materials that cast

Chiang in a favorable light. Although his work presented a comprehensive (albeit favorable) public face, it fell short of a compelling story.

Of the three secretaries, Wang is the only one for whom any personal information is available. His decade-long service in Chiang's secretarial retinue was an anomaly in his career as a doctor, professor, and editor of medical journals. Several factors made him a likely candidate to organize Chiang's *shilüe* and his other chronologies.[19] Wang came from Chiang's hometown of Fenghua, and these native place ties were important for fostering loyalty and trust. Moreover, as an expert on Chinese medicine, Wang had extensive knowledge of literary Chinese, which represented competence in the Chinese language. Although he was promoted and given responsibility for the national archive following Japan's defeat, in 1949 he decided to return to Ningbo, Zhejiang, to continue practicing medicine rather than follow Chiang to Taiwan.[20] The little we know about these secretaries' background appears to suggest that the genres of historical writing were in flux during the Republican era and the requisite training therefore ill-defined and the pool of qualified talent small.

Despite writing in the stereotypical inscrutable handwriting of his profession, Wang clearly selected materials that were either important to history or necessary for understanding Chiang's leadership, juxtaposing materials that perceptively demonstrated the interrelations between the two.[21] For instance, he included excerpts from the avenging humiliation entries if they involved a concrete method of avengement or reflected an important aspect of Chiang's leadership. Examples include Chiang's struggle to curb his temper, his anxiety over Japan's aggression, and his reaction to advice about confronting Japan from warlord Feng Yuxiang (1882–1948).[22] Yet Wang refrained from questioning whether these topics truly belonged in the avenging humiliation entry. Nor did he omit Chiang's frequent complaints or expressions of frustration because they might reflect badly on his leadership.

At the same time, he avoided quoting from these entries if he thought they lacked substance. For the first half of 1931, for instance, Chiang, who was then more concerned with domestic disunity than with Japanese aggression, simply repeated several motivational four-character phrases in his avenging humiliation entries, such as "man will overcome nature" (*rending shengtian*) or "be determined and cultivate one's spirit" (*lizhi yangqi*). Wang simply quoted these phrases once and indicated that they made up the avenging humiliation entries for this six-month period, thereby avoiding the repetition of unimportant details.[23]

Compared with Sun and Yuan, Wang appeared best able to integrate the raw *shilüe* materials to deliver a compelling story about Chiang to posterity. Perhaps counterintuitively, this may suggest that a leader's ability to preserve his or her story and secure a legacy may depend on compilers and historians who seek to place their day-to-day words and actions in that of the broader, complex, and often difficult context within which they lived and led, instead of presenting leaders as heroes in the annals of history.

At the end of 1948, just before surrendering to the Chinese communists, Chiang ordered his *shilüe* and other personal archival materials shipped to Taiwan, along with gold ingots from the Central Bank.[24] Once retaking mainland China became unlikely, Chiang, in 1958, appointed Qin Xiaoyi to be his head secretary and tasked him with continuing the work on the *shilüe*. In exquisite calligraphy, Qin made editorial comments across all of the *shilüe* volumes—sometimes directly in the volume and sometimes on attached pieces of paper, and his remarks are easily distinguishable from the work of the earlier secretaries. Because several of his attached notes were removed or folded out of the way (presumably so the underlying text could be read) in preparation for photo-reproducing the *shilüe* for publication, this book references both the *shilüe* volume and the published volume whenever possible. In ensuring that events covered were accurate (especially in Sun's volumes) and historically important, Qin ultimately transformed the 300-volume *shilüe* chronology into an 8-volume official biography that was modeled after the veritable records of past Chinese leaders.

Materials

Chiang's diaries were the anchor that guided the secretaries' selection of the other materials that would make up a *shilüe* entry. In dynastic times, court diaries or "diaries of activity and repose" (*qijuzhu*) were the analogous component in the veritable records. Two court diarists were chosen for their supposed moral rectitude and were expected to voice praise or blame when needed, both in person and in their record of the emperor's words and actions.[25] Although Chiang wrote his own diary entries, he similarly suffused them, as he did his speeches and other communications, with Confucian moral precepts.[26] Drawing from the neo-Confucian tradition of self-cultivation, he often invoked past Chinese and foreign role models to motivate himself and his soldiers and to encourage good and discourage bad behavior.[27] In starting his diary in 1917 and continuing it until 1972 despite other demands on his time and attention, Chiang once remarked to his son, Chiang Ching-kuo (1910–88), that his diaries greatly helped him in policymaking and self-cultivation.[28]

In keeping with the Republican trend toward vernacularization, Chiang's diary writing was more revelatory, undigested, and unvarnished compared with the court diaries, disclosing his personality as a modern national leader who was more accessible to the masses, in contrast to the emperors of the past. He used a preformatted diary booklet that included a quotation of the day printed at the top of each page and several preset categories, such as "main points" (*tiyao*), "weather" (*qihou*), "temperature" (*wendu*), and "location" (*didian*). To these, Chiang added some categories of his own, such as "pay attention" (*zhuyi*), "schedule" (*yuding*), and "reflections" (*fanxing*). Of particular relevance to this study is the category of "one method to avenge humiliation" (*xuechi zhidao*; sometimes shortened in text to "avenging humiliation" (*xuechi*)), which was the only added category for which he made a daily entry (fig. 1.2).[29]

From these diaries, the secretaries generally chose excerpts that featured different facets of Chiang's internal workings as a leader, such as his reactions to events and subsequent efforts to respond. Secretaries also followed Chiang's diary lead by recording his routines and habits, such as the time of day he awoke, what book he was reading, how he felt physically, and where and how he was traveling. To learn that he read daily in the early morning may be of little consequence, but to find out that over time he read one book at a time, in systematic fashion, suggests that Chiang had a persevering and somewhat regimented vision of his responsibilities and leadership. By also including his thoughts about and quotations from the books he read, the secretaries reflected the process by which Chiang drew inspiration from these texts to confront his day-to-day problems. Aware of the importance of the Confucian concept of *chi* to the didactic purpose of the *shilüe* and to Chiang's notion of leader-

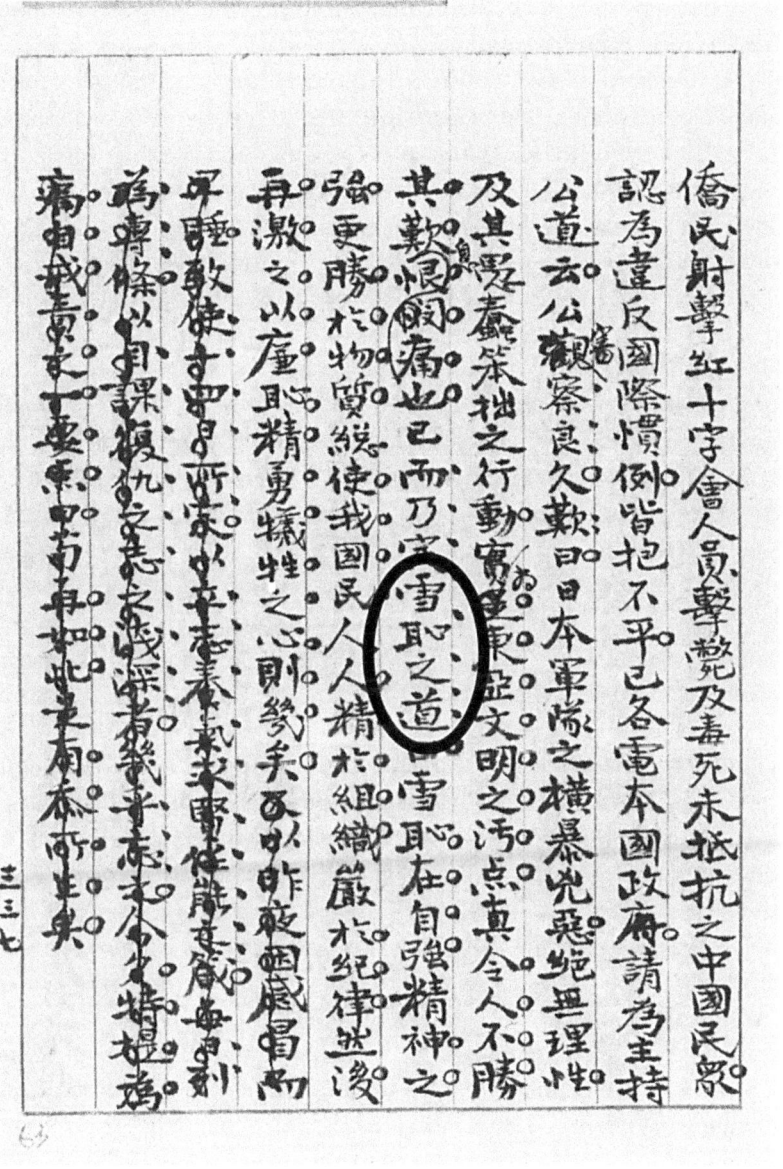

FIGURE I.2: "One method to avenge humiliation" (*xuechi zhidao*) from Wang Yugao's compilation of the *shilüe*. Secretaries often concluded a *shilüe* daily entry by quoting from this section of Chiang's diary. May 16, 1928, *JZZDSG*, 2003, 3/362–63. Courtesy of Academia Historica, Taipei, Taiwan.

ship and narrative for China, the secretaries quoted almost daily from his avenging humiliation diary entry.[30]

If secretaries relied on diary excerpts to anchor posterity's understanding of Chiang's thinking with respect to daily living and events, they drew from his telegrams, reports, and speeches to complete the picture. By juxtaposing the raw materials of his public interactions with that of his private diary reflections, the secretaries reveal Chiang's ongoing formulation of his approach to leadership and his construction of the collective story in response to outside feedback.

Secretaries typically included excerpts from telegrams on a daily basis, which usually contained direct orders or requests by Chiang (such as to move troops from position A to B) or his replies to other people's telegrams. They included reports sparingly, some of which Chiang authored, such as the pamphlet on the New Life Movement.[31] Although the degree of Chiang's authorship was often in question, the secretaries included such materials because of their significance.[32] At times, a secretary might include a report that Chiang had no hand in creating because it helped contextualize events that were historically important in retrospect, such as accounts about the Wanbaoshan and Korean incidents discussed in chapter 3.[33]

Chiang's speeches were the final other major component of the *shilüe*. Here the secretaries tended to include his so-called moral instruction speeches, known as *jiaoxun* or *xunlian* speeches. Although Chiang lacked a flair for public speaking—accounts from those subjected to his speeches describe them as long and tedious, his words indecipherable through his thick Zhejiang accent—the content of his speeches often revealed a blunt honesty about what he viewed as the defects of the Chinese national character. In one speech, he noted that upon entering the auditorium, he had been disgusted by the spit and snot on the main doors. Putting his audience to shame, he reprimanded, "What would an American or Italian think? That we are barbarians!"[34] In another, he mentioned that he had heard Western military and ancient Chinese music being played at a funeral and saw participants wearing ritual clothing but riding in modern cars. He lamented the chaos (*luan*) that now afflicted funeral rituals.[35] By shaming his various audiences (and his words were neither modified nor tempered by a secretary in the *shilüe*), Chiang underscored the Confucian didactic intent in his leadership and, by extension, the collective story about China he wanted to convey to his various audiences—one that respected public spaces and would be more intentional about performing important rituals in the new era.

Credibility

In addition to modeling Confucian rectitude, Chiang's secretaries also had to navigate between the competing goals in traditional Chinese historiography of ensuring objectivity and of positively reflecting the political goals of the current regime. Moreover, secretaries sometimes altered Chiang's words to achieve a better alignment with historical reality and create a unified tone or mood (*yuqi*) in their compilation of excerpted materials.[36] These competing goals and changes to the *shilüe* warrant a closer examination as they speak to issues concerning the document's credibility.

Regarding historical objectivity, the *shilüe* secretaries appeared to follow the principles set out by the Qing historian and philosopher Zhang Xuecheng (1738–1801): "the historian's greatest concern is to avoid having himself as the authority for anything he writes. . . . If he himself is the authority for any statement, then that statement is without evidence . . . [and] will not be credible to posterity."[37] In keeping with this idea of recounting rather than originating, the three *shilüe* secretaries did not alter quotations from Chiang's diaries, speeches, and telegrams to mask any potentially embarrassing aspects of his leadership, such as his strong emotions, insecurities, and critical thoughts about other leaders. Because they were literally recording Chiang's words and actions, they had little room for manipulating the text for propagandistic purposes or creative interpretation. Undoubtedly aware that the veracity of much of their record could be checked against other sources—for instance, diary excerpts could be compared with the actual diaries—they avoided inserting their own opinions or interpretations about Chiang.

Nevertheless, the goal of maintaining historical objectivity was sometimes in tension with that of attempting to conform to the political goals of the current regime.[38] Like historians of the past, to resolve this tension in part, the secretaries could purposely omit details that put Chiang in an unfavorable light; indeed, none of them gave an account of any obviously inappropriate, illegal, or cruel action by Chiang.[39] Yet the draft nature of the document (*gaoben* in *shilüe gaoben* means "draft manuscript") mitigated the problem of purposeful omission. Even when a secretary crossed out (in part or in entirety) speeches or quotations from Chiang that might have cast him in an unfavorable light, *shilüe* readers can still see what has been crossed out. Yuan, for instance, drew a thin black line through the final clause of the following remark from one of Chiang's speeches: "Sun's knowledge is based on Western science and Chinese culture, *whereas I think Chinese culture is more important than science.*"[40] That the omitted passage might be perceived as a sign of disrespect to the founding father of the Kuomintang is also suggested by Qin's decision to omit this speech entirely from his 1978 official biography.

Moreover, the materials were supposed to be kept confidential within the party, and this presumably allowed greater freedom for the *shilüe* secretaries to relax the criterion of loyalty to Chiang by experimenting and including an array of exceptionally candid materials, so frank that probably no one expected them to make the official published record. Wang, for instance, included Chiang's unflattering impression of his most viable rival for leadership of the Kuomintang after Sun Yat-sen's death, Wang Jingwei (1883–1944): "When speaking with [him], I always feel he is really boring."[41]

Secretaries did sometimes revise Chiang's words to align them more closely with historical reality, but again, the draft nature of the *shilüe* makes this process transparent. In responding to an unforeseen military conflict with the Japanese while trying to unify China in 1928 (the subject of chapter 2), Chiang wrote, "To put right the educational system, to tighten organization, to use people of talent, these are the important things to implement in order to destroy the Japanese."[42] When Wang selected this excerpt, he crossed out the word "destroy" and wrote "resist" in its place, purposely revising the text to reflect the reality of China's relative strength compared with Japan's and perhaps make Chiang appear more realistic in his expectations to posterity.

Specifically in the case of Chiang's diary excerpts, secretaries sometimes altered his words to provide context and uniformity in the tone or mood while staying within the spirit of Chiang's meaning. For example, in a bizarre twist of events, Chiang's subordinate Zhang Xueliang (1901–2001) kidnapped Chiang on December 12, 1936, in an attempt to force him to change his policy of quelling internal rivals before confronting Japan. In this crisis, Chiang's wife and brother-in-law, Song Ziwen (T. V. Soong, 1894–1971), flew into Xi'an to negotiate his successful release.[43] Describing his response to his brother-in-law's visit in his diary, Chiang wrote: "At eleven o'clock in the morning, I was sleeping when Ziwen suddenly came through the door. I felt as if my eyes were peering through a dense fog. I couldn't recognize that it was Ziwen. In less than a moment, I awoke, and I started to recognize that it really was Ziwen."[44] Wang made several changes in his version of the excerpt in the *shilüe*: "Gong [a respectful term for Chiang] is still at Gao Guizi's residence. This morning, Gong slept most soundly. At eleven o'clock, Song Ziwen opened the door and peered in. Gong's eyes were still blurry and he couldn't recognize who was at the door. After a while, he awakened and was able to recognize that it was Ziwen."[45]

As was sometimes the case, Wang chose not to enter this excerpt as a direct quotation but changed it from a first-person, subjective point of view to a third-person, objective one. Beyond that alteration, he provided context by noting that Chiang was at Gao Guizi's residence and inferred from Chiang's entry that he was sleeping soundly when Song appeared. Such changes demonstrate Wang's understanding that the *shilüe* was meant to be more than just a copy of the diary. Although by altering Chiang's words he ran the risk of overlooking or misrepresenting subtle nuances of intent, his changes added context and detail that clarified the narrative and unified the tone of the *shilüe* entry by phrasing it into a third-person view.

The draft nature of the *shilüe* and the ability to compare it with the actual diaries, telegrams, and speeches help mitigate concerns about secretaries potentially manipulating the content of the raw materials. Moreover, because the *shilüe* was never meant for public consumption, the criterion of creating a favorable public face was not foremost in the compilers' minds. Finally, because these changes are made transparent in the draft *shilüe*, they provide a unique window into the compilers' process of seeking to create a credible narrative to posterity.

Narrative

Although the *shilüe* secretaries did not systematically incorporate what the public thought of Chiang or what fellow party members or officers wrote in their telegrams or felt in their interactions with Chiang, they often included Chiang's reaction to other leaders and to public opinion as recorded in his diaries, speeches, or telegram responses. As such, the secretaries provided evidence of Chiang reworking the face of his leadership and the collective story he was putting forward in reaction to daily feedback from the public and from those interacting with him. Thus they captured the process by which Chiang constructed his collective narrative, one that took pains to legitimate his leadership and justify an agenda that would ensure China's survival. This narrative creation, as we shall see in the following chapters, often followed the intensity of Chiang's reactions to events and efforts to make sense of them and did not necessarily correspond to the magnitude of the event's significance as judged by Qin Xiaoyi or later historians.

Although Chiang was the main contributor to this narrative, the *shilüe* secretaries also assisted as his agents. In the *shilüe*'s initial compilation, for instance, the secretaries appeared uncertain as to how Chiang should be depicted when paraphrasing his words and actions in the third person. In Sun's 1927 volume, for instance, he or Qin inserted the editorial reverse order marks to every joint reference of Wang Jingwei and Chiang (WangJiang) to indicate that Chiang should be considered the more important of the two.[46] In the 1929 *shilüe*, Yuan originally referred to Chiang as "mister" (*xiansheng*) but later systematically crossed out and replaced each instance with the more respectful *gong*.[47] By the time he compiled the 1934 *shilüe*, Yuan not only began referring to Chiang as *gong*, but he also left one blank space before writing his name. Like the other secretaries, however, he avoided leaving two spaces before Chiang's name, a designation reserved solely for Sun Yat-sen and which Kuomintang members would likely have viewed as a sign of disrespect and arrogance by equating Chiang with the father of the party. Thus the *shilüe* reveals an important developmental arc of the secretaries grappling with how to capture Chiang's status that has been largely erased in Qin's official 1978 chronological record.

The *shilüe* secretaries' handiwork provides a relatively unfiltered version of how Chiang sought to legitimate his leadership and put forward his version of the Chinese national narrative. For instance, the entries included by the secretaries suggest that Chiang's victory in the Central Plains War (Zhongyuan dazhan) was critical in bolstering his confidence as a leader and in forging a different path from Sun Yat-sen.[48] Before this battle, those excerpts show, Chiang had excessively referred to Sun Yatsen and the Three People's Principles (*Sanmin zhuyi*) in his speeches, as if he wished to strengthen his legitimacy with continual association with Sun.[49] After this battle, the *shilüe* selections reveal that Chiang referred to Sun less often and reinterpreted Sun's thinking as similar to that of Dai Jitao (1891–1949), the conservative political ideologue of the Kuomintang.[50] Yet this development in Chiang's confidence and leadership is more difficult to discern in Qin's severely abridged official history, in which Qin understandably sought to eliminate repetition. Qin's version also omitted a telling comment by Chiang, as alluded to earlier, in which he had disagreed with one of Sun's beliefs.[51] Liu Weikai, a contemporary Kuomintang historian, considers many of Chiang's recollections of conversations with his wife in the *shilüe* as unnecessary, reasoning that these conversations had no direct relevance to historical events.[52] Yet their inclusion in the *shilüe* provides a more personal window into Chiang the man and reflected a view of marriage that appeared more equitable and modern.[53] Given the necessary ellipses in any official history, the *shilüe*'s more inclusive version better captures Chiang and his development as a leader, and by extension, the story he attempted to construct about China.

In an attached note that is not visible in the photo-reproduced version of the *shilüe*, Qin suggested that Wang's inclusion of a 1928 skirmish in Xuzhou that involved 6,000 or 7,000 enemy warlord troops be omitted from his official draft in favor of the more historically significant 1938 Battle of Xuzhou that involved approximately 300,000 troops against the Japanese. Qin's retrospective assessment, however, had the potential of inadvertently eradicating important developments in Chiang's narrative creation.[54] As chapter 2 reveals, from a historical perspective, another skirmish in Jinan was considered insignificant compared with the eight years of the Sino-Japanese War, and indeed, most histories (as we shall see) treated it as such. Yet from the perspective of the *shilüe*, the incident was of utmost importance in galvanizing Chiang to create a narrative that drew heavily on shame and humiliation. Significantly, the *shilüe* can convey this process-oriented view of Chiang's leadership and efforts to construct a narrative.

For the purposes of this book, the *shilüe* volumes of the early years, 1927 to 1936, are especially useful for tracking Chiang's narrative creation, as the materials from which they were created are less self-conscious, more experimental, and more directly reflect Chiang's earnest efforts to legitimate his authority and create a collective story for the nation.[55] The following chapters particularly rely on Wang's volumes because they are the most helpful in conveying the ongoing, open-ended stories filled with contradictions, tension, and changes over time. Because Yuan's loyalist slant was not yet in full force during these years and his original versions are still visible in the *shilüe*, his volumes also assist in crafting the full story of Chiang's development as a leader. Unfortunately, the poor quality of Sun's work may leave potential gaps or obscure nuances in this volume's analysis of the chronological record.

Ultimately, the *shilüe* offers an intriguing and revealing first draft of the didactic narrative that Chiang sought to construct about his leadership and about Chinese nationalism and identity that continues to resonate today. By tracking his uses of *chi* in the *shilüe* and comparing it with that of other leaders, the following chapters reveal that Chiang's deployment of this Confucian cultural resource did not form a solidified, coherent story that worked in every circumstance. Yet his efforts at narrative creation exemplify a critical and creative aspect of his leadership that provides readers a window into important, though often ignored, alternative understandings of leadership, nationalism, and modernity.

CHAPTER 2

Enduring Humiliation in Jinan

In May 1928, Chiang Kai-shek started a new heading in his diary titled "one method to avenge humiliation" (*xuechi zhidao*). With rare exceptions, he wrote a daily entry under this heading for almost two decades. The trigger that started this occurred toward the end of the Northern Expedition military campaign, in which Chiang sought to unite China. In 1921, Sun Yat-sen had set up a base in southern China with the goal of bringing the country under Kuomintang control.[1] He distinguished himself from other warlords of this period by promoting a unifying ideology for China under the Three People's Principles, which was meant to guide the Kuomintang and the new republic in the areas of nationalism, democracy, and the people's livelihood.[2] Because the Nationalist government was militarily weak compared with other warlords, Sun sought Soviet help to reorganize the party and train a military that could defeat the northern warlords. He established the Whampoa Military Academy in Guangzhou in 1924, which was funded mainly by the Soviets, and he made Chiang its first commandant.[3] Because Moscow felt that the Kuomintang had the best chance of unifying China, it forced the Chinese communists to join the Kuomintang in planning and executing the Northern Expedition, and this cooperation became known as the First United Front.[4]

Sun died in March 1925, but Chiang continued with Sun's plan by launching the Northern Expedition in July 1926. By May 1928, Chiang seemed to be on the verge of completing the northern campaign. His next task was to take over Jinan, the provincial capital of Shandong. The city was critical to the success of the Northern Expedition because it was strategically located at the intersection of the north–south Tianjin-Pukou railway and the east–west Jiaozhou-Jinan railway.[5] When Chiang's troops entered the city on May 3, a military skirmish ensued between the Chinese and Japanese armies, the latter having been sent into Jinan to protect Japanese nationals living there. Although Chiang and his army eventually continued northward to complete China's unification, they experienced a string of humiliations at the hands of the Japanese, including having to abandon Jinan to the imperial power.

Major Western accounts of modern Chinese history mention the Jinan (or Tsinan) Incident only briefly, if at all. The military clash was but a ripple compared to subsequent battles with Japan in the 1930s and 1940s and was a seemingly minor hitch in Chiang's attempt to unify China through the Northern Expedition.[6] Yet the *shilüe*'s account of the incident provides a markedly different perspective. The Jinan Incident spurred Chiang to begin an avenging humiliation entry and was the catalyst for him to construct a national humiliation story that would inform and legitimate his political agenda over the next two decades. Advocates of the May Fourth Movement criticized aspects of Confucianism as being clearly inadequate for training officials to run a modern bureaucracy and containing values about obedience to authority that were antithetical to those in a liberal democracy. Yet Chiang's deployment of *chi* in response to foreign imperialism has been curiously absent from this discussion by May Fourth advocates and by scholars who have analyzed Chiang's uses of Confucianism.[7] It deserves further investigation because it helps to reassess the importance of the Jinan Incident and opens a window into how Chiang adapted and wielded a traditional resource to construct a powerful story to achieve his political agenda despite confronting a new and difficult situation that threatened to derail it.

The Jinan Incident

The Northern Expedition lasted from July 1926 to December 1928 and was a key event that solidified Chiang Kai-shek's leadership in the Kuomintang. Launching the expedition from Guangzhou in 1926, Chiang and his troops pressed northward with the aim of unifying all of China under the Nationalist flag. Within a year, the Kuomintang government was installed in Wuhan with Wang Jingwei as its leader; however, right-wing party members decided to set up a rival government in Nanjing with Chiang as the leader. When taking over Shanghai in April 1927, Chiang and the right wing of the party decided to purge the Chinese communists from the Kuomintang despite opposition from Wang and his followers. Nevertheless, by July 1927, Wang's Wuhan government faltered because of its military weakness (the army tended to support Chiang) and economic woes. Reversing course, it purged the Chinese communists from its ranks and rejoined the right wing of the Nationalist Party with Wang temporarily fleeing to Europe. By February 1928, the First United Front had collapsed, some of the northern warlords had become Chiang's allies, and Chiang had become the most influential member in the Kuomintang.[8]

The forces at play in the Northern Expedition, however, were not just domestic in nature. Since the Opium Wars and the signing of unequal treaties with imperial powers in the mid-nineteenth century, a sizable foreign presence had become ensconced in China. In the post–May Fourth era, anti-imperial sentiments flared more visibly and regularly—the May 30th Incident in 1925, for instance, started with some striking Chinese workers at a Japanese cotton mill in Shanghai and eventually resulted in a large-scale, nationwide boycott of Japanese and British goods. Although the Northern Expedition depended on popular forces to undermine warlord control and secure the newly conquered territory, these domestic forces were also prone to anti-imperialist and anti-Christian attacks.[9]

The Nanjing Incident in March 1927 is important to note because it influenced the unfolding of events in Jinan a year later. As the northern troops (Beiyang) were leaving the city of Nanjing, having conceded defeat, and Chiang and the National Revolutionary Army were entering the city, Chinese soldiers (likely from both northern and southern sides), students, and others began rioting against the foreign soldiers stationed in the city to protect foreign nationals doing business. This violence soon turned to foreign civilians, including missionaries.[10] National Revolutionary soldiers were accused of looting the British, US, and Japanese consulates and attacking and robbing foreign nationals in the city. They were also blamed for killing two Englishmen, an American vice president of Nanjing University, and a Japanese naval officer. The Americans and British responded by bombing the area to assist in the evacuation of some fifty foreigners, mostly British and American.[11] From this point on, foreign governments had heightened concern about the safety of their citizens in China. This was especially true of the Japanese, as additional violence occurred in the Japanese concession in Hankou (one of the three cities that form modern-day Wuhan), ten days after the Nanjing Incident, resulting in deaths on both the Chinese and Japanese sides.[12]

In this context, in December 1927, Japanese Prime Minister Tanaka Giichi (1864–1929) informed Chiang and former warlord-turned-coalition leader Feng Yuxiang that he hoped their advancing forces would avoid Jinan so that his government would find it unnecessary to send Japanese troops to protect the roughly 2,000 Japanese nationals residing there. Although Chiang assured Tanaka that his Nationalist troops and the coalition's armies would protect Japanese nationals, he stopped short of explicitly promising to bypass the provincial capital.

By April 1928, the National Revolutionary Army had made their way northward close to Beijing. Unlike the three leaders of the coalition forces (Feng Yuxiang of the Second Army Group, Yan Xishan [1883–1960] of the Third Army Group, and Li Zongren [1890–1969] of the Fourth Army Group), whose troops advanced northward without going through Jinan, Chiang decided that his First Army Group would pass directly through Jinan. Fighting between the coalition forces and the northern armies near Jinan was already causing concern, so Prime Minister Tanaka responded by sending 5,000 troops to Tianjin on April 18, purportedly to protect the 2,000 Japanese nationals in Jinan rather than interfere with the civil war, claiming the troops would be withdrawn once they were no longer needed.[13] On April 25 and 27, General Fukuda Hikosuke (1875–1959) and his troops landed on Qingdao in Shandong Province and, without awaiting further instruction from the Japanese government, proceeded into Jinan.[14] Following their arrival on April 30, the Japanese troops set up barricades around the area of the city where most of the Japanese nationals resided and forbade Chinese troops from entering (map 1).[15]

On May 3, fighting broke out between Chiang's army and the Japanese troops. Conflicting reports were given as to how this clash began.[16]

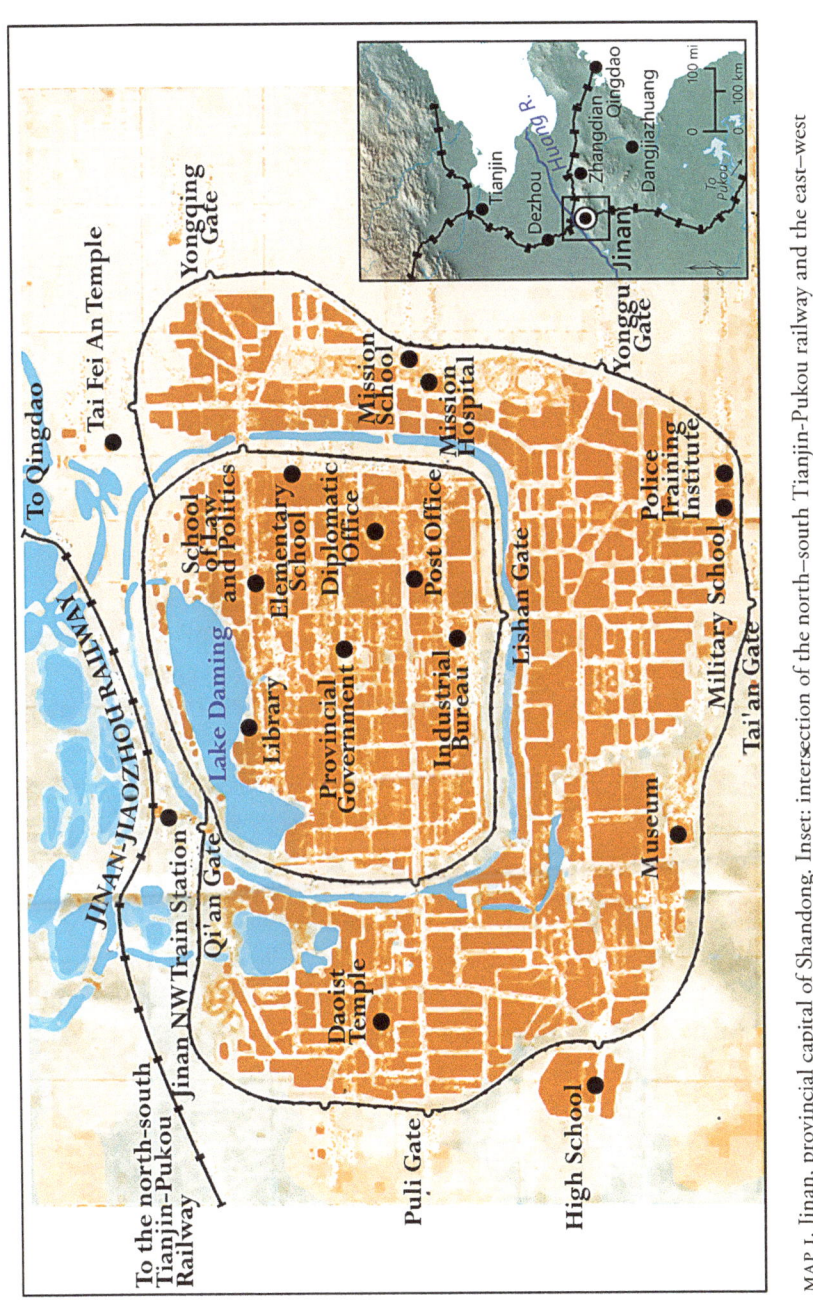

MAP I. Jinan, provincial capital of Shandong. Inset: intersection of the north–south Tianjin-Pukou railway and the east–west Jiaozhou–Jinan railway, with locations mentioned in the text. Cartographic design by Scott Walker.

FIGURE 2.1: Japanese troops after occupying Jinan. Published in the Japanese newspaper
Asahi Shimbun in Osaka, May 1928. Image source: Wikimedia Commons.

Chiang sent a group of negotiators to find a peaceful resolution, but they
were tortured and killed. On May 7, the Japanese commander presented
Chiang with an ultimatum that Chiang eventually accepted with some
revisions. By May 11, the Japanese succeeded in driving Chiang's troops
out of the city.[17] Although the National Revolutionary Army had approximately 100,000 troops in the area, far outnumbering the Japanese,
Chiang concluded that superior weaponry and probable willingness to
send reinforcements made fighting the Japanese ill-advisable.[18] Chiang
thus decided to leave Jinan and continue with the Northern Expedition. Nevertheless, the Chinese suffered casualties with over 3,000 dead,
whereas the Japanese had 230 soldiers and 16 civilians who were killed.[19]
In the end, Japan occupied Jinan for almost a year (fig. 2.1), only returning the city to the Kuomintang government under pressure from Western governments.[20] The outcome of the Jinan Incident was clearly worse
than the one in Nanjing—the latter was still in Chinese hands—yet
Chiang's response to the incident, as we shall see from the *shilüe*, forcefully connected his personal story to the collective one to legitimate his
leadership (despite his failure to secure Jinan) and reaffirm his political
agenda for China.

Deploying Humiliation

Three days into the Jinan conflict, Chiang left the city to meet with coalition leader Feng Yuxiang and his troops in Dangjiazhuang. At one point, in reference to the humiliations occurring in Jinan, he stated resolutely in front of them: "If I am able to lie on brushwood and taste gall, then there is nothing difficult about avenging this great humiliation."[21] His words, "to lie on brushwood and taste gall" (*woxin changdan*), might present an odd metaphor in translation, but they were not his own words, nor were they an obscure reference from a long-forgotten history. They were a well-known proverb that had even been written in bold black characters on the front entrance of the Whampoa Military Academy, and Chiang went on to reference it repeatedly in the days after the Jinan Incident.[22] Feng Yuxiang's troops would have easily recognized that the proverb alluded to a well-known story and that Chiang was conveying a response to the Jinan humiliation whose meaning could only be deciphered within the context of the story.

The proverb was inspired by the actions of an ancient king named Goujian (d. 465 BCE), who reigned from 496 to 465 BCE. A brief retelling of his tale follows to highlight some of the main themes that Chiang appeared to invoke in his response to the Jinan Incident.[23] One theme that emerges from the tale is that King Goujian willingly endured humiliations for the sake of his country's survival. The story thus emphasizes the details of the humiliation because they were to be construed as a character strength of Goujian's leadership rather than an embarrassment. In Zhao Ye's recounting of the story in *Wu and Yue in the Spring and Autumn Period* (*Wu Yue Chunqiu*), he notes that in 494 BCE, the country of Wu conquered the country of Yue and the king of Wu (Fuchai, d. 473 BCE) made the king of Yue (Goujian) and his wife his slaves. Wearing coarse clothing, Goujian and his wife worked diligently and without complaint for three years tending to his enemy's horses. When Fuchai fell sick one day, Goujian demonstrated his "loyalty" by telling him that he had some medicinal knowledge and could diagnose Fuchai's condition based on the flavor of his stool. After tasting it, Goujian pronounced that the king would soon be well, and when he indeed became well, Fuchai, touched by such loyalty, set the couple free.[24] The endurance of these humiliations (and thus their elaborations in the story) ultimately enabled Goujian to survive.

Despite being set free and allowed to return home, Goujian's country was still under occupation. A second theme that surfaces is that to avoid complacency about Yue's defeat, Goujian created reminders of his goal to take revenge on Wu. If he was sleepy, he would use the sharp smell of knotwood to keep his eyes open. By the Song dynasty (960–1279), the recounting of the story noted that he hung bitter gall by his bedside and tasted it every time he entered or left his room and he slept on a pallet of brushwood in a thatched hut. This version of the reminder led to the phrase that became closely associated with Goujian in the late imperial and Chinese Republican era, "to lie on brushwood and taste gall" (fig. 2.2).[25] Because Goujian performed this ritual for two decades, the phrase came to symbolize a capacity and perseverance to remember humiliation to accomplish a greater purpose.

A third theme that appears in the story is that the point of enduring humiliation is to build collective strength to avenge it. According to Zhao's account, Goujian took specific measures to strengthen Yue, including exempting farmers from taxes for seven years, recruiting scholars and people of talent to serve him, and instituting policies to grow the population, such as rewarding parents for the birth of each child. Through these steps, King Goujian "pooled together and trained for two decades" (*shinian shengju, shinian jiaoxun*) the people of Yue—words that also became another well-known and inspirational phrase. After many years of strengthening the country of Yue and undermining the country of Wu, Goujian finally dared to wage war against the king of Wu, emerging victoriously nine years later.[26]

A fourth and final theme that emerges is that King Goujian's personal story coincided with his country's collective story. To achieve personal and collective salvation, it was imperative for Goujian to lead his country to take revenge on Wu because his individual and the country's collective humiliation were the same.[27] Another recitation of the story by an anonymous author in the Southern Song period (1227–79) further reinforces this necessity to avenge humiliation by the idea of "returning (*bao*) what someone had done [to one's sense of honor]."[28] If one is shown kindness, one must return that kindness; if one is shown hatred, one must return that hatred. In essence, this interpretation argues that Gou-

FIGURE 2.2: A drawing of King Goujian "lying on brushwood and tasting gall." Image source: Zhao Longzhi, *Goujian*.

jian's particular response was not only to be admired for its own sake but a necessary and the only honorable response.

The Chinese public in the Republican era was familiar with the Goujian story. Indeed, the phrase "to lie on brushwood and taste gall" was already a popular allusion to China's humiliation by foreign powers ever since the Opium War. Not only was the phrase prominently displayed at the Whampoa Military Academy, it was also pictorialized by the Nanbao Tobacco Company to advertise their Golden Dragon cigarettes in 1925 and 1926.[29] Chiang's call to withstand this humiliation in the midst of the Jinan humiliation undoubtedly took on heightened significance for his various audiences and bolstered his legitimacy as a leader. But just as the story is much more complicated than the themes drawn from it, Chiang's deployment of *chi* with signifiers from the Goujian tale had to be strategized, adapted, and modified to work in a very different set of circumstances and goals.

Recording the Humiliations of the Jinan Incident

For audiences to appreciate the humiliation of the Jinan Incident, the magnitude of the disgrace had to be conveyed. Just as the Goujian narrative detailed the stunning defeat of Yue and the king's humiliating servitude to the enemy ruler, Chiang and his secretaries systematically painted a picture of wrongdoings and abuses by the Japanese that Chiang, his subordinates, and his troops had to withstand. At the same time, they had to use this cultural resource with political nuance to advance a storyline that portrayed Chiang as a strong and loyal leader to the Chinese people.

In helping Chiang construct the narrative of the Jinan Incident for posterity, secretary Wang included a report in the *shilüe* to establish that by stationing its troops in the provincial capital, Japan was clearly in the wrong. According to a treaty agreement at the Washington Naval Conference (1922), Japan had returned the Jiaozhou-Jinan railway to China, for which China had paid Japan in government bonds. Thus, Japan had no basis to send troops to Jinan on this railway.[30] Moreover, the commercial port in Jinan was not a foreign concession, and therefore the conditions of the treaty port agreements for places like Shanghai and Hankou were inapplicable.[31] In addition, Wang noted that not only were the Nanjing and Beijing governments and Chinese students in Japan protesting Tanaka's decision, even the Japanese opposition parties responded to Prime Minister Tanaka's decision to send troops with a vote of no confidence.[32]

A new aspect about the recording of the Jinan Incident, as compared with the telling of the Goujian story, was that Wang added excerpts from Chiang's diary, revealing the leader's personal response to the unfolding events. On May 1, 1928, for instance, as Chiang was on a train heading into Jinan, he described having tossed and turned as he tried to sleep and reminded himself that when "in danger, pay attention to detail. . . . Be firm in the overall goal [in reference to completing the Northern Expedition despite potential troubles he might face in Jinan]. Do not veer to the left or right."[33] By including a diary passage in which Chiang revealed his fears about a potentially volatile situation and his need for self-encouragement, Wang signaled Chiang's resolve to do what he thought was strategically best for the country and humanized him as a leader, a quality absent in the Goujian story and the veritable records for the emperors of the past.

The *shilüe* also shows that in response to Japanese actions, Chiang was modeling Goujian's ability to withstand humiliations. Upon arriving in the city the following morning, Chiang recorded his indignation on seeing the barbed wires, sandbags, and Japanese troops: "The dwarf pirates (*wokou*) [a derogatory term Chiang used for the Japanese] are displaying this kind of perverse tyranny! For the time being, I can only endure [this humiliation] and stay calm to take care of this situation. To my loyal and faithful soldiers and civilians, who are extremely angry, I can only, with a mind of great sincerity, exhort them to calm down."[34] After hearing that Japanese soldiers had killed, injured, and captured some Chinese soldiers, according to the same diary entry, Chiang responded, "If one does not bend, how can one extend? . . . Lack of forbearance in small matters will upset great plans. The sages warned against this."[35]

In case posterity should look negatively on Chiang's lack of immediate protest toward the Japanese actions, Wang included a report that when Cai Gongshi (1881–1928), the Chinese foreign affairs commissioner, had identified himself to the Japanese soldiers and directly protested their presence in Jinan, the Japanese soldiers proceeded to cut off his ears, nose, and tongue and gouge out his eyes before shooting him to death.[36] That macabre turn of events made the wisdom of Chiang's outward nonresponse evident.

As in the case of the Goujian story, the *shilüe* recounted in detail the humiliations committed by the Japanese throughout the Jinan Incident, starting with the fate of Cai Gongshi and his team of negotiators. Next, Wang included a description of the Japanese ill treatment of the Nationalist foreign affairs minister, Huang Fu (1883–1936), whom Chiang had sent to negotiate a ceasefire with Fukuda. After Huang had been forced to sit alone in a small room for an hour, a platoon leader entered and pressed him to sign a document acknowledging that the Chinese army had started that day's conflict by looting and beating up Japanese nationals. When Huang refused, a squad leader threatened him with a pistol. Even after being detained for eighteen hours, Huang refused to concede and wrote only "I have read this" on the document and was let go.[37] The details of this humiliating treatment, one might surmise, was to interpret Huang's actions as demonstrating resolve to maintain China's honor and refusal to put the Chinese side at a disadvantage.

In further cataloging the humiliation, the *shilüe* noted that in the midst of Huang's ordeal, Fukuda suggested another meeting to which Chiang agreed but asked Fukuda to send a representative to meet with him. After waiting several hours, Chiang finally received news that Fukuda instead wanted him to send a representative to Japanese military headquarters. According to an excerpted diary entry, Chiang angrily responded, "Fukuda has no sincerity. He sees me as an enemy. I refuse to send a representative over to the Japanese military headquarters and humiliate the country's national prestige (*guoti*) in the process."[38] In relaying his refusal to send a representative to the Japanese headquarters, Chiang signaled his determination to maintain China's honor. When Fukuda more reasonably suggested a neutral location, Chiang agreed and sent his general, Xiong Shihui (1893–1974).

These ceasefire negotiations nevertheless failed. Bolstered by the arrival of Japanese reinforcements in Jinan, Fukuda delivered an ultimatum on May 7 to the interim Chinese commissioner of foreign affairs, who had replaced the murdered Cai Gongshi.[39] Wang included the egregious aspects of this ultimatum, which, among other things, forbade the Chinese army from coming within twenty *li* (six miles) of the city and twenty *li* along the Jiaozhou-Jinan railway. It further stipulated that all high-level

Chinese officers involved in the Jinan disturbance be punished and that the troops responsible for the disturbance disarm in front of the Japanese army, the latter an acutely demeaning demand. If these conditions remained unfulfilled within the time limit, Fukuda implied, his army would do as it pleased.

Wang portrayed Chiang as responding to the ultimatum with reasoned calm while protecting the progress of the Northern Expedition and the honor of his soldiers. Chiang told Fukuda that if, after an investigation, he found that some of his soldiers were guilty of causing the disturbance, he would punish them, but he also requested that the Japanese do likewise. Although he agreed to make sure that Chinese soldiers abided by the twenty *li* distance from the Jiaozhou-Jinan railway and Jinan, he asked for permission simply to move troops on the railway.[40]

An important difference between the fate of Yue in the Goujian story and that of China in 1928 was that in the latter case the occupier's victory was only local to Jinan. As will be seen in the next two chapters, this difference between the ancient and modern cases had repercussions for the ways Chiang could deploy the Goujian template of success. Chiang finally commanded his troops to leave Jinan on May 10 to continue with the Northern Expedition, but he paid homage to the remnant troops by noting in a diary excerpt:

> I do not know whether my loyal and courageous officers and soldiers are dead or injured. *Wuhu* ["alas," but indicating a graver state of affairs]! Wen Wenshan's [better known as Wen Tianxiang, 1236–83] *Song of Righteousness* [*Zhengqi ge*] represents the traditional spirit of the Chinese people. Those who have presently died under the bombing of the Japanese may be nameless heroes, but they fall into the same historical category as Wen Wenshan. Since I have personally experienced this tragedy, how can I not feel the suffering of my subordinates?[41]

On May 11, the remaining officers and troops attempted to escape Jinan, only to meet Japanese troops outside the city.[42] Chiang knew that the left-behind regiments, with a combined total of about 3,000 soldiers, were no match for the Japanese, but by asking them to wait three days before abandoning the city, their heroic sacrifice would reveal Japan's ambitions to invade China to the world and posterity.[43]

Even after the Japanese occupied Jinan, Wang still included reports that emphasized continued Japanese humiliation. The Japanese, he noted, had planted their flag in the city and continued to harass the Chinese in Jinan and in neighboring areas. A few days into the occupation, near the Jinan commercial port, the Japanese looted more than ten stores. On the pretext of making a search, Japanese soldiers began ransacking the Lucky Health Cookie Corporation, and when a civil militia intercepted them, the ensuing fighting resulted in injuries and casualties. In another report, a Japanese plane had flown over Jieshougu Mountain and hurled poisonous bread out the window.[44] The Japanese destroyed farmland in Zhangdian to make an airstrip. Revealing his connection to the people in Jinan and the surrounding areas and the collective humiliation they suffered together—at least to posterity—Chiang exclaimed in a diary excerpt, "My people are innocent. Yet they already have met with a destroyed country's disaster. This humiliation must be avenged. Without avenging this humiliation, one is unable to be a person."[45]

Wang's narrative of the Jinan Incident, however, had some omissions, one of which is important to note. The secretary avoided mentioning Chiang's back-channel negotiations to offer a personal apology to the Japanese in exchange for not interfering with the Northern Expedition. Instead, he painted a picture in which the apology appeared forced on Chiang, thus suggesting certain limits on a leader's public acceptance of humiliation. In the May 15 entry of the *shilüe*, Wang reported that the Japanese chief of staff had telegraphed a new set of conditions to conclude peace that surpassed Fukuda's ultimatum and included a demand that Chiang personally apologize.[46] According to Wang, Chiang responded that "if the Japanese still require that the Chinese commander-in-chief must apologize to Japan, this humiliation, I can personally take, but the humiliation to the country, how can I forget?"[47] Presented in this way, Chiang signaled that he would not forget or forgive the injustice of the demand when China was in the right.

According to Yang Tianshi, Chiang had in fact offered to apologize. A week before the Japanese demanded an apology, Chiang had sent one of his generals to speak with Prime Minister Tanaka, who had assured the general that although Fukuda was still responsible for protecting Japanese nationals, the Japanese had no interest in protecting northern warlord Zhang Zuolin (1875–1928) or interfering with the Northern Expedition. Apparently satisfied that Tanaka intended to stay out of China's internal affairs, Chiang telegraphed Huang Fu on May 10 to relay the message that if the Japanese were willing to leave the Tianjin-Jinpu railway unobstructed, allowing the Northern Expedition troops to use it freely, Chiang would suppress the anti-Japanese movement. To show his sincerity and to enhance the friendship between the two nations, he would personally apologize to the Japanese army. He telegraphed Huang a second time, asking that Huang use his own name to relay the message.[48]

After the Japanese announced their conditions on May 15, including calling for Chiang's personal apology, Chiang fired Huang on May 20. Chiang apparently made the strategic decision to trade an apology to ensure the success of the Northern Expedition and to let his subordinate take the fall—after all, the record would show, it was Huang's idea to have Chiang personally apologize. Even though secretary Wang was the most realistic compiler of the *shilüe*, he chose to omit this political use of humiliation, perhaps because it detracted too much from the portrayal of Chiang as China's noble leader withstanding Japanese incursion. Even given that these contradictory facts found their way into our understanding of the incident via another outlet, the overall story constructed by Wang is still persuasive, as one can still make the case that even though Chiang had resorted to such underhanded tactics, his actions were in the service of the larger mission of uniting China.

Leveraging the Jinan Humiliation

Cognizant that abandoning the civilian population of Jinan could undercut Chiang's legitimacy as a leader, Wang included a diary excerpt in which Chiang justified his decision to leave the city. Upon recalling the barbed wires and sandbags, Chiang realized he needed to make concessions for the greater cause of completing the Northern Expedition.[49] To bolster this line of reasoning, Wang noted several days later that the expedition's success seemed imminent, as the previous day Chiang had received news that coalition forces had taken over the northern armies' first line of defense, Dezhou, a city along the Tianjin-Pukou railway north of the Huang River.[50] Chiang's deployment of *chi* thus deviated from the Goujian story by positing an important intermediary goal—unifying China first through the Northern Expedition was imperative to avenge the humiliation by the Japanese in Jinan. Hence, Wang's portrayal of the Jinan Incident also sought to justify Chiang's acceptance of humiliations because of this larger intermediary goal and to show how he further used *chi* to mobilize potential allies and the public to his cause.

Although the Jinan Incident ended in utter defeat for the Chinese, the narrative of the event in the *shilüe* focused on China's honorable resistance to the Japanese throughout the incident until the very survival of the Northern Expedition (and hence of the country) was at stake. In the early negotiations, for instance, the Japanese had demanded that Chinese officers and soldiers be prohibited from passing through Jinan's commercial port and from transporting soldiers on the Jiaozhou-Jinan or Tianjin-Pukou railways, but because these demands would severely hamper the progress of unification, the Chinese negotiators refused.[51] When these demands were reported to Chiang, he expressed outrage. He asked his foreign affairs minister, Huang Fu, to register a direct protest to Prime Minister Tanaka, and he sent a telegram to the Nanjing government, stating that if the Japanese continued their violent behavior, he would fight to preserve his people's spiritual strength.[52] For the time being, he declared, his troops would remain in Jinan because he refused to succumb to Japanese demands.

To further signal Chiang's willingness to stand up to the Japanese and protect China's interests, Wang noted that only after hearing that the fighting had stopped did Chiang reverse course several hours later. According to Yang Tianshi, Fukuda had agreed to a truce, stating, "Concerning yesterday's situation, it was our own subordinates who started the conflict. We [the Japanese] had misunderstood."[53] In the *shilüe*, Wang attributed this turn of events to the Japanese army hearing that Chiang had decided to fight back.[54] At the time, Chiang was unaware that at Fukuda's request, Tanaka and his Cabinet had authorized reinforcements.[55] Given the lull in fighting, according to Wang's account, Chiang ordered his troops to retreat across the river. By May 10, however, no more than half of the Chinese troops had managed to cross the Huang River when the Japanese began to attack them. Twenty-one soldiers and a platoon leader were killed.[56] At this point, the survival of the Northern

Expedition—and by extension, that of China—seemed threatened. Only at this dire moment, according to the *shilüe*, was Chiang willing to endure the most distasteful conditions of the ultimatum. Indeed, his troops would stay twenty *li* away from the Jiaozhou-Jinan railway, although he requested that armed police be allowed within Jinan and its outskirts to maintain order and ensure the safe departure of the Chinese soldiers. He ordered that all anti-Japanese propaganda be suppressed and that the soldiers in the nearby military barracks depart. Finally, Chiang requested that the Japanese return the Chinese soldiers (and their weapons) who had disarmed in front of the Japanese soldiers.[57]

The Jinan narrative Chiang sought to construct was intended to persuade various audiences (and posterity with the help of secretary Wang) that he had put forward his best efforts in accordance with correct actions despite China's comparative weakness, and thereby they could feel pride in their identity as Chinese citizens. At the time, the National Revolutionary Army felt a surge of patriotism in response to this confrontation, as did the Chinese body politic, which was moved by photographs of the gory event. By contrast, the northern Chinese army suffered a blow to their morale because of the increasing sympathy for the National Revolutionary Army in the press, which had previously referred to them simply as "southerners," and suspicions grew that the northern armies had been colluding with the Japanese. In these ways, the encounter with the Japanese, along with Chiang's strategic deployment of *chi* in response, may have sped up the completion of the Northern Expedition.[58]

Always cognizant of a fine line between enduring humiliation in the Goujian sense and plain weakness, Wang notes in the *shilüe* that the ultimate resolution of the Jinan Incident did not happen in its immediate aftermath. In fact, Chiang had begun to see the benefits of avoiding a resolution altogether. Rather than formalize his defeat, Chiang employed delaying tactics, stating in a diary excerpt, "The Japanese policy of invading China involves threatening our country, misleading the international community, and misleading their own public (on the true situation). . . . The Japanese personally think they have a good plan, but I have already seen through to their true intentions. Therefore they are unable to sign an agreement with me. I delay day by day, thereby enabling their genuine abominable actions to manifest themselves. This is currently one method to confront the Japanese."[59]

Not only did Chiang justify his acceptance of humiliation in terms of completing the Northern Expedition, but he also deployed *chi* to mobilize party leaders and potential allies to help him complete the campaign. For each audience, Chiang tried to turn the liability of abandoning Jinan into an asset by emphasizing the scope of the humiliation and the need to endure it. After learning that the Japanese had killed approximately 2,000 Chinese soldiers and civilians in Jinan, Chiang compared the incident to a much earlier one from Chinese history in a diary excerpt: "Wuhu! The humiliation and pain of the ten days in Jinan greatly surpasses *The Record of the Ten Days in Yangzhou*."[60] Although the incidents are hardly comparable—the Yangzhou reference was to Wang Xiuchu's harrowing account of Ming resisters battling Manchus in 1642, resulting in 80,000 dead—Chiang declared that the Jinan humiliation was greater.[61] Rather than feel immobilized by the news, Chiang swiftly absorbed it, correlated it in his mind to the Yangzhou Incident, and dashed off a telegram to party leaders inspired at least partly by Wang Xiuchu's account.[62]

In this telegram, which Wang included in the *shilüe,* Chiang called on the party to unite behind him, explicitly linking the Jinan debacle to the Yangzhou Incident by "describing in detail these ten days that he personally experienced," even though he had left Jinan after forty-eight hours and his troops after nine days. Although he provided none of the harrowing specifics that Wang Xiuchu had, his description of the "extreme suffering" and "poisonous ferocity" of the enemy were intended to generate feelings similar to those of the earlier account. Emphasizing his own feelings and personal sacrifices, Chiang assured the leaders that although they must feel "extreme indignation" over the incident, their feelings could not compare to his own anger from experiencing it personally. Indeed, he claimed that the harms and humiliations he had encountered since devoting himself to the revolution could not compare to his current feelings of outrage.[63]

In addition to making the Jinan humiliation palpable to Kuomintang leaders, Chiang justified the need to endure it in political terms with the following logic: "To take on the responsibility of the country, I wish to commit suicide, but because the Northern Expedition is not yet successful, the faltering wicks of the warlords will have an opportunity to re-light. For the sake of the party, country, and citizenry, I temporarily must endure not dying and continue to move forward with the Northern Expedition."[64] By connecting his enduring of the Jinan humiliation to completing the Northern Expedition, he appeared to take responsibility (i.e., he felt that he should commit suicide for having failed to avert the humiliation in Jinan) and act courageously (i.e., even though he wished to die, he would press on for the sake of the Northern Expedition).

His deployment of *chi* in this way might be analogous to that of a Chinese historian of the early Han period (202 BCE–9 CE), Sima Qian (135–86 BCE). Sima Qian suffered the punishment of castration and imprisonment for defending a military officer that had fallen out of favor with the emperor. On release, the expected course of action for a gentleman-scholar disgraced with castration was to commit suicide. Yet as Sima Qian explained in a letter, he felt it would be a greater humiliation that his writings would not be completed and known to posterity. Hence, he willingly endured the humiliation of castration and of not committing suicide to finish a monumental work of history known as *Records of the Grand Historian* (*Shiji*), which covered a 2,500-year period and became known as "a foundational text in Chinese history."[65] Analogously, Chiang's use of humiliation in his letter to party members echoed that of Sima Qian in that withstanding the great humiliation of Jinan was necessary for achieving the greater goal of Chinese unity under Kuomintang leadership.

Chiang also tailored his use of *chi* to attract potential allies to his cause. Losing no time to see how he could leverage the Jinan Incident for military advantage, on the day he abandoned the city he telegraphed a subordinate to pursue such a strategy: "The Jinan Incident has been China's largest national humiliation. There must be some generals in the Fengtian army, headed by [northern warlord] Zhang Zuolin [1875–1928], who have patriotism for their country and who have sympathies for our side. We could perhaps take this opportunity to see if some of these generals of the Fengtian army are willing to cooperate with us to rescue the country. . . . We do not wish to be 'killing each other and letting the foreigners benefit' (*yubang xiangzheng, yuren deli*)."[66] The idiom referred to a well-known story about a fight between the snipe and the clam in which both ended up captives of the fisherman. The Jinan humiliation, Chiang knew, could be an important rallying point to persuade the remaining northern armies to come under the Nationalist umbrella without shedding further blood on the battlefield.

In a miscalculation, the Japanese military assassinated Zhang Zuolin on June 4, 1928, despite the imperial power backing Zhang since 1921 as someone who could protect Japan's interests in Manchuria. Concerned that this northeastern area of China would come under Nationalist domination and that Zhang appeared no longer capable of protecting Manchuria, the Japanese army leadership decided to eliminate him. His son and successor, Zhang Xueliang, was more independent and skilled than the Japanese leaders had expected, and in December 1928, he declared his allegiance to the Kuomintang, thereby marking the successful completion of the Northern Expedition.[67] The father's assassination, coming on the heels of the Jinan humiliation and Chiang's appeal to the northern armies to unite in the face of Japan, apparently convinced the son to cooperate with the southern enemy.

In addition to reaching out to party members and potential allies, Chiang attempted to suppress and dissuade the public from protesting by appealing to the idea of enduring humiliation. When students called on the Kuomintang government to break off diplomatic ties with Japan, boycott Japanese goods, and urge Chiang to negotiate rigorously with the Japanese, Chiang instructed his troops to suppress their slogans and declarations.[68] In an excerpted telegram to the minister of internal affairs, Chiang justified his actions by saying that he wanted the public to understand that avenging the humiliation might take at least ten years, and in the meantime, the country needed to concentrate on science, organization, and statistics and on producing more steel, iron, medicine, electricity, machines, and railroads. The people, he further declared, needed to rely on the spirit of lying on brushwood and tasting gall. By doing so, he claimed, the public would begin to "'know *chi*' [*zhichi*] and to avenge humiliation."[69] By enduring the humiliation and keeping in mind the bigger picture of the need to self-strengthen, Chiang implied, the public would have better chance at restoring its honor.

Chiang even sought to indoctrinate children into his definition of humiliation. Two weeks after abandoning Jinan, Chiang telegrammed the minister of education directing him to issue new school books that emphasized national humiliations. In addition to the Jinan Incident, he wanted to include the awarding of the Liaodong Peninsula and the valuable harbor city of Port Arthur to the Japanese in the 1895 Treaty of Shimonoseki.[70] Although Japan ultimately returned the peninsula at the urging of Russia, France, and Germany, it demanded 50 million taels for the return in addition to the original indemnity of 200 million taels for having lost the first Sino-Japanese War (1894–95).[71] By pointing out the unfairness of having to pay indemnities to Japan when the land was China's to begin with, Chiang wanted the Chinese youth to make the connection between the unreasonableness of Japan's actions three decades earlier with the current situation.

Modeling Goujian

In addition to detailing the Jinan humiliation and deploying it in service of his political agenda, there was a third and more personal way Chiang employed the humiliation. After accepting the Japanese ultimatums, he noted in his diary that he found this particular humiliation hard to endure: "This is too tragic . . . if I am unable to withstand these humiliations in the short term, then I am not a rational person. In the end, I will fail to avenge humiliation. Right now I can only bear the humiliation that the common people are unable to endure."[72] Like his hero Goujian, Chiang understood the necessity of enduring before avenging humiliation and thus encouraged himself to bear the burden. The incident, as revealed in the *shilüe*, not only critically influenced the advancement of Chiang's political agenda more than has commonly been acknowledged, it also enabled him to connect his personal story to the collective one he sought to construct about China.

To become the twentieth-century analogue of Goujian, Chiang appeared to emulate Goujian's decision "to lie on brushwood and taste gall" by adopting a daily reminder and practices he believed would help him become the leader who would avenge the Jinan humiliation. A week after the start of the incident, Chiang began a new daily reminder, stating in his diary, "From this day on, I will rise out of bed at six o'clock. I will remind myself of [the Jinan] humiliation and continue to do so until the national humiliation is wiped away completely."[73] Four days later, Chiang added substance to the reminder by creating a "method to avenge humiliation" heading in his diary: "Every day, [I] will record/call to mind a method on how to destroy the dwarf pirates to avenge national humiliation. [Today's stated method is] to put right the educational system, to tighten organization, to use people of talent, these are the important methods to destroy the Japanese."[74] Although Wang tempered his language for posterity (he crossed out "destroy the dwarf pirates," and he replaced the second "destroy" with "resist"), Chiang clearly linked his personal reminder to realize a collective story of avengement.[75]

An initial task for Chiang was to maintain the avenging humiliation entry faithfully. The few exceptions of when he did forget appeared to have reinforced his commitment to the task. When he failed to make an entry on May 15 after going to bed early with a cold, he castigated himself the next day for so quickly forgetting the daily task.[76] Three years later, Chiang similarly berated himself for having been so preoccupied with a crisis in Guangdong—Wang Jingwei had set up an anti-Chiang government in the provincial capital—that he had almost forgotten the anniversary of the Jinan Incident. He wrote, "What day is today?! Is not this the day that Japan massacred our soldiers and people in Jinan? Today, Guangdong is on the brink of chaos. In putting all my efforts into thinking about this, I almost forgot the national humiliation. How can I face my father and mother and the soldiers and citizens who died a martyr's death? I am recording that I made an enormous mistake!"[77] True to his word, Chiang rarely forgot to make an entry, maintaining the avenging humiliation column faithfully for almost two decades.[78]

The avenging humiliation entry, like Goujian's daily gall and brushwood, appeared to keep Chiang's focus on the big-picture goal of freeing China from foreign influence. Eight days after surrendering Jinan to the Japanese, for instance, Chiang and his wife were landing in Zhengzhou, the provincial capital of Henan, when they heard bombs go off, shaking the city with their blasts. After learning that the Chinese side had accidentally set off the bombs, resulting in some deaths and injuries, Chiang angrily declared, "Because these various military units are disorganized, they have been careless in securing munitions, and therefore these accidents happen. If they are careless even in these matters, how can we avenge humiliation? Regarding this matter, I must rigorously put things in order."[79] Already, he was framing day-to-day events in terms of whether they contributed to or detracted from the goal of avenging the Jinan humiliation.

Entries under his avenging humiliation heading revealed that Chiang was thinking about concrete methods to confront the Japanese. For example, in one entry he reported a discussion he had with the coalition leader, Feng Yuxiang, concerning the organization of the first and ninth

armies, in which he approved Feng's ideas of siphoning off surplus soldiers to be construction workers, policemen, or railroad guards; of taking care of families whose sons were killed or injured; and of improving
the hospitals. "To do these tasks," he noted, "is ultimately to avenge humiliation."[80] He also spoke of modernizing China's educational system,
logistics, weapons, transportation, and health care, among others. Ultimately, as he wrote in his diary, "To avenge the [Jinan] humiliation, we
must rely on real strength and real strength derives from our getting
stronger."[81] Hence, whether consciously or otherwise, Chiang drew on a
second theme in the Goujian story of "ten years to grow the population,
and ten years to train the population" (*shinian shengju, shinian jiaoxun*)
to apply to modernizing China.

Moreover, Wang's selection of the diary excerpts showed that Chiang tried to cultivate in himself the qualities of a leader who was capable
of avenging humiliation. He particularly emphasized two goals—
controlling his behavior and pursuing learning—which reflected a Confucian understanding of leadership and self-cultivation.[82] Regarding his
behavior, Chiang recounted having lost his temper twice on June 15,
1928. The first occurred after seeing his bodyguards behaving improperly. He berated them terribly and then lectured them to correct their
behavior. Later, when passing through Golden Mountain Temple on
their way to Sweet Dew Temple, Chiang lost his temper when he observed
soldiers occupying the temple also behaving badly. Upon returning to
his lodgings, he reflected in his diary, "I can so easily and suddenly get
angry until I lose all composure. This is often hard for people to take.
This benefits neither others nor myself. The ancient sages said that joy,
anger, sorrow and delight should be expressed in a harmonious matter. I
am unable to do this. I warn myself."[83] Under the avenging humiliation
heading, Chiang then wrote, "Do not lose temper; do not scold people;
and, do not be discouraged. [I must] cultivate myself so that when [the
anger] is forming in my heart, I am able to transform it into something
harmonious. I should be able to do this."[84]

Often upset that he had fallen short of how a Chinese leader should
behave, Chiang drew on the neo-Confucian practice of recording his wrong
behavior and warning and encouraging himself to avoid repeating the
mistake. In fact, the frequency with which he followed this Confucian practice led his secretaries to compile a separate chronology titled *Reflections on*

Overcoming Difficulties (*Xingkeji*) to collect these entries.[85] These entries portrayed a leader who not only drew on Confucian methods but appeared similar to (and perhaps more flawed than) the ordinary Chinese, further cementing the connection between the fates of the leader's personal story and that of the body politic in the collective story.

For Chiang, avenging the humiliation of the Jinan Incident would also require continuous learning. Wang wrote in the *shilüe*,

> Because Gong [respectful term for Chiang] was occupied with urgent military matters on the Northern Expedition, and the Jinan tragedy had increased his being pressed with work, he had no free moment to read books. Nevertheless, he knew that an important method of avenging humiliation was to pursue learning. He therefore swore an oath: "From now on, I must read ten pages a day. If in the process, there is a break, then I am a person who has forgotten the hatred and who is without shame."[86]

Chiang further developed his leadership by using the Jinan Incident to commit to a reading regimen. He later shared his rather ordinary approach to reading books with army cadets: first browse the table of contents to get a general idea, finish one book before starting another, read broadly, and apply what one reads to practical matters.[87]

As a result of reading ten pages a day, Chiang read many books, and his thinking about *chi* would be influenced by these varied sources across time and geography. The books included the biography of Goujian and biographies of political leaders such as Vladimir Lenin (1870–1924), Otto von Bismarck (1815–98), and Zeng Guofan (1811–72). They included history books about the West, the French (1789–99) and Russian (1917–23) revolutions, World War I (1914–18), the transition from the Ming (1368–1644) to the Qing dynasty, and the Spring and Autumn period (771–476 BCE). Finally, they included the Bible and works by philosophers such as Guan Zhong (720–645 BCE), Sunzi (544–496 BCE), Confucius (551–479 BCE), Mencius (372–289 BCE), Zhu Xi (1130–1200), and Wang Yangming (1472–1529).[88]

Chiang often wrote insights and reflections from these books into his avenging humiliation entry. A month after abandoning Jinan, he culled several statements from Chinese classics on the importance of knowing *chi*. From the *Analects of Confucius* he transcribed, "One's behavior must display a sense of shame," and from the *Doctrine of the Mean* (*Zhongyong*) he copied, "To know shame is to be close to courage." From the *Spring and Autumn Annals*, he quoted, "One must prepare if one wishes to humiliate the common person; imagine the preparation for humiliating a country?" and observed General Wu's principle regarding shame: "if a country has a deep knowledge of shame, they can do battle, but if they have only superficial knowledge, then they only can defend."[89] These observations about shame and humiliation in relation to human and state behavior that Chiang transcribed from the classics led him to conclude that the process of avenging humiliation must begin with him. On July 17, 1928, Chiang wrote in his diary: "This word, *chi*, is the hinge upon which we will recover the country. But we must start with my behavior of knowing *chi* as the foundation." Wang added, "Therefore, [Chiang] wrote in his avenging humiliation column, 'Don't follow others. Don't give up.'"[90] By adapting a Goujian reminder, Chiang was able to reimagine what was necessary for the education of the modern Chinese leader. While still drawing from the Confucian tradition, he also drew from Western history and leaders and from Christianity. In these ways, Chiang was laying a groundwork for a Chinese story and identity that spoke of the country's modernization without dismissing its traditional cultural and political heritage as irrelevant to a new world order of nation-states.

· · ·

In responding to the Jinan Incident, Chiang adapted from the Goujian template of success in three ways: by constructing a moral and strategic framework for understanding the Jinan Incident, by leveraging the incident to persuade others to follow the direction in which he wanted to lead the nation, and by developing his leadership skills through the practice of keeping an avenging humiliation column in his diary. These various ways of using *chi* worked in tandem to build a persuasive story about China and its leader enduring humiliation with the promise of capably building strength from weakness.

The *shilüe* portrays the Jinan Incident as crucial in the development of Chiang's leadership, as the event galvanized him to subsume all of his subsequent goals, such as "exterminating the communist bandits" (*jiaofei*) and strengthening the country, under the overarching goal of "avenging

national humiliation" (*xue guochi*) by Japan and other imperialist countries. Whether this narrative, the cooperation of his compatriots, and his
embodiment of the Goujian hero could still be sustained when China's
unification proved to be a mirage is the subject of the next chapter. From
the point of view of the *shilüe*, the incident served as a potent impetus for
Chiang to accomplish a twentieth-century version of what the *Strategies of
the Warring States* (*Zhan Guo Ce*) had observed more than two millennia
earlier: "The spirit of 'returning hate' and of 'avenging humiliation' of
former kings was thus able to make a strong country of 10,000 carriages
surrender and to receive 800 years of savings and collections."[91] At the
time the documents were written from which the *shilüe* was composed,
the imminent prospect of completing the Northern Expedition appeared
to bring that possibility within reach.

CHAPTER 3

Diversifying His Uses of Chi

Domestic Disunity and Foreign Conflict

When the Japanese Kwantung Army invaded Mukden on September 18, 1931, Chiang Kai-shek gave strict orders for the Chinese soldiers not to fight back. This response was part of a policy that became known as "internal pacification before external resistance" (*xian annei, hou rangwai*), where Chiang prioritized domestic unity over military confrontation with an imperial power like Japan. Although the policy was uncannily similar to his response in the 1928 Jinan Incident—endure the humiliation for the sake of uniting China through the Northern Expedition—Chiang was inhabiting a more precarious political position in 1931. Domestic unity appeared unlikely, the Mukden incursion was considered the gravest threat to China's autonomy since the nineteenth century, and his policy toward the Japanese was wildly unpopular. Any of these factors could have undermined his leadership. Instead, as we shall see, Chiang confronted the deepening internal divisions and the attack on Chinese sovereignty by diversifying his uses of *chi* to invoke a seemingly counterintuitive alternative national path—one that shamed the Chinese population for its shortcomings, attempted to avenge humiliation from a position of weakness, and distrusted the efficacy of popular protests as a method to confront Japan—to solidify the case that he was the legitimate leader of China.

Deploying Shame

The Northern Expedition did not unify China for very long. Warlords with whom Chiang had allied to complete the expedition turned against him, and a series of civil wars ensued. One battle had the Nanjing government pitted against an alliance between northern warlords Yan Xishan and Feng Yuxiang, and some 250,000 casualties resulted over a four-month period. Chiang was saved only because the northern and southern warlords were unable to act in concert to overthrow him.[1] The Chinese communists also continued to pose a threat, and in October 1930, Chiang began the first of his annihilation campaigns to rout them out. Even the Guangdong faction in Chiang's own party challenged his leadership. In May 1931, the faction proclaimed to the world that it, and not the Nanjing government, was the legitimate center of authority in China.

Scholars have tended to emphasize humiliation in the national narrative, but there is an equally important, overlooked aspect of shame, which Chiang advanced in the narrative as a way to confront the chaotic domestic context and unite China under his leadership.[2] As alluded to in the introduction, in the Confucian hierarchical order, one deploys *chi* differently based on whether one is a superior or an inferior in a relational dyad; as leader of China, shaming is considered an appropriate method to guide the inferior (in this case, the people) toward proper behavior. Chiang thus deployed *chi* as shame to bend his subordinates, including the military, Kuomintang officials, and the public, toward realizing his political agenda of uniting China under his leadership.

Before drawing on shame, Chiang sought to define the "standard" by which to measure proper state functioning. It had never been Chiang's intention to allow the continued existence of autonomous sources of power, such as that of the warlords, many of whom had been co-opted into the revolutionary movement rather than defeated on the battlefield and who had no affinity with Kuomintang ideology.[3] Taking this context of divided sovereignty into account, Chiang appeared to argue that a proper state consisted of a centralized authority under a unified ideology. In a January 19, 1931, speech given at the Sun Yat-sen Memorial, Chiang gave an example of the "wrong" kind of criticism of the state. Referring to a newspaper article that disparaged the Kuomintang's Foreign Affairs Bureau, he declared, "Our government desires that people criticize . . . [however] if the newspapers depart from the Three People's Principles or from the concept of National Revolution, this is being counter-revolutionary."[4] In this case, Chiang might have rejected criticism of the Foreign Affairs Bureau because he distrusted various groups that were jockeying for power and he wanted to legitimate his leadership even if the original criticism was justified.

Having defined the legitimate state as one that upheld Sun Yat-sen's ideology and was consolidated under his authority, Chiang counterintuitively (from a Western perspective) shamed his various audiences for China's current disunity. In a January 12, 1931, speech to members at Nanjing's Central Military Academy (Zhongyang junxiao), Chiang noted that even though Japan had only one-tenth of China's population, its patriotism (*aihu guojia*) enabled it to become capable of invading China. By contrast, the Chinese still acted based on selfish motivations (*zisi zili*), which prevented them from becoming strong and invited insults from foreign countries.[5] In speeches like this one, Chiang highlighted the Chinese people's role in contributing to the country's disunity and, by extension, China's weakness.

Just as Chiang used humiliation by invoking the familiar and relevant ancient hero Goujian to help the Chinese public make sense of the state's weak international status, he also trod on familiar ground with his uses of shame. Chinese intellectuals before him had remarked on the shame of disunity since the Sino-Japanese War of 1895. In 1904, a member of the editorial staff of a prominent magazine, *Eastern Miscellany* (*Dongfang zazhi*), noted that when the Germans destroyed a Confucian temple in Shandong in 1897, the Chinese offered no protest. By contrast, he noted, the Japanese united in their anger over the humiliation of their "defeat" by the Russians (giving up the Liaodong Peninsula after winning it from the Chinese). Even the Koreans, the author reminded his readers, forced the Russians to retreat when they violated Korean borders, but when the Russians occupied Manchuria, China offered no resistance, treating a hostile act as if it were a friendly one.[6]

Intellectuals similarly bemoaned that vigorous protests of Japan's 1915 Twenty-One Demands to the Chinese government quickly lost steam. One had even initially warned the public to avoid the scenario where "once the situation slightly improved, people forgot their hard times."[7] Leaving no doubt that the blame for this passivity rested with the Chinese people as a whole, the editor of *Eastern Miscellany* declared, "The fact that today the powers dare to impose humiliations on us and add to our burdens with impunity is surely something we have brought upon ourselves."[8] The source of shame in these criticisms was not China's humiliation at the hands of an imperial power (for other countries experienced humiliation, too), but, as Paul Cohen notes, the *"quality* of the remembering, the persistent indifference and passivity they detected in the mood of the Chinese people."[9]

By tapping into this long-running critique, Chiang arguably could preserve the integrity of his leadership by deflecting the blame for his inability to unify the country after the Northern Expedition onto the collective. Expanding on this critique in a speech he gave in Nanchang, Chiang complained that even his party lacked respect for the country's flag since members at headquarters left it flying at all times and ignored protocols for raising or lowering it. Such neglect, he claimed, invited foreigners to "chuckle and sneer" when they saw the flag still flying in the evening.[10] By offering a shameful example of even the Kuomintang headquarters' neglect of the country's quintessential national symbol, Chiang urged all Chinese to respect the flag and see themselves as a nation under Kuomintang rule.

In other speeches in the *shilüe*, Chiang exhorted the Chinese people to treasure their culture and history. Pointing to Korea as a worst-case scenario, he noted that since their annexation to Japan in 1910, Koreans had been forced to learn Japanese language and history and dramatically claimed that as a result, Korean culture no longer existed. Drawing on a Confucian classic, *The Great Learning* (*Daxue*), he clarified that he was exhorting the Chinese not to reject everything foreign but to revere their culture and history before venturing outward to learn from foreigners.[11] If the Chinese believed that everything foreign was good to the neglect of their own heritage, he argued, they might as well subjugate themselves to foreigners.[12] Chiang also recommended books that he thought captured Chinese culture by including not only classics like *The Great Learning* but also works by Sun Yat-sen and Dai Jitao—the latter had elaborated on Sun's ideas in a more conservative direction.[13]

Chiang also spoke of the disgrace of the Chinese people in failing to comport themselves as modern citizens. In this case, he appeared to deploy shame to encourage various subordinates to perform their roles well, as befitting a modern Chinese state. In an exhortative speech to the military police on April 26, 1931, for instance, Chiang urged them to be "models of the nation" and "teachers to the ordinary citizen."[14] The military police needed to respond to the public's current disdain of them by respecting themselves and ending corrupt or lazy behavior so as to gain the respect of their fellow citizens, who were always observing their actions.[15]

Chiang even shamed children. In a speech to elementary school students in his hometown of Xikou, he chided the children for their bad habits of yelling and hitting. By avoiding such habits and conducting oneself properly by listening to teachers and parents and doing their part to keep the environment clean, he told them, they could accomplish the important task of making China strong and independent and forcing "foreigners to respect and admire us and no longer humiliate us."[16] Such attention to proper behavior and dress, Chiang declared, was even more important than book learning.[17]

Whether intentional or otherwise, Chiang addressed only behaviors and outward appearances during this period and thereby glossed over the fact that China's infrastructure and resources for educating and training its citizens lagged far behind those of the imperialist countries. Perhaps because 1931 was ill-suited for implementing Goujian's "ten years to grow the population, and ten years to train the population," Chiang emphasized this more superficial method as a way to establish unity first under his control. The following example particularly captures his characteristic response to situations that might be attributed to this resource gap between China and the imperial powers. On July 27, Chiang was sleeping on a boat that departed Zhangshu at four in the morning, only to travel for about an hour before hitting shallow water. Chiang later erupted about this event in his diary: "Yesterday, the rower made no mention that the water would be shallow and that it would be difficult to row. Therefore, today, in the middle, we must stop. My plans are ruined through mismanagement. . . . Chinese people cannot be trusted. They often are despised and insulted by foreigners because of incidents like this. Today, [the rower] even treats me like this. How must he treat others? I must let my people wake up and get rid of bad roots such as this!"[18] Although this mishap might have been avoided with better equipment or intelligence about river conditions and contingency plans,

Chiang concluded that the rower was untrustworthy, possibly because he had no time to address the root causes of the mismanagement.

As indicated in the *shilüe* for 1931, Chiang's imprint on the national story focused on how China was bringing shame on itself instead of on concrete steps toward true self-recovery via the Goujian model. As such, Chiang may have aimed to reflect a pragmatic understanding of what was possible, deflect the blame of China's failures away from his leadership, and ultimately presented himself as a virtuous and concerned (if also frustrated) legitimate leader of China, motivating his people to become proper citizens of a unified state.

Whither Enduring Humiliation? Resisting from a Position of Weakness

Although he continued to deploy *chi* as humiliation during the three-year interlude between the 1928 Jinan and 1931 Mukden Incidents, Chiang appeared to depart completely from his original Goujian template that would make avenging humiliation possible. In the wake of the Northern Expedition's failure, Chiang abandoned the "lying on brushwood and tasting gall" part of the template and instead actively resisted imperial incursion onto Chinese sovereignty. In the face of continued domestic disunity, Chiang was also unable to realize the second part of the template of "ten years to grow the population, and ten years to train the population." Because China was neither fully conquered (like Yue) nor was Chiang the undisputed leader (like Goujian), he clearly had to improvise on the Goujian template to pursue and legitimate his political agenda.

Turning the Goujian template on its head in the aftermath of the Northern Expedition, Chiang sought to avenge humiliation from a position of weakness by wresting Chinese autonomy from imperial control. In a January 5, 1931, speech at the party headquarters in Nanjing, he asserted that a priority for that year was to abolish the unequal treaties.[19] Through his Foreign Minister C. T. Wang (Wang Zhengting, 1882–1961), Chiang had already begun an aggressive "revolutionary diplomacy" as a way to distinguish the Nanjing Kuomintang authority as the true head of the state. In 1930, at Chiang's prompting, Wang began pressing imperial countries to give up their extraterritorial rights. By January 15, 1931, Belgium gave up its concession in Tianjin, and by April 23, Norway and the Netherlands also conceded.[20] In addition to revolutionary diplomacy, in June 1931 Chiang slapped new import tariffs that specifically discriminated against Japanese economic interests in Manchuria.[21] No longer would Chiang tolerate unfair imperial privileges in China in his quest to unify and strengthen the country.

But revolutionary diplomacy and aggressive tariffs negatively affected the Sino-Japanese relationship as Japan's interest in Manchuria cannot be overstated. As a latecomer to the imperial game, Japan had acquired Liaodong Peninsula (the southeastern section of Manchuria) from China after its victory in the Sino-Japanese War in 1895, but the three powers (Russia, Germany, and France) intervened to demand that Japan "return" the peninsula, a humiliating loss to Japan. Rubbing salt into the wound, the Chinese granted the Russians a railway concession through Manchuria the following year—the Trans-Siberian Railway—in exchange for protecting them from the Japanese. After emerging victoriously in the Russo-Japanese War in 1905, Japan acquired Russia's long-term leases on the Liaodong Peninsula and the expensive railway concessions and finally felt that it was given its due.[22] Decades later, the Great Depression cemented Manchuria's importance in Japanese eyes as US demand for Japanese silk instantly dried up, devastating the Japanese economy.[23] By 1931 Manchuria was indisputably Japan's "jewel in the crown": "Manchuria," according to David Gordon, "became so important that many economic and military planners linked its preservation to the survival of Japan itself."[24]

Hence, the Japanese, especially the military, were alarmed when the Nanjing government declared in May 1931 that all negotiations over extraterritoriality would be terminated and that the regulations of foreign nationals in China would go into effect on January 1, 1932.[25] Clearly the idea of giving up its sphere of influence in Manchuria, including its rights to operate the South Manchurian Railway, did not sit well with the Japanese.[26] Although Chiang was distinguishing his government from rival ones, he also contributed to the deterioration of Sino-Japanese relations in the first half of 1931.

Japanese army leaders responded to Nanjing's May pronouncements by concluding that force was needed to protect Japan's interests in Manchuria. To avoid interference from Western powers, they decided to simulate a Chinese attack on the South Manchurian Railway so that their use of force would appear to be a "defensive act" under the League of Nations definition. Although the General Staff in Tokyo thought that spring 1932 was a practical time to strike, those within the Japanese Kwantung Army pushed for an earlier date, believing that the disunity in China offered the best opportunity.[27] Only an appropriate excuse needed to be found. With many low-level squabbles occurring in China between the Chinese and Japanese, one was bound to become that excuse.

WANBAOSHAN AND KOREAN INCIDENTS

A low-level row came quickly in the form of a clash between farmers in Wanbaoshan, a village in Manchuria just outside the provincial capital of Jilin and about 300 miles from the Korean border. There were Koreans living in Wanbaoshan, as they had remained in this area even after the Manchus tried to drive them out in the seventeenth century. Moreover, after Japan annexed Korea in 1910, these Koreans often came to represent "a displaced expression of Sino-Japanese competition."[28] A further strained dynamic existed between Chinese and Korean farmers. Because the latter worked for less, Chinese landlords preferred hiring them over Chinese farmers.[29] With this background in mind, in April 1931, a Chinese villager leased a plot of land to nine Koreans without authorization from the county magistrate.

According to a detailed report Wang included in the *shilüe*, a conflict arose when these Koreans needed water to irrigate their land and therefore proceeded to build a dam in the Yitong River and dig a thirteen-foot-wide channel across the land of forty Chinese farmers. The affected Chinese farmers appealed to the local authorities to no avail. Meanwhile, under the protection of the Japanese consular police, the Koreans continued shoveling and completed the canal and dam by the end of June (fig. 3.1).[30]

On July 1, between 300 and 400 angry Chinese farmers began tearing down the dam and pushing the embankment back into the channel. When the Chinese farmers showed up to continue their work the next

FIGURE 3.1: The narrow channel dug by Koreans in Wanbaoshan. "History of the Founding of Manchukuo and the Shanghai Incident," *Richu xinwen she*, May 1932. Image source: Wikipedia Commons.

morning, Japanese soldiers and the Chinese police were on the scene. Some injuries occurred on both sides, but there were no casualties and the farmers abandoned their efforts.[31] After reading the report, Chiang acknowledged the mistakes made on the Chinese side by saying, "Unfortunately, when people do things, they forget procedures, making it easy for others to take advantage."[32]

The Wanbaoshan Incident likely would have been relegated to the hundreds of other nameless disputes between China and Japan. However, because of Chiang's revolutionary diplomacy and Japanese military leaders' response to it, propagandists in the Japanese Kwantung Army and sympathizers in Japan's Korean Army seized on this incident to provide exaggerated accounts in the Korean press of Koreans being brutalized by the Chinese.[33] According to a report included by Wang, on July 3 news stories in the Korean press falsely alleged that Chinese farmers had killed 200 Koreans in Wanbaoshan, a number that later rose to

800.[34] In reaction to these sensationalized reports, the Koreans began attacking Chinese merchants and residents in Korea, which resulted in 119 Chinese deaths, 370 injured, 82 missing persons, and Chinese property losses of more than 3 million yen.[35]

Just like the Jinan Incident, the Korean Incident was brimming with potential to paint the Japanese as morally wrong. Secretary Wang made sure to highlight these instances in the *shilüe* by including reports blaming Japanese inaction for the harm done toward the Chinese, as when the Japanese police only half-heartedly attempted to stop the Koreans who attacked the Chinese in Seoul. On July 5, Wang noted that Chiang had also read that Koreans had attacked the Chinese in Pyongyang, and because the Japanese police had delayed intervening, more than thirty Chinese people were killed. Moreover, even though the Japanese police had captured more than 100 Koreans, more than 5,000 Koreans continued attacking the Chinese for several more hours.[36] Chiang reacted to the Korean Incident by calling the Japanese "barbarous" and "despicable" and accusing them of using methods that were "violent and crafty."[37] For the Japanese to say that they were unable to control the Koreans making retaliatory attacks on Chinese was hard to believe because usually they were quite effective in "nip[ping] in the bud" any signs of rebellion in Korea.[38] Even though it had been Koreans who lashed out against the Chinese, Chiang expressed some sympathy for them, believing the Japanese had duped them.[39]

Yet these developments did not convince Chiang to begin enduring humiliation again. Instead, when the Chinese in Shanghai organized a boycott against Japan, Chiang remained publicly silent about it. Strategically, he was signaling to the Japanese that the riots were out of his government's control, but he was tacitly supporting the riot for the domestic audience. The Guangdong faction of the Kuomintang rightly accused him of taking advantage of the Korean Incident to centralize power and entrench himself more firmly as China's leader. Although the Guangdong faction suppressed local riots as a way to gain rapprochement with the Japanese, when one of its leaders, Eugene Chen, attempted to meet the Japanese with a message of goodwill, the Japanese received him as an unofficial visitor, not as a foreign minister representing China.[40] Despite China's domestic disarray in 1931, Chiang's Nanjing government appeared more legitimate in international eyes.

Continuing in the spirit of revolutionary diplomacy, Chiang's government eschewed responsibility regarding the Wanbaoshan and Korean Incidents. When the Japanese ambassador to Mukden demanded that the Chinese government guarantee the lives and property of the Koreans in Wanbaoshan, compensate them with one year's salary, give them the right of residence in Jilin, and allow them to cultivate rice, Chinese Foreign Minister C. T. Wang refused, insisting that the Japanese consular police and Korean farmers leave Wanbaoshan.[41]

The Chinese side also made demands. On July 7, the Chinese Foreign Ministry protested against the Japanese government for failing to control the Koreans. It entreated the Japanese government to adopt precautions against future anti-Chinese riots and reserved the right to demand full compensation for losses sustained by Chinese victims. The Japanese countered by denying responsibility for the Korean Incident, leading the Chinese side to launch a second protest by asking for international arbitration.[42] The Japanese responded on August 12 by reiterating that the Wanbaoshan Incident was responsible for the Korean Incident and refused to participate in outside arbitration. The Chinese launched a third protest along similar lines, but to no avail. In these interactions, the Chinese government was clearly conducting itself as an equal to imperial Japan.

The problem, however, with pursuing a more aggressive policy with the Japanese from a position of weakness was that Japan might force a military solution. With no forthcoming resolution, Chiang (and the *shilüe*) began building a case that the Japanese were planning to invade China. Upon hearing that Japan had refused international arbitration on August 12, Chiang claimed, "These strong words are irrational. [The Japanese] badly want face. We can see their desire to expand. . . . I only worry that there is too little hope for peace in East Asia."[43] After reading another report about the Wanbaoshan and Korean Incidents on August 16, Chiang was even more convinced that Japan's desire to expand their influence in Manchuria included a military solution: "On the one hand, [the Japanese] negotiate; on the other hand, they attack abruptly to cover their ambitions to invade. Regarding their cheating and cruel method, humankind has never seen this kind of ugly technique before. When their objective is reached, they pretend to retreat. But step-by-step they are spiraling toward invasion."[44]

NAKAMURA INCIDENT

The *shilüe* included a third incident, apparently to provide additional evidence of Japanese designs to invade northeastern China. In June 1931, the General Staff Office in Tokyo sent Captain Nakamura Shintaro on a reconnaissance and map-making mission, with orders to travel incognito through Manchuria accompanied by a Japanese guide and former cavalry sergeant-major, Isugi Entaro, and two assistants, one Mongolian and one Russian.[45] In late June, Chinese soldiers killed the four men on the reasonable assumption that they were spies.[46] Although the precise details of what followed are unclear, what was not in dispute was that the Chinese soldiers killed the captives and burned their bodies, their horses, and their possessions, with the exception of two notebooks and two military maps.[47] When the Japanese inquired about the killings, the Chinese were uncooperative. After a two-week investigation, the Chinese vaguely reported that some Mongolians had heard of an injury, but the Mongolians provided no concrete proof. The story about the Mongolians attacking the men was doubtful given their strong animosity toward the Chinese in the area. The Chinese provincial officials were probably guilty of the Japanese accusations of insincerity and procrastination, given their dismissive attitude toward resolving the incident.[48]

When the Japanese government made the incident public on August 17, the Japanese media seized on the news as yet another outrageous provocation by the Chinese. Chiang, observing that the Japanese had made the Nakamura Incident into an even larger media spectacle than the Wanbaoshan Incident, concluded that "Every day is closer to invasion."[49] On September 4, he noted that a Japanese political faction had hardened their stance; on September 7, he claimed that Japanese military leaders were vigorously supporting a forceful solution in Manchuria. To substantiate Chiang's thoughts, the *shilüe* included a report that the Japanese army and navy were already conducting war games in Korea.[50]

On September 13, Chiang received a report that the Japanese consul in Mukden had made a formal request to the head of Liaoning Province, Zang Shiyi (1884–1956), that the government in Manchuria apologize, severely punish those involved in killing the "mapmakers," provide compensation for the lives and property of those harmed, and guarantee that a similar incident would not happen again. After reading this, Chiang responded angrily, "The Japanese people desire to take over Northeast China, and their clever method is like this. Who are they cheating? They are cheating heaven. I hate what is currently happening in China. Wuhu! Is it that heaven wants our country to be destroyed?"[51] Because a military incursion seemed credibly imminent, the Manchurian governor, Zhang Xueliang, signaled a change in attitude regarding the investigations. On September 18, Chinese governmental officials finally confessed to killing Nakamura and his team.

The events of the summer, as reflected in the *shilüe*, indicated that Chiang (and all levels of government for that matter) was not enduring humiliation but resisting foreign privileges. By avoiding responsibility for any wrongdoing in the various incidents and refusing to cooperate with the Japanese to resolve these issues, Chiang reflected a leadership and country that was standing up to Japan. It also lent credibility to Chiang's government as the default government when dealing with international relations and further delegitimated his rivals, whether they were other warlord leaders, factional leaders within the party, or Chinese communist leaders. Moreover, the *shilüe* diligently highlighted Japanese inaction toward the killings of Chinese people in Korea and the audacity of sending a spy to map Manchuria to reinforce the national narrative that China was confronting an untrustworthy imperial power with designs on wresting Manchuria away. A trade-off for Chiang's strategy in resisting from a position of weakness, however, was that the imperial powers might attempt to "teach" China a lesson, and, as the "default" leader of a weak state, Chiang would be blamed for any additional humiliations.

The Mukden Incident and Chiang's Politics of Selectively Enduring Humiliation

On September 18, 1931, the Kwantung Army set off a bomb on its own South Manchurian Railway tracks near Mukden (map 2). The damage was so minor that twenty minutes later, an express train passed over the tracks without incident.[52] Nevertheless, the Kwantung Army alleged that Chinese soldiers had attacked them and proceeded to occupy a dozen Manchurian

MAP 2. Mukden Incident, Manchuria, along with locations for the Wanbaoshan and Korean Incidents. Cartographic design by Scott Walker.

cities throughout the night. Because Zhang Xueliang, with Chiang's support, had ordered the Chinese soldiers to withhold fire, the Japanese military easily established all of Manchuria under a puppet government within weeks. Military nonresistance was the Chinese response across Manchuria, with the exception of one local general who resisted but failed.[53]

Outrage concerning Chinese inaction was initially directed toward Zhang, but the public eventually shifted its anger toward the Nanjing government as the scope and permanence of the incursion became clear.[54] In the *shilüe*, Wang included a report of students attacking the Foreign Ministry building in Nanjing as early as September 26 and more students arriving from Shanghai in uninterrupted succession.[55] Indeed, in Shanghai, all sectors of the population from labor unions to university associations and even the Christian salvation societies submitted circulars and telegrams (totaling 543) demanding that the government take action before the end of the year. One member of the Kuomintang even asserted that an "overwhelming majority" of the population disliked this policy of nonresistance.[56]

It appeared Chiang had painted himself into a corner with his policy of "internal pacification, then external resistance." The more the Japanese pressed forward, the stronger the public's anti-Japanese sentiments. Chiang's strategy was becoming increasingly incompatible—instead of fostering unity, which fighting Japan would have spurred, he seemed to encourage the opposite by focusing on routing out domestic rivals.[57] He appeared to "alienat[e] the flower and hope of Chinese nationalism" and to widen the chasm between the government and people.[58] Although Chiang could have wielded nationalism as a mobilizing, energizing force to connect the people with the Nanjing government, his policy, according to Parks Coble, killed this possibility by preventing him from attracting the talent of these student demonstrators, salvationist supporters, and the politically active members of the public into his administration.[59]

But Chiang did in fact harness nationalism. The Mukden Incident complicated matters but did not convince him to alter his approach since the Jinan Incident of prioritizing domestic unity under his leadership: "The dwarf pirates," he noted in his diary, "have had plans for invading the eastern provinces [Manchuria]. Unfortunately, the invasion is now a fact. At the moment, I feel there is no way to emerge victoriously from this predicament. However, if from now on our country is unified, we will have the opportunity to turn this disaster into fortune."[60] As in the Jinan case, Chiang invoked a nationalism that was specifically adapted from Goujian—writing in his diary that he would endure the Mukden humiliation by "lying on brushwood and tasting gall."[61]

The expression of this kind of nationalism (unlike in the form of protests) is less visible but no less significant. By connecting the attack to the Jinan Incident, which he had personally experienced, Chiang signaled that he was deeply affected by the events in Mukden: "Since the May 3, 1928, massacre," Wang wrote, based on Chiang's diaries, "Gong has written in his avenging humiliation column daily, swearing to eradicate this humiliation. And now, the September 18 humiliation has added such an insufferable pain to his heart that [he] is unable to write about it."[62] Wang further included a diary excerpt from September 22 in which Chiang remarked, "My suffering has never been as terrible as today."[63] In the ensuing weeks and months, Chiang continued to convey his emotional response to the event in words and actions.

In revealing his internal anxiety over the Mukden Incident, even if it was just toward his close associates and to posterity, Chiang presented an alternative to the suggestion that his policy of nonresistance reflected a leader unconcerned about ceding territory and interested only in gaining power. He candidly admitted his anxiety but signaled his willingness to take on the responsibilities of the country. Three days after the Mukden Incident, after suffering a bout of insomnia, he encouraged himself by saying, "for the sake of avenging national humiliation, there is no other who can help me carry heaven's duty."[64] After another sleepless night six days later, he reiterated the sentiment: "the danger and urgency of the situation has never surpassed this day, and the responsibility of the difficulties and dangers posed by the Japanese is something that only I can take on."[65] In voicing his fears and a desire not to give into them, Chiang reflected his conviction that he was the "right" leader for China despite the deepening chaos surrounding him.

Given his choice to endure the Mukden humiliation, Chiang sought to portray an outwardly calm demeanor rather than protest and lash out in anger as an expression of "appropriate" nationalism. Although he was not entirely successful, ironically, it was in moments of losing his composure that he appeared to bolster his legitimacy as a leader. An incident occurred on September 22 that Wang felt was worth recording in the *shilüe*. At a Kuomintang conference, Chiang noted that if international arbitration were to fail and there were no more peaceful solutions to pursue, his government would go to war to protect the country's character. He declared, "I, Zhongzheng, devote my life to the revolution. . . . During this difficult time of the country's survival or death, naturally I will live or die with the country."[66] After he said "live or die," an audience member blurted out that Chiang was exaggerating and promising more than he could deliver. In response, Chiang reprimanded the audience member by saying, "Has our country's essence already died? If this is true, then [we] will be quickly destroyed!"[67] Chiang then knocked over his tea cup by accident and began sobbing until he could make no sound.

After recovering his composure, he reminded the audience of his credentials in Jinan: "I have been under artillery attack by the Japanese more than once. The dwarf pirates used cannons and planes in Jinan, but I managed to survive . . . I swear I will live or die with the country!"[68] At this point, Wang noted in the *shilüe* that audience members expressed their disapproval toward the critic in the audience and their sympathies toward Chiang.[69] In momentarily exhibiting strong emotions in words and demeanor, he conveyed that he felt the same pain of the humiliations that his compatriots did and reminded them that he had personally experienced Japan's attacks before. In doing so, Chiang wielded *chi* as a political tool by showing that he was a sincere nationalist and, by extension, a credible leader of the nation.

By choosing to endure the humiliation, Chiang also critiqued the national response that promoted mobilization and protest. Wang noted that when Chiang heard that students were protesting the Mukden invasion in Nanjing and Shanghai on September 28, he sighed and wrote in his diary that although his main objective was to resist Japan and save the country, this kind of idle and violent protest would do the country no good and was probably politically instigated by the Guangdong faction of the Kuomintang.[70] He further remarked on his disappointment: "the courage and resolve of my country's people have long been lost, relying only upon a moment's excitement and unable to stick to a long-term resolve. This gives no benefits to the country. In addition, it further hastens the country's destruction."[71] Having met with some of the student protesters on December 14, he noted, "There are quite a few students who are reasonable, but there are a few rotten apples, like the rotten horse who harms the whole herd. If we don't get rid of them, then everything will be indiscriminately destroyed, and as [they are] the foundation of the country, this hurts me."[72] From Chiang's perspective, although the people's protests reflected a momentary awakening from their usual passivity, he believed they were likely to relapse into it rather than use their anger to unite in their resolve to endure and ultimately prevail.

Like his uses of shame, Chiang defined humiliation according to his goal of consolidating state sovereignty under his rule. When the Chinese public diverged from the path he was setting for them, he appeared to think of them as ignorant children, unable to see the "correctness" of his envisioned goals. In his view, the people were also supposed to endure the Mukden humiliation to unite under his leadership. Given the sharp disagreement toward Chiang's policy by a swath of the Chinese population and even members in his own party, Chiang drew on *chi* to adhere to his unpopular path.[73] To fulfill his duties as a filial son and a loyal disciple to Sun Yat-sen, he needed to honor his betters by remaining steadfast to his policy of nonmilitary resistance and (as we shall see) international arbitration even if it drew ire from all quarters: "Today, I am pressed close to a dangerous environment. In case of something unpredictable, when I see the danger, I will accept responsibility. In the end, I refuse to be a child that shames his mother and father and a disciple [that shames] Sun Yat-sen."[74]

JAPAN, THE INTERNATIONAL COMMUNITY, AND THE POLITICS OF NONRESISTANCE

Even though Chiang suddenly reverted to enduring the humiliation after the Mukden military incursion, he nevertheless pursued tactics of nondirect negotiations and noncooperation, which he had honed from the summer events of the Wanbaoshan and Korean Incidents and the Nakamura spy incident. Although some have his policy of "internal pacification then external resistance" as simply meaning nonresistance at all costs, in fact, he was only selectively enduring.[75] In outlining Chiang's thinking in the *shilüe*, Wang reflected the nuances with which Chiang wielded humiliation to justify his actions. As a result, a more complete picture of his leadership can be gained that, like his more quiet expression of nationalism, again stressed alternative methods of standing up to an imperial power from a position of weakness.

In a diary excerpt from September 21, Chiang laid out his rationale for avoiding direct dealings with the Japanese: they "will not retreat willingly. I know that Japan has designs on our Manchuria in their hearts. They are willing to let their own three islands be destroyed, but they still will not leave Manchuria automatically."[76] Hence, when Zhang Xueliang lobbied for a speedy resolution to the Manchurian crisis, Chiang explained his reasoning for giving the problem to the League of Nations: "The international situation still offers public justice. The position of Manchuria should be dealt with in its entirety. [We] should not negotiate independently and sign treaties randomly where we lose land and humiliate the country."[77] By avoiding direct negotiations that might result in formal economic or territorial concessions, Chiang apparently hoped to postpone a certain victory for Japan and preserve China's honor and his own legitimacy. If the arbitration failed, he vowed to "go ahead and fight the Japanese. Even if we lose, we still have honor."[78]

Chiang was nonetheless taking a risk because he had no assurances of achieving a favorable outcome through international arbitration. Foreigners, including diplomats, generally agreed that in 1931, China was no innocent victim because the so-called 300 pending issues, including the Wanbaoshan and Nakamura Incidents, could be interpreted as China actively checking Japanese interest in Manchuria. They initially condoned Japanese behavior, feeling that Japan was teaching China a "necessary lesson."[79] On the other hand, although the Japanese Kwantung officers had calculated correctly that they did not have to fear European military intervention in Sino-Japanese affairs in 1931, they had not calculated on other forms of international interference.[80]

The League of Nations adopted a resolution on September 30 to take some interim measures to prevent the situation from growing out of hand in the aftermath of the events at Mukden.[81] Despite the fact that Japan ignored the League's request to leave Manchuria on October 25, Chiang reacted favorably to the resolution, noting in a diary excerpt that at least "public justice and correct reason have been made manifest."[82] On December 10, the League adopted a second resolution to form the Lytton Commission, headed by Victor Bulwer-Lytton (1876–1947) of the United Kingdom, to investigate the incident and come to a final determination

FIGURE 3.2: The Lytton Commission inspects a section of the South Manchurian Railway that was bombed on September 18, 1931, to investigate the causes of the Mukden Incident. Image source: Chronicle of World History/Alamy Stock Photo.

(fig. 3.2).[83] A year later, the commission concluded that both sides were to blame—the Chinese for their anti-Japanese propaganda and uncompromising attitude, and the Japanese for being the aggressor.[84]

Whereas the Japanese summarily rejected the report, left the League of Nations in protest, and found themselves with few international supporters, the Chinese approved the report and found themselves in international favor.[85] The impressions that respective representatives of each side imparted to the commission had mattered. According to Lord Lytton, writing to his wife in Shanghai, "The Chinese are so articulate—they talk beautiful English and French and can express themselves clearly. With the Japanese it was a surgical operation to extract each word."[86] Moreover, the difference in international perceptions of the two countries, according to Ian Nish, was due not to a tremendous expenditure in propaganda but to the international community's increasing sympathy toward the Chinese case; after all, China was the one being invaded.[87] At least in the eyes of the international community, Chiang's choice to offer no military resistance in the form of "enduring humiliation" helped establish China's "innocence."

Although the outcome appeared to work in China's favor, the *shilüe* reflected that Chiang had expressed doubts about pursuing international arbitration in the first place. Only a week after the Mukden Incident, Chiang in fact noted in a diary excerpt, "If I cannot self-strengthen, and rely completely on foreign power, how can this be helpful? I am scared of this. I am scared of this."[88] He returned to this theme on November 5: "People must help themselves, and then later, others will help. Today, my people do not yet know how to help themselves. This is regretful."[89]

While Chiang was "resisting" humiliation outside of military conflict, he nevertheless chose to endure it when further military skirmishes occurred. When the Kwantung Army clashed with China's Nineteenth Route Army over a scuffle that originated between Chinese workers and Japanese monks in a Shanghai factory, Chiang and Wang Jingwei negotiated with the Japanese to conclude the Shanghai Truce (May 5, 1932), which stopped the fighting in Shanghai but left the Manchurian question untouched.[90] The truce, however, did not prevent the Kwantung Army from encouraging provinces in North China to secede from the Nanjing government, and a crisis brewed in early 1933 when the army occupied a strategic pass in the Great Wall at Shanhaiguan. Here, Chiang and Wang negotiated the Tanggu Truce (Tanggu xieding, May 31, 1933) in which a demilitarized zone was to be established along the Great Wall and North China. In a telegram to the nation, Wang emphasized that this truce was only a military agreement to end the armed conflict and not a political one that would compromise China's sovereignty.[91] In these cases and others, Chiang made sure that nothing was put in writing with his name attached that would formally give Chinese territory away.

DOMESTIC DISUNITY

The Japanese invasion of Mukden also necessitated that the factional struggle in the Kuomintang be resolved because the public demanded that the division cease and because the credibility of the Kuomintang was undermined when one voice in Nanjing and another in Guangdong each claimed to speak for China in the international arena. Had there been no Mukden Incident, this intraparty conflict (according to Lloyd Eastman) presumably would have been fought on the battlefield, with provincial militarists of Guangdong and Guangxi backing the Guangdong faction.[92] In the aftermath of the incident, however, the Guangdong faction continued to attack Nanjing's foreign policies, which undermined Nanjing's diplomatic efforts by causing Western powers to question whether China was a bona fide state that could make claims on Manchuria. The attacks also weakened a united response to Japanese aggression.[93]

Since the rival Kuomintang factions were unable to resolve their disagreements on the battlefield, Chiang chose the seemingly passive approach of enduring the humiliation of accusations and criticisms directed toward him. He explained the logic behind this approach in an April 1931 speech to a group of young men preparing to propagandize the need for the communist "extermination" campaigns in Henan, Hubei, and Anhui. Offering advice that he seemed to take to heart himself when dealing with party divisiveness, Chiang warned the young men that they might encounter humiliations because of their mission or their youthfulness. Rather than feel troubled by this, they should think of it as an opportunity to alter their audience's perception and eventually command their respect. To become a person of talent and help China complete the revolution, he declared, a person had to undergo extraordinary danger and humiliation.[94]

Following this logic, Chiang remained determinedly silent as fellow party members attacked and criticized him in the aftermath of the Mukden Incident. In one diary excerpt, he said, "I am willing to take on the responsibilities for all of these calamities. Otherwise, other than myself, there is no one who can carry this responsibility. Therefore, concerning this, I can only endure the humiliation, carrying this responsibility to death. I encourage myself."[95] A month later, with no signs of rapprochement between the Nanjing and Guangdong factions, Chiang seemed to almost calmly accept that he had "the misfortune of accepting all this dirtiness; I now feel even more sympathy for the wise men of the past."[96]

Chiang remained steadfast in prioritizing domestic pacification. When an opportunity arose to free his son, Chiang Ching-kuo, he declined. Although his son had been forced to remain in Russia as a hostage after the First United Front split in 1927, Chiang refused a prisoner swap that would free his son in exchange for a Chinese communist leader and his wife. He reasoned that if 300,000 of his soldiers and officers had perished, he could not put his own need above that of his country.[97] He justified his decision based on the political legacy he sought to impart: "When I think about what we pass on to future generations, [I believe that our legacy] derives from one's occupation and behavior, not from one's descendants. In reading about the lives of past sages, outstanding men of talent, loyal officials, and martyrs, no one really comes to know their children. But [in terms of these outstanding people], we clearly know their occupation and moral behavior . . . for ten thousand autumns."[98]

Like his role model King Goujian, Chiang saw that his fate and China's were one and the same. Although he announced his resignation from power on December 15, 1931, "in the interest of national unity and the fight against the Japanese—and to leave the way open for 'more competent men,'" when he attended a meeting a week later, he felt that it marked "the beginning of commemorating the death of the country."[99] At the same time, because he was unable to fulfill his duties as a leader, he reflected, "I am frustrated. No matter how sad I am about the fate of the country, I am unable to be completely loyal to it. Toward my children, I lack benevolence. Toward my family, I have not done my best to take care of them. . . . I have shamed my parents. Isn't this something to be upset by?"[100] Rather than seek compromise, Chiang chose to step away and highlight the shame of his inability to realize his goals. This path, counterintuitively, helped shore up his legitimacy.

The Whampoa generals signaled that they would take orders only from Chiang, and the provinces withheld their salt tax revenue from the new government until he was restored. Even some of the student associations called for his return. The rhetoric of protest and resistance to Japan by Chiang's opponents seemed less palatable in his absence. "Nobody in a position of responsibility," Youli Sun notes, "believed that China could defeat Japan militarily."[101] Goats fighting wolves was just too unrealistic, according to Jiang Tingfu (1895–1965), a mainstream intellectual who had become less enamored with the imported ideologies of the May Fourth Movement and was persuaded by the idea that a strong, viable state was needed before considering something like a liberal democracy.[102] In the end, the Guangdong faction ultimately capitulated, acknowledging that Chiang was indispensable. Chiang was thus back in power forty-five days later after making a power-sharing deal with Wang

Jingwei, who had remained neutral in this factional fight.[103] Apparently, his exhortations to the young men promoting the communist annihilation campaigns had worked for him: to accomplish something extraordinary, he had to experience danger and personal humiliation.

•   •   •

Scholars have noted that Chiang tolerated no loyal opposition and mistrusted initiatives outside of his control, such as jailing students who protested the Mukden Incident.[104] Such observations have led some commentators to label him a fascist, dictator, or militarist. Yet such labels only partially capture the complexity of his behavior. Given the highly divisive environment that Chiang inhabited, his actions might also be interpreted as attempting an all-or-nothing approach: either all had to be on board with his leadership and policies of enduring the Mukden humiliation and avoiding the signing of formal treaties with Japan as a way of preserving China or he would resign. Unlike the charismatic leader who inspires followers toward a desired outcome as Max Weber envisioned, Chiang seemed to offer the inverse of an inspirational leader who quietly endures the humiliation of disagreements and protests to prevail in the end. Even if the Goujian template appeared to apply only to himself by the end of 1931, the end result was that Chiang managed to secure his leadership in the Kuomintang more firmly and increase China's favorability in the eyes of the international community.

CHAPTER 4

The New Life Movement in Context

Deploying Shame to Modernize China

By 1934, Chiang Kai-shek could be more confident about leading China. His battles against warlords were over, his fifth and final "annihilation" campaign against the Chinese communists had concluded successfully at the end of the year, and he had no direct military conflict with Japan. Nevertheless, Chiang continued to use *chi* to construct China's national story and identity, and he did so by shifting its focus domestically onto citizens, soldiers, party members, students, and even rival challengers to his authority. Adapting from Goujian's "ten years to grow the population, and ten years to train the population," Chiang primarily deployed shame to motivate his "inferiors" and rivals to become part of the modern China he envisioned.

One area where Chiang mobilized shame was in launching the New Life Movement (Xin shenghuo yundong) on February 19, 1934, at his military headquarters in Nanchang, Jiangxi. He sought to resurrect traditional Chinese morality as a way to build a new national consciousness, direct energy toward modernization and nation-building, and promulgate directives to achieve a "New Life," which included fifty-five rules related to orderliness (e.g., when you bump into someone, excuse yourself) and forty-one rules on cleanliness and health (e.g., open your windows often). Through lectures, radio broadcasts, newspaper and journal essays, social programs and displays, voluntary organizations, posters, and mass rallies in the early months of the movement, Chiang appealed to his audience's sense of shame to realize these objectives.[1] By the end of

1935, the New Life Movement and its directives had spread to nineteen provinces, five municipalities, twelve railway centers, and ten overseas communities. Its administrative reach extended to 1,132 counties (*xian*).[2] With help from military leaders like Xiong Shihui, Chiang promoted and oversaw this movement for three years.[3]

Previous scholars have criticized the path Chiang took to modernizing China, especially when comparing it with the seemingly more progressive approach advocated by Chinese students and intellectuals in the aftermath of the Treaty of Versailles at the end of World War I.[4] Members of the resulting May Fourth Movement, such as Lu Xun (1881–1936), Chen Duxiu (1879–1942), and Hu Shi (1891–1962), chose to embrace global and Western standards based on science and democracy. By contrast, Chiang appealed to seemingly outdated Confucian and pre-Confucian moral precepts to define and implement a new China. Scholars have tended to describe the New Life Movement as counterrevolutionary, superficial, and an abysmal failure.[5] This characterization of Chiang and his modernization efforts, however, is incomplete at best.

For one thing, as Lloyd and Susanne Rudolph have argued in the case of India, the categories of modernity and tradition are not mutually exclusive, and the tendency to separate them conceptually when studying a non-Western country can easily fall into normative conceptions based on Western identity and fail to notice ways—as in Chiang's case—"tradition" can serve as a conduit into the "modern."[6] The privileging of the May Fourth revolutionary narrative and the nearly unanimous dismissal of a Confucian alternative in Western scholarship suggest that observers saw Chiang's efforts to draw on traditional sources as a deficient approach to modernization. In viewing China through a lens of Western achievements and standards, Western scholarship may have overlooked some of the preconditions necessary to replicate the Western path, namely, a functioning, autonomous, unified state. By making a leap to what China should be without deeper investigation into what it actually was and an openness to potentially multiple paths going forward, the analyses of Chiang's leadership in the New Life Movement inadvertently shortchange Chiang's creative agency and contributions during this period.

This chapter looks at the contingent factors in 1934 that shaped Chiang's understanding of *chi* and how he used it in culturally inflected ways to define and implement his vision of a modern China. Despite the limited success of the New Life Movement and his attempts to modernize the military and infrastructure, it will show, Chiang actually had a broader intent of constructing and advancing a strategic national identity that deliberately aligned his idea of modernity with his international and domestic political goals. As a result, he not only put his imprint on the Chinese national identity, he also offered a more multifaceted and consequential path to modernity than has been previously acknowledged.

Global Trends

In observing the conjunction of several pending political events in 1934, Chiang believed that a world war would break out within three years.[7] This reading of the global context profoundly shaped Chiang's policies and his uses of *chi* to realize those policies. In a 1934 speech to provincial directors and senior officials, Chiang noted that the 1922 Washington Naval Treaty (or Five-Power Treaty) limiting Japan's navy to only three major battleships for every five operated by Great Britain and by the United States would expire in 1936. This treaty, along with the Four-Power and Nine-Power Treaties, was put together after World War I at the Washington Naval Conference by the major nations who had won the war in an effort to discourage an arms race and relieve tensions in East Asia. Chiang, knowing that the Imperial Japanese Navy was indignant about this battleship ratio, believed it was eager to resume and escalate the naval race.[8] Furthermore, Japan's rights and privileges in the League of Nations were to end in 1936, which would force Japan to relinquish its governing privileges in the South Pacific. Last, the Soviet Union appeared likely to complete its second five-year plan a year early in 1936, thereby turning its attention toward increasing its military capabilities. Chiang believed that this confluence of events would lead the imperial powers to begin fighting over China, most likely in a clash between the Soviet Union and Japan over Japanese-occupied Manchuria. Such a war, he believed, would either spell China's doom or provide it with the opportunity to gain its autonomy from foreign control.[9]

Chiang was close to the mark in his analysis. Indeed, shortcomings in the Washington Naval Treaty contributed to an inability to check Japan's aggression in Asia and thus to the eventual outbreak of World War II in Asia. As Chiang predicted, when the treaty expired in 1936, the Japanese began building the *Yamato* and *Musashi* battleships, which were nearly twice the displacement of any existing ship.[10] Furthermore, by the time the United States formally recognized the Soviet Union in 1933 and encouraged it to join the treaty system, the Soviets refused to accept the constraints placed by the treaties and, as Chiang had anticipated, decisively switched to arms production at the end of their Second Five-Year Plan in 1937.[11] Although the United States was a signatory of all three of the aforementioned Washington treaties, it was not a member of the League of Nations, the umbrella institution meant to resolve disputes. The United States therefore had no direct way to advocate punishing Japan for invading Mukden three years earlier.[12] Because the treaty system lacked enforcement mechanisms and did not include all the major players, it hampered the United States' best efforts to secure global peace through liberalism.

Thus, in a 1934 speech titled "The Essentials of Recovering the Citizenry," Chiang noted that China lacked King Goujian's luxury of growing the population for ten years and training it for another ten. Given his global timeline, he wanted China to stabilize its foundations to begin its recovery within three to five years.[13] In another speech to senior officials, Chiang declared that China had only about 1,100 days to prepare for inevitable war and laid out a strategy by which the country could rid itself of foreign influence.[14] Because he operated in a divided state with limited resources and three years' time was inadequate to reversing China's weak state, Chiang sought to construct a national identity that would *appear* worthy of autonomy in the short term in an effort to gain the support of the Chinese people and sympathetic international allies in the long run. His continued work in consolidating the state, his New Life efforts, and his deployment of shame in both these areas must thus be considered within this urgent global timeframe.

Defining the Legitimate Political
Elite through Shame

Chiang's goal of unifying China clearly preceded the New Life Movement, but it continued during and after the movement itself. Rather than focus solely on the New Life Movement to understand Chiang's modernization path, as Western scholarship has tended to do, it is important to also analyze his consolidating efforts as part of his overall plan. Indeed, his uses of *chi* connected various efforts inside and outside the movement to form a strategized national narrative and identity. An examination of the *shilüe* reveals that Chiang gave leaders certain labels as a way to legitimate some domestic conflicts with rival leaders and delegitimate others. This approach had Confucian and (by extension) *chi* overtones, as suggested by a passage from the *Analects of Confucius*. In response to a question about governance from Duke Jing of Qi, Confucius responded, "Let the lord be a lord; the subject a subject; the father a father; the son a son." The duke then replied, "Excellent! If indeed the lord is not lord, the subject not a subject, the father not a father, the son not a son, I could be sure of nothing anymore—not even my daily food."[15] Recognizing that strategic naming could ensure appropriate action and convey legitimacy, Chiang deliberately identified his domestic rivals and foes with specific terms that signaled who belonged to the nation and who did not. In the process, he advanced a national story to strengthen his legitimacy by defining the appropriate political elite who would help him rule.

During periods of irreconcilable differences with challengers to his authority, Chiang, as revealed in the *shilüe*, consistently applied the label *ni* 逆 to people with whom he thought he could ultimately cooperate. These included fellow warlords, party members, and members of his army. He thus referred to the warlord Feng Yuxiang as Feng *ni* Yuxiang during the Central Plains War in 1930, which pitted Chiang and various warlords in a civil war, and the party leader Wang Jingwei as Wang *ni* Jingwei during the Nationalist Party split in 1931. Likewise, when members of the Nineteenth Route Army rebelled in Fujian in November 1933, Chiang labeled them the *ni* army.[16]

Ni is a word used to describe a brother who has gone astray and can potentially come back to the family fold. It can also mean "going against the current." When Chiang invoked *ni*, he was suggesting that warlords and party and army members were outside the body politic because of their actions, and they were making things unnecessarily difficult for themselves by going against his leadership. However, because he believed that they were still valued members of the Chinese collective, his use of *ni* was also a way of shaming them back into the national fold.

Indeed, Chiang had allowed the northern and southern warlords who fought and almost eliminated him in 1929 and 1930 to stay in their territories. Despite Feng's failed military challenge to Chiang's authority in the spring of 1933 and Bai Chongxi's (1893–1966) challenge in the summer of 1936, both eventually cooperated with Chiang again. By the same token, the severe intraparty power struggle that led Chiang to resign temporarily at the end of 1931 did not prevent him from returning in early 1932 with greater legitimacy when party members such as Wang Jingwei and Sun Ke (1891–1973), who had vociferously attacked Chiang, once again became his allies. In fact, when Feng and Wang returned to the same side as Chiang, he referred to them with the respectful term "older brother" (*lao*).

By contrast, Chiang unfailingly called the Chinese communists *fei* 匪, or "bandits," inserting the label into the names of communist leaders, such as always referring to Mao as Mao *fei* Zedong. The word *fei* typically refers to people who roam the outskirts of towns and villages harassing others and causing chaos. Viewed as forces of disorder, their conduct placed them outside of the Chinese collective and perhaps even outside the realm of being human. Chiang often discussed the Chinese communists as if they were rodents or pests and his campaigns against them as "exterminating" (*jiao*) them, rather than shaming them back into the fold.[17]

Although groups and individuals had been labeled bandits in China for several millennia, most commonly using the terms *dao*, *zei*, or *kou*, the term *fei* was a relatively recent one. Originally coined to describe the White Lotus sect, which rebelled against the Qing dynasty in 1794 and arguably began that empire's downfall, the term became more widely used during the nineteenth century. For the late Qing regime, concerned about bolstering its legitimacy, the word served the dual purpose of denigrating a given group—*tufei*, for instance, played on the idea of "local," which could also mean "scum of the earth"—and of designating it a law-breaking group.[18]

Through *fei*, Chiang and the Nationalist government promoted the idea that the communists could hardly be rulers of the new China but were simply common bandits who must be suppressed by the legitimate authority of the Nationalist government. Moreover, Chiang gave no option of rehabilitation through an appeal to their sense of shame to change their "deviant" ways. Despite being labeled bandits living outside the Chinese collective, the Chinese communists clearly were the most formidable opponents to Chiang's rule, and the Nationalists' fifth attempt to exterminate them in 1934 ultimately failed.

Thus, in addition to battles in the field to unify the state, Chiang waged an ideological battle by deploying shame to define who constituted the legitimate national leadership. When he used it, challenges to his leadership entailed the possibility of rejoining him in the common endeavor of freeing China from foreign influence. When he did not, Chiang revealed a perhaps prescient understanding that such challengers could never be shamed into being a part of the same collective as the Nationalists.

Inculcating a Knowledge of Humiliation in the Modern Citizen

Another often overlooked use of Confucianism outside of the New Life Movement was in Chiang's effort to sensitize Chinese citizens (and posterity) to the humiliations visited upon them by imperial powers. These efforts would help imbue a collective identity with a sensitivity to humiliation that, along with defining the legitimate leadership of China, he could deploy to realize China's autonomy with himself in charge.

Chiang's attempts to shape this knowledge among the Chinese often began with his mulling over an event or policy to see whether it counted as a "humiliation," his idea being that once a humiliation was identified, the courage to avenge it would follow. For instance, he noted in a diary entry that at first glance, the Nine-Power Treaty of 1922 seemed advantageous to China. In addition to China, Belgium, the United Kingdom, France, Italy, Japan, the Netherlands, Portugal, the United States, and Japan had signed on to "stabilize conditions in the Far East, to safeguard the rights and interests of China, and to promote intercourse between China and the other Powers upon the basis of equality of opportunity."[19]

The treaty formalized the tenets of the Open Door policy toward China, which had been articulated by US Secretary of State John Hay at the turn of the century. The other signatory countries pledged to avoid seeking special rights and privileges to enable equal access to economic trade in China.[20]

When reflecting on the treaty in 1934, Chiang noted with dismay that none of the signatories had punished Japan for invading Manchuria in 1931; only the United States had protested and called for economic sanctions. He concluded that the treaty constituted a humiliation, even more so than the Japanese Twenty-One Demands in 1915 (discussed in chapter 5), and a humiliation that was now his responsibility to bear and avenge.[21] In reflecting on the treaty days later in his diary, he remarked that the people should also feel shame: "To rely only on others to speak in accordance with justice and to forget to seek after self-strengthening, this is the country's greatest worry and humiliation."[22]

After deciding that something constituted a humiliation, Chiang then thought about getting the public to feel the same way. On March 27, 1934, after noting in his diary that the people had "accumulated too much weakness" and "were confused with stupidity," he telegrammed Xiong Shihui to publish a textbook on common sense.[23] He further specified that it would include thirty-eight items encompassing a basic knowledge of world affairs, science, the environment, and the people's obligation and responsibility to the country. Several items incorporated descriptions of humiliations: item 4 would be a brief history, including the year and month, of the territories China lost; item 26 would describe the foreign concessions and China's powers to deal with foreigners; and item 29 would give a short history of avenging humiliation throughout the Chinese dynasties.[24] The next day, he telegrammed Xiong again with orders to form a special committee of old Confucian scholars to gather examples from history of people who stood up to barbarians and refused to bow to foreigners, and to submit the materials to him within a few days.[25] Through indoctrination, Chiang intended to provide and widely disseminate a shared worldview about the trajectory of modern China.

Chiang also offered role models. On February 11, 1934, Chiang entered in his avenging humiliation column a reference to Yue Fei (1103–42), a hero of the Southern Song dynasty who fought valiantly against the minority nationality, the Jins, but was betrayed by Qin Hui and executed. "To have Wumu's [Yue Fei's] patriotism, one can therefore complete Goujian's enormous task. Goujian's success and Wumu's martyrdom, these two things are the same in terms of the pride of the people."[26] After later noting in his diary that the people should be aware that the path to recovery from imperial influence was through the examples of Goujian and Yue Fei, he asked his chief secretary, Chen Bulei, to compile a single edition on the biographies of Goujian and Yue Fei.[27]

By inculcating this sense of national humiliation, Chiang appeared to strengthen and provide articulation to some themes already latent in Chinese society. In spring 1936, the Literary Society (Wenxue she) and the editorial board of the project "One Day in China," headed by Mao Dun (1896–1981), advertised in magazines and newspapers asking Chinese people from all walks of life to record their observations of a particular day—Thursday, May 21, 1936—to capture what was happening in the country, whether at sea, on land, or in air, on that day.[28] One contribution came from a Shanghai policeman, Wu Jun, who recounted that he met a Japanese couple on the train platform, whose little boy was "very clever and cute!"[29] The little boy was imitating Wu Jun's movements, causing everyone to laugh. The boy's father gently reprimanded him in fluent Mandarin and conversationally complained to the policeman about his child's naughtiness. Wu Jun reported that he had warmly responded by noting that naughtiness was a sign of intelligence, but when the father seemed to want to continue their conversation, he remembered that the father was Japanese and a flood of painful events suddenly came to mind: "the extinction of Korea, the Twenty-one Demands, the four northeastern provinces, the January Twenty-eighth Incident, the establishment of the illegitimate state of Manzhouguo [Japanese-occupied Manchuria], the Tanggu Truce, and problems of North China, etc."[30] This recitation of humiliations, which so clearly coincided with Chiang's list, indicated that the police officer was certainly agreeable to Chiang's delineation of the recent past and perhaps amenable to avenging these humiliations Chiang-style with the initial step of abruptly halting his conversation with the Japanese man.

The former premier of Taiwan, Hao Baicun (Hau Pei-tsun, 1919–2020), recalled in a 2003 interview that in his middle school years in the 1930s, he read histories about avenging humiliation (which were probably the works prescribed by Chiang) that made him angry about foreign concessions. These works, which impressed on him China's lack of independence from foreign interference, had fueled his growing sense of nationalism, and he decided to join the army to fight the Japanese.[31] Hao seemed to buy into the narrative Chiang created, reflecting some success Chiang had in shaping the kind of citizen he wanted for a new China.

A Strategized Story about a New China

Chiang began the New Life Movement in regions the Nationalists had recently recovered from the Chinese communists, believing that these areas would serve as a model for the rest of the country. Moreover, Chiang initiated the movement to realize Sun Yat-sen's Three People's Principles, which shaped Nationalist politics and government structure under Chiang's leadership on the mainland and later in Taiwan.[32] The New Life Movement can thus be situated within the stage of tutelage rule, an intermediary stage to prepare the people to eventually realize Sun's second principle, democracy.[33] Although Chiang ambitiously wanted to implement democracy and remake the newly recovered areas into "a shining, new, glorious, civilized, advanced modern country," he had to square these lofty goals with the more immediate objectives of consolidating sovereignty and wresting China from foreign influence.[34] Given his urgent timeline and the constraints of starting a movement where state institutions were weak, one of Chiang's goals, which has been underappreciated, was to define a strategized vision of the modern citizen that would inform the Chinese national story and identity.

CONNECTING WITH GUANZI AND THE FOUR VIRTUES

When launching the movement, Chiang drew inspiration from a pre-Confucian political philosophical work called the *Guanzi*. Although the *Guanzi* is usually associated with the Legalist tradition, Chiang's use of its ideas supports translator W. Allyn Rickett's argument that the book can more faithfully be described as "realistic Confucian," in the vein of Confucius's disciple Xunzi (310–235 BCE) rather than the more idealistic philosophies of Confucius or Mencius. Moreover, the work is compatible with a Confucian approach of promoting change through rites and people's morality rather than through coercion and bribery.

Six days before officially launching the New Life Movement, Chiang reviewed this ancient treatise on leadership in earnest. In it, philosopher and statesman Guan Zhong advises Prime Minister Duke Huan of Qi (Qi Huan Gong, d. 643 BCE) that a leader should rule his country through the Four Virtues: propriety, justice, integrity, and sense of shame (*liyilianchi*).[35] As defined by one of the chapters, "Propriety consists in not overstepping the bounds of proper behavior. Righteousness consists in not pushing oneself forward [at the expense of others]. Integrity consists in not concealing one's faults. Having a sense of shame consists in not following those who go awry."[36] In this quartet of virtues, which Chiang adopted to define the modern citizen and state, *chi* played the critical role of engendering a sense of shame when one strayed from the first three principles.

An examination of Chiang's personal copy of the work shows that he engaged the text methodically and intensively. On the first page of each of the four slim paperback volumes, he noted when and where he started and finished the volume; for instance, he started the first volume on February 13, 1934, in Nanchang, and finished it twelve days later. He had completed all four volumes by April 21, 1934. In the tables of contents, he used a calligraphy brush to rate each chapter, awarding four black circles to the chapters he deemed most important, "On Shepherding the People" and "On the Cultivation of Political Power"; three to "On Overseeing Government" and "The Seven Standards"; and two or one to the remaining chapters. Given the multicolored underlining and notes in the margins, Chiang appeared to have read extensive portions of the *Guanzi* multiple times.[37]

Chiang recorded his reflections on the text and transcribed more than twenty quotations into his diary. He stated at one point that the *Guanzi* was to politics as Sun Tzu's *Art of War* was to military affairs.[38] He thought so much of the work that he also wrote in his diary, "If politicians neglect to read the *Guanzi*, and they only seek after new books, I am afraid that they will fail."[39] About a month after launching the New Life Movement, Chiang further reported in his diary that his thoughts had led him to burst into song spontaneously: "Propriety, justice, integrity, and a sense of shame are China's Four Virtues. Let the Four Virtues expand and let the country be healthy. . . . This morning," he continued, "I sang something on a whim and drafted a national song to eradicate the shame of not having one."[40]

The *Guanzi* gave Chiang inspiration, support, and even a sense of delight. Such devotion to this major work of Chinese thought gave credence to his seemingly counterintuitive use of an ancient text to define the modern citizen. It created a bond between his private and public persona that followers, audience members, and observers undoubtedly recognized as authentic. Chiang could thus bolster his legitimacy by presenting himself as a conduit of traditional wisdom, enabling others to appreciate the relevance of this ancient source for modern times.

ADAPTING THE FOUR VIRTUES TO DEFINE
THE MODERN CITIZEN

Chiang often used the Four Virtues in the *Guanzi* as a springboard to think about the kind of citizen he believed would allow China to seize the opportune moment to become independent from foreign influence and attract allies to help the nation in that effort. In line with a Confucian outlook on how best to effect transformation, Chiang approached the New Life Movement as a spiritual revival to restore traditional Chinese morality based on the Four Virtues and legitimate his leadership by responding to the perceived corruption of his government.

In his inaugural speech of the movement, Chiang argued that because of the people's "spiritless" psychology, citizens were unable to discriminate between good and evil, public and private, and primary and secondary.[41] Lacking such discernment, Chiang claimed, the Chinese people fell short of fulfilling their social roles in a morally correct fashion. No one escaped his criticism: officials were dishonest and avaricious, the youth degraded and intemperate, the rich extravagant and luxurious, the poor mean and disorderly.[42] By adopting the Four Virtues, he argued, the people's spiritlessness, and thus their inability to behave like a modern nation, would be cured.

Importantly, in the same speech, Chiang stressed that the Four Virtues must be observed even in the minor details of life. Quoting verbatim from the four-black-circle chapter "Cultivation of Political Power," he said, "Since those who would shepherd the people desire them even in minor matters to be meticulous in observing propriety, practicing righteousness, cultivating integrity, and displaying a sense of shame, they must prohibit even the slightest beginnings of evil . . . such is the basis of good order."[43] "If one is unable to manage a household," he elaborated, "how can one manage a country? To attain what is far, one must pay attention to what is near."[44] Here Chiang referenced Chen Ping (d. 178 BCE) as an example of a practitioner of the Four Virtues, a commoner who managed his locality well and eventually became a chief minister during the Han dynasty (202 BCE–220 CE).[45] By performing small tasks well, Chiang implied, China could demonstrate that it would eventually accomplish large-scale tasks well.

One way Chiang leveraged the fourth virtue, shame, in this framework of starting small was to point out minor deviances in citizens' appearances and behaviors. In speaking to graduating air force cadets in Hangzhou, Chiang observed that nine out of ten Chinese people ate, sat, or stood improperly. He felt bothered by people who left their top shirt button unbuttoned.[46] Speaking to Nanchang's school principals and various party, government, and military officials, Chiang called junior high school students' red and green clothing "barbarian" (*yemanren*) or clearly uncivilized.[47] Addressing student athletes at a Jiangxi sports event, he exhorted them to keep their nails and hair cut short. Although he conceded that girls could keep their hair longer than the boys', which he limited to a thumb's width (*cun*), he argued that excessively long hair made them look like ghosts and that permed hair resembled the hairs of a beast.[48]

Despite focusing on minor details, Chiang also tried to convey a larger message. When speaking to the Jiangxi student athletes, he criticized the expense and time that some boys invested in caring for their hair because "if this same person did not have long hair, we could take the money spent on perfume and oils to buy a few books that would be beneficial, and the time he takes to comb his hair can be put towards learning and acquiring skills."[49] By the same token, by keeping up their appearance, starting with their hair, the girls would become models for all Chinese women and girls.[50] By ignoring the Four Virtues in seemingly small matters, Chiang implied, the Chinese youth would lack the competence to tackle the bigger issues of educating themselves, developing skills, and becoming models for their community. The failure to practice these virtues reflected shame on the country, and he contrasted this with students in strong countries who embraced these virtues.[51] Although some critics have ridiculed Chiang in his obsession with such minutiae as the hemlines of women's dresses and blouses, he was also using them to signal larger issues and his stance on them. Regarding women's roles in modern China, for instance, Chiang felt that the "modern girl," who symbolized urban consumerism and cosmopolitanism in cities like Shanghai, was the antithesis of his vision of the modern patriotic female citizen and thus undermined China's national salvation.[52]

Chiang appeared to focus on minor matters rather than confront the larger issues associated with modernization that they suggested, perhaps because he recognized he had neither the time nor the resources to fulfill such goals. Taking the latter route with a potential world war on the horizon, for instance, may have opened up a Pandora's box of demands that Chiang was unlikely to resolve that would therefore undermine his credibility. Instead, he sought to increase national pride, start the modernization process, and enlist new audiences toward his goals (not just military and political leaders), thinking this was the best way to achieve national salvation and consolidate power.

Another way Chiang adapted the Four Virtues to his political and cultural ends was to incorporate behaviors he admired in foreigners into his idea of the modern Chinese citizen. He noted in his inaugural speech that foreigners (i.e., the imperial powers) practiced the Four Virtues better than the Chinese did. The Japanese, he noted, showed frugality by washing with cold water and eating cold food, and they exhibited respect for public spaces by spitting into a bag or handkerchief.[53] In another New Life speech, he noted that the revolutions in Turkey, Germany, and Italy succeeded because those citizens applied the first virtue, propriety, by obeying rules and regulations.[54] The implied corollary was that these foreign citizens would feel a sense of shame (the fourth virtue) if they deviated from this proper behavior, as should the Chinese. By emulating these behaviors, Chiang argued, China could also produce modern citizens.

Chiang further shamed the Chinese about their failure to dress and act as modern citizens by claiming that foreigners looked down on them, like the Chinese did on people from Taiwan or other uncivilized nations (*yeman minzu*).[55] He thus exhorted his audiences to remove the shame of foreigners' ill judgment of the Chinese by behaving and dressing well. In this use of the Four Virtues, Chiang appeared to draw on the colonial critique of "John Chinaman," a stock backward Chinese character, and he implicitly promised that if John Chinaman rectified his faults and made the necessary improvements, he could get his country back. Sun Yat-sen had similarly adapted this critique ten years earlier when, in his lecture on the Three People's Principles, he told his audience to avoid spitting and burping in public, reframing a trope of colonial racism as an act of political resistance to imperialism.[56] In applying the Four Virtues, Chiang similarly merged this critique into his program by reminding the people of larger matters of hygiene, health, and education and thereby resisting imperialism through focus on minor, accomplishable details.

Because Chiang often drew his examples from fascist and fascist-leaning countries, some have suggested the fascist nature of his leadership. Indeed, he did declare the militarization of society as a central tenet of the New Life Movement, and he gave the Blue Shirts (Lixingshe), a group associated with fascism, the responsibility of implementing the movement.[57] But while the New Life Movement exhibited some characteristics of fascism, so did many national organizations around the world whose countries were also in crisis in the 1930s.[58] In addition, this analysis overlooks how Chiang's obsession with people's daily living was consistent with Confucian tradition. As Jennifer Lee Oldstone-Moore notes, "The theory of transformative action and imposition of public morality is firmly rooted in the Confucian tradition, recorded first in the *Record of Rites* (*Liji*)."[59] Furthermore, his promotion of the virtues of militarization—frugality, discipline, and asceticism—could also be attributed to his admiration of King Goujian and his reading of China's chaotic milieu and weak state. Finally, as will be elaborated on in the next section, rather than adapt and enforce fascism wholesale, Chiang's approach to implementation made it quite unlike the German and Italian versions.

In drawing broadly from foreign ideas, Chiang also borrowed from Christianity to refine his adaptations of the Four Virtues to define the modern citizen. Having converted to the faith after his marriage to Song Meiling in 1928, Chiang believed that Christianity was consistent with the teachings of Confucius and even viewed Jesus in Goujian terms, particularly admiring Jesus's ability to endure great humiliation.[60] The church, he felt, served as a unifying force for England and the United States, whereas the Kuomintang fell short of supplying this energy for China. The local missionaries and members of the Young Men's Christian Association (YMCA), he believed, could help the Kuomintang become that integrating force. Chiang made clear, however, that the Chinese were not giving up their identity by accepting this influence. Rather, he viewed the Christian "attitude toward life" as simply "sane and sensible": "I am not urging that we become foreignized, that we eat foreign food, wear foreign clothes and live in foreign houses, but rather that we live that rational sane life that the [Christian] Movement and its principles call for."[61]

Nor was Chiang enamored of all foreign ideas about modernity. Indeed, he used the Four Virtues to cement a vision of citizenship that rejected Western-originated communist ideology. In a speech to provincial administrative officials, Chiang argued that the Chinese communists had rendered the Four Virtues meaningless because they wanted the people to recognize the Soviet Union as their homeland and Marx and Lenin as their ancestors. It was as if the Chinese were facing foreigners and performing the special rite of kneeling three times with the head touching the ground nine times (an ancient ritual performed by a subject during an audience with the emperor). Although they were performing the ritual correctly, the overall act lacked propriety. In fact, Chiang pointed out, this kind of "propriety" was synonymous with being a traitor. Only by knowing genuine propriety as he defined it, he argued, could one come to understand a sense of shame.[62]

Chiang's Four Virtues had their naysayers among Chinese observers at the time. They argued that the Four Virtues were insufficient to rescue the country or improve China's knowledge and technology, which remained inferior to that of foreigners. In response, Chiang argued in a pamphlet titled "An Outline of the New Life Movement and the New Life Essentials" that these skeptics misunderstood the origin and consequence of things: the virtues needed to be adopted before seeking knowledge and skills because otherwise those might be used as tools for malevolent purposes.[63]

To skeptics who also argued that the Four Virtues were useless in shielding against cold and hunger, Chiang argued that they misinterpreted a passage from the *Guanzi*: "Only after one has adequate food and clothing will one know glory and shame. Only after the grain house is full does one know the requirements of decorum."[64] Chiang interpreted these lines to mean that only in a society with the Four Virtues could one rely on the strength of the people to make adequate clothing and food. Without the virtues, he claimed, fighting, robbing, stealing, and begging would result. Indeed, without these virtues a society could begin with an abundance of food and clothing but quickly degenerate into scarcity.[65]

Like the May Fourth intellectuals, Chiang wanted to remake Confucian familial authority; unlike them, he privileged national salvation over Enlightenment principles or material improvement of the masses in his path to modernity. Moreover, the "morality" he promulgated was intended to reorient citizens' allegiance firmly to the nation-state rather than the family. Given Chiang's timeline of global events, he believed that some semblance of a modern Chinese nation had to come into being, and the Four Virtues, with the *Guanzi*'s emphasis on meticulously practicing them in minor matters, were the appropriate method by which to forge that shared national consciousness.

Implementing Modern China in 1,100 Days

Of course, the critique in Western scholarship of Chiang's path to modernity also spilled into its analysis of the New Life Movement's accomplishments. As we have seen, Chiang appeared to believe that inculcating the Four Virtues would help the people better internalize a sense of duty to the state. To better understand how this Confucian-like approach worked in practice, I borrow a theological term that has found its way into scholarly discussions regarding practices of Chinese governance that draw from Confucian ideas: orthopraxy.[66] Chiang appeared to rely on an orthopraxic (as opposed to orthodox) approach to modernization. Instead of stressing that correct beliefs will lead to correct actions (orthodoxy), he appeared to underscore that correct actions will lead to correct beliefs (orthopraxy). That is, by promoting the correct practice as exemplified through the Four Virtues, Chiang hoped that the desired beliefs would in time correspond to practice, even if local practices varied in a unifying structure of what was deemed correct practice.[67] Through this approach, Chiang could promote support and compliance among the people, even if it was only tacit.[68] Practically speaking, given his timeline, Chiang arguably had a better chance of modernizing some external behaviors than the people's internal belief systems. His practice of orthopraxy in the New Life Movement and with regard to the military and national infrastructure, as this section will suggest, contrasts Confucianism with Christianity and Western ideologies like fascism and communism. It raises questions as to whether Western assumptions about Chiang's effectiveness were based on underappreciating the possibilities of applying a Confucian orthopraxic approach to modernization within a context of divided sovereignty and weak state.

IMPLEMENTING THE MODERN CITIZEN

At first glance, the New Life norms Chiang tried to instill appeared to be ignored and therefore ineffective. Wu Jun, the Shanghai policeman mentioned earlier, reported hearing people making flippant remarks about the New Life pronouncements (fig. 4.1) as he directed them to exit left:

"Ah! I forgot, I forgot."
"Oh, New Life!"
"Why aren't you letting me by?"
"Oh, are going to frisk me?"[69]

Yet increasing coercion was unlikely to compel people to follow New Life rules.[70] For one thing, Chiang would, like bursting into song about the Four Virtues, impulsively add to the ninety-six directives mentioned at the beginning of this chapter. Moreover, so particular and detailed were these added guidelines that enforcing all the rules seemed impossible. On February 27, 1934, for instance, Chiang telegrammed Xiong that at 1:15 p.m., he had seen bus no. 345 pull into the Qingyun stop and a man climb out of the window with his luggage. He noted that this was a barbarous act that had occurred more than once and for which he blamed the president of the bus company, the station manager, and the driver.[71] About a week later, he telegraphed Xiong to direct that all buses in the provinces of Jiangxi, Zhejiang, Anhui, and Hubei post the following rules:

1. Sit straight on the bus, not crooked.
2. Speak cautiously, not loudly.
3. Do not smoke.

FIGURE 4.1: New Life Movement wall poster, stating "Walk on the Left Side." Published by the Commercial Press. China Inland Mission Collection, CIM 425/32. Courtesy of SOAS University of London.

4. Do not spit.
5. Do not climb out the window.
6. Do not lean against the window.

Chiang declared that bus station workers and drivers should be trained in these rules and punish passengers who broke them.[72] Yet it seems unlikely that people actually stopped climbing out of windows, especially if the behavior stemmed from overcrowding. The punishments also seemed difficult to enforce. How was a bus passenger to be punished for slouching? How about a passenger who fell asleep and accidentally leaned against a window?

By using moral persuasion rather than coercion to encourage correct practices, Chiang left room for people to adhere to the New Life directives in their general form but adapt the practice of them to their specific interests. For instance, people swept the streets only when Chiang and his wife visited, and restaurant owners got around the limit in the number of dishes by serving several dishes on extra-large plates and pouring alcohol in teapots.[73] According to Carlton Benson, sellers of foreign silks savvily sidestepped New Life calls for frugality, spartan living, and buying Chinese-made goods. The Shanghai manager of Lao Jiu He Silk and Foreign Goods Emporium swiftly adopted a patriotic front by substituting "Woolen" for "Foreign" in the store name and argued that consumerism constituted patriotism because it contributed to national wealth and power. Another silk retailer hired a songwriter to compose a ditty to advertise the store. Adhering to the tone of the New Life Movement, the songwriter appealed to women's sense of shame by encouraging them to avoid decadent Western customs such as perming their hair or wearing high heels but made a clear exception for silk, citing none other than Chiang's hero as justification. Buying national goods, including silk, he claimed, was an act of sacrifice, "so lie on your thorns and taste your gall; study Gou Jian's [example]."[74] All of these examples appear to show that even if the people ignored the New Life rules, they acknowledged them in parts, which was a step toward internalizing Chiang's collective vision for the modern Chinese nation that included frugality, hygiene, and patriotism and thus lent legitimacy to Chiang's government.

Perhaps the biggest challenge to implementing this vision was overcoming the perception that Chiang was seemingly privileging the population's spiritual regeneration over its material well-being, even though both were important forms of modernization and not necessarily opposed to each other. Given the obviously more difficult and financially costly route of the latter, the New Life Movement accomplished little to improve material conditions in the rural areas.[75] Still, Chiang attempted to ameliorate peasant conditions by launching a People's Economic Reconstruction Campaign in 1935 to complement the New Life Movement's emphasis on the spiritual foundation of the Chinese nation.[76] Even though he failed to accomplish rural reconstruction in Republican China before the outbreak of war in 1937, he successfully did so in Taiwan after 1949, suggesting that it was exigencies and lack of resources, not a lack of concern, that kept him from substantively addressing China's material well-being.[77]

Chiang's gradualist approach, while undeniably slow, stopped short of the violent coercive approaches that Mao later advocated to implement rural construction, in which 800,000 landlords died in the Land Reform campaign of 1950–52.[78] Although Chiang was disappointed that the "result of three years of the New Life Movement has merely been a temporary and superficial renovation without attaining a fundamental reform," he avoided a more fascist path of intensifying coercive measures to militarize his citizens and continued to rely on such methods of persuasion as appealing to the people's sense of shame.[79]

Furthermore, by pursuing an orthopraxic approach, Chiang demonstrated that practices could cultivate belief and changes could be effected. The Nationalist government invested in rural education, for instance, doubling state funding from 23 million to 46 million yuan between 1933 and 1934. The curriculum incorporated New Life principles of cleanliness and orderliness and the symbols and mannerisms of modernity that had been promoted since the beginning of the Republican era in 1912.[80] Elementary school primers, for instance, showed students bowing to their teachers and taking off their hats, while their teachers wore Western-style suits. These investments enabled rural students to become knowledgeable about national symbols and rituals and orient themselves into a new imagined community.[81] Other signs of transformation included street cleaning in Nanchang, which resulted in more hygienic conditions, and by 1936, each of the counties within Jiangxi province had established a health clinic. Women also became important leaders in the New Life Movement (including Song Meiling and Madame Xiong Shihui) and joined organizations like the New Life Women's Labour Corps (Funü Xin shenghuo laodong fuwutuan), which had registered 737 members.[82]

As often occurs in an orthopraxic approach, many of the discussed governmental proposals were scrapped or only partially implemented. Yet there were some notable successes. There was a plan in Nanchang, for instance, to eliminate flies because they were considered a health hazard, especially in shops selling food. Shortly after instituting a week-long campaign to exterminate flies, the Public Security Bureau of Nanchang noted that the situation was controlled in groceries, bakeries, and stalls and peddlers selling cold food.[83] Chiang's approach might be contrasted with Mao's Four Pests campaign at the start of the Great Leap Forward in 1958. In his zeal to kill sparrows, Mao produced an unintended ecological imbalance that resulted in an overabundance of mosquitoes, which then necessitated pesticides.[84] Chiang's mini-campaigns to kill flies and rats and to sanitize public areas, although on a more localized level, managed to make modest gains in public safety, health, and hygiene. Whereas moral persuasion and shaming generally led people to honor the rules sporadically and somewhat haphazardly, that alone led to some changes in behavior and improvements.

IMPLEMENTING THE MODERN MILITARY

Chiang also perceived a wide gap in cohesiveness, professionalism, and resources between the Chinese army and the armies of the imperial powers.[85] Just as he applied shame to citizens in the New Life Movement, Chiang similarly pointed out deficiencies in the military to improve it. Given his global timeline, Chiang tended to ignore the underlying sources for problems cropping up in the military and instead concentrated on alleviating their symptoms. Moreover, the *shilüe* reveals that Chiang acknowledged the problems more candidly in his telegrams to military officers compared with his New Life speeches.

The content in Chiang's telegrams and speeches did reveal one similarity in that he was sensitive to details in appearances. Just as civilians climbing out of bus windows was unacceptable, soldiers should not be behaving inappropriately in public. In one telegram to Xiong, Chiang described seeing two soldiers sleeping in the middle of Zhongshan Road in front of the Jiangxi Affairs branch office who were so disheveled that their state left him speechless. Rather than ask why these soldiers were so unkempt and sleeping in the road, Chiang only demanded that the head of the branch office and seventy-ninth division commander be reprimanded and this not happen again.[86]

Diverging from his New Life speeches, in his telegrams Chiang also called attention to the shame of more serious deviations from professional competence and discipline. In a March 11, 1934, telegram to Jiang Dingwen (1895–1974), one of his high-ranking army generals, Chiang reviewed the army's behavior during the quelling of the anti-Chiang Fujian rebellion instigated by the Nineteenth Route *ni* Army. Chiang complained that even though the entire tenth division was sent to defend a narrow road at Yiban, the *ni* army still escaped. Furthermore, when the soldiers reached Quanzhou, they sought prostitutes, gambled, forcefully entered homes and boats to rape and pillage, and urinated into water wells, behavior that he claimed demonstrated no sense of shame and prompted him to ask, "How can we call this a revolutionary army?"[87] He demanded that Jiang get to the root of this incompetency and breakdown of military discipline.[88]

These problems went beyond just one division. Chiang wrote to Hekou's twenty-first division commander, accusing several of his soldiers of secretly leaving their posts and entering the village, where they harmed residents and travelers and then lied to their superiors when they returned. Unable to determine which soldiers committed crimes, the officers randomly beat the soldiers. These officers also fired and hired soldiers arbitrarily, neglected to report soldiers who fled, and even put soldiers on a ghost payroll, believing such acts were normal.[89] Chiang further noted to Tang Enbo (1898–1954), his General Office commander, that the fourth and eighty-ninth divisions had the worst disciplinary problems, followed by the tenth and eighty-eighth divisions. The various division commanders had to assume responsibility because otherwise, he declared, one would be unable to control the people's mouths, tongues, eyes, and ears. By highlighting the army's misbehaviors and the impression people might have about it, Chiang appeared to use shame as a method to motivate his officers to improve professionalism.[90]

This breakdown in military discipline was due at least partly to how Chiang chose to expand the army to fight the communists. He ordered villages to form civil volunteer units, which the government would train and arm, but rather than recruit willing volunteers, the government relied on local elites to dragoon people. Rather than morally persuade villagers to join, as in the case of improving hygiene among the citizens, Chiang allowed brute force to be applied on them; soldiers shot confirmed communists and implemented ruthless repression. British writer Peter Fleming, who witnessed the fighting firsthand between Kuomintang and Chinese communists troops in Jiangxi, commented that Chiang's method of expanding his troops not only led to its deteriorating quality but also alienated the locals from the Kuomintang.[91]

Chiang made no mention of such serious problems in his New Life speeches. But the strategy behind the speeches was to focus on the implementable details that would make China appear modern. Hence, in one excerpted selection from a New Life speech, Chiang alluded elliptically to the breakdown of military discipline but focused on a small detail that if accomplished, could arguably enable the Chinese army to appear like its modern imperial counterparts. In a March 5, 1934, speech at the military headquarters in Nanchang, Chiang observed:

> Let us say that an army member must salute his superior. What is having propriety without rhythm? He is someone who puts his hand down before the superior finishes his salute. This is not having rhythm, and so, propriety is not realized. The subordinate is not saluting the superior. One might as well say that the superior is saluting the subordinate. Can we call this propriety? You must wait until the superior receives the salute, his eyes looking at yours, and finishes his salute, and then you can respectfully and solemnly put your hand down.[92]

Chiang further pointed out that such salutes were performed smoothly in foreign countries with several hundred troops. The reason the Chinese army was trained badly and lacked spirit, he argued, was that when the superior gave orders, he neglected to see whether the soldiers followed them through.[93] Although the more euphemistic example of the salute is hard to square with the scope of the actual breakdown of military discipline on the ground, Chiang seemed to believe that the correct knowledge of the salute by both officers and troops was an important first step toward enabling the Chinese army to become a modern army.

Although scholarly studies on Chiang's New Life efforts have predominantly focused on the citizenry, his uses of shame make evident that the deeper problems of modernizing the state were with the military and the peasants who were dragooned into military service and suffered the consequences of the military's misbehaviors. Unlike the case for citizens, the contradictions between prescribed and actual practice were more consequential for affecting the legitimacy of the Kuomintang regime. At the same time, one must recall that Chiang was not operating with an already unified, well-paid, and technologically advanced military. Although he advocated "disciplined efficiency," in his writings, speeches, and orders, as Jay Taylor observes, he encountered fierce resistance from his Nationalist army commanders, especially in the area of centralizing military financing, which forced him to tolerate a certain amount of corruption in exchange for retaining cohesion and loyalty.[94] But this arrangement was fragile. While the state may have been unaffected by and perhaps indirectly benefited from retailers covertly selling luxury silk goods, it could ill afford breakdowns in military discipline or insubordination by officers. In this, Chiang was not alone, as forging a national army with a strong esprit de corps continued to be difficult in China throughout the twentieth century.[95]

IMPLEMENTING THE MODERN
INFRASTRUCTURE

One final area Chiang sought to modernize, which made little headline in his New Life speeches, was infrastructure, and he approached this task in a strategized manner as well. Certainly, Nanchang, where Chiang housed his military headquarters, had to appear like a modern city, presumably to impress local and international visitors. Quick to point out the shame of deviating from his ideal vision for Nanchang, Chiang indicated in a telegram to Xiong that the electric poles outside of the city were always crooked and slanted, and the height of the wires followed no rules. Someone, he felt, should inspect and correct this situation.[96] When Chiang observed disorder in other cities, he was quick to point them out, too. He later notified Xiong that the Fuzhou city government had neglected to clean the streets and alleyways, that drainage pipes were still exposed, and that some electric poles had fallen outside the city gates that had yet to be repaired.[97]

Although there were inadequate resources to neaten the landscape all over China, Chiang did channel available funds into building roads, which were important to his thinking about national defense, consolidating authority, and preparing China for another world war. In fact, when pursuing the Chinese communists to Yan'an, in the northwestern part of China, Chiang was able to assert control over more parts of the country by constructing and repairing roads. As with the citizen and soldier, he revealed his attention to details in his telegrams to Xiong, such as pointing out a shameful litany of incomplete and decrepit roads. He noted that the paved stone road that passed through Chengtian, Yongfong, and Badu was in such bad shape that when it rained, no one could drive on it. Chiang requested that this road be fixed within ten days. He then stated that if construction workers were ineffective, the weak ones could be let go while the strong ones kept to reduce meal expenses. At the same time, he insisted that the road from Suizhou to Ganzhou be finished by the established date. Finally, there was a section of road from Shangrao to Guixi that was still incomplete. Chiang demanded that a date be set immediately to repair it, and he would personally inspect the two roads.[98]

Perhaps because building roads was easier than changing citizen psychology or restructuring the Chinese army, it appeared that in this case, Chiang did create a national infrastructure of roads based on his attention to minor details. Even so, the government had to conscript peasants to get the job done. While some developmental economists have claimed that conscription was a rational approach to economic construction for countries that were capital poor, Lloyd Eastman has argued that these roads served little economic advantage, as they were built without a coherent plan for feeding into major railways, and they sometimes duplicated existing cart paths or waterways. It also did not help that the government mistreated the peasants.[99] Nevertheless, given Chiang's global timeframe, his conception of infrastructure projects in national defense (not economic) terms, and the cheapness of highway construction (it was one-twentieth the cost of building new railroads), the regime achieved notable results. By 1936, China had 115,703 kilometers of highway, compared with only 1,000 kilometers in 1921.[100]

Although road construction served as a source of pride for Kuomintang partisans, it arguably came at a political cost to the regime's legitimacy. Peasants went unpaid, and the government often seized land with little or no compensation or forced peasants to work at harvest time. Perhaps the dragooned road construction workers summed up the costs well: "Those mothers! [referring to Chinese government officials] When the XX (Japanese) [*sic*] come, it will be no worse than this."[101] The trade-offs Chiang made to modernize China's infrastructure, however, were meant to achieve the overall goal of unifying the country under his leadership and wresting China's autonomy from foreign control.

• • •

Analyzing Chiang's use of *chi* to modernize China in the context of an urgent timeline and a somewhat flexible implementation reaffirms several of the negative evaluations of previous scholars: Chiang's gradualist policies were ineffective in bringing genuine rural transformation; his policies tended to treat symptoms, not causes; and participants could subvert his policies and generally get away with it. In addition, his privileging of state-building and national salvation put an undue burden on peasants, who were always shortchanged by being dragooned into the military and coerced into doing the heavy lifting of modernization tasks.

Missing from the discussion of Chiang's leadership during his drive to modernize China has been an awareness that he was attempting consciousness building on a much broader level than has generally been recognized. Beyond his specific attention to matters of dress, snappy military salutes, and perfectly aligned telephone poles, his underlying mission was to sensitize the country to its weaknesses, relentlessly pointing out deviations from his ideal vision of China. He shamed not only citizens but rival warlords, fellow party members, the military, and the population to bend their efforts toward his agenda of a modern country. In the process, he offered a vision of a national identity that some Chinese embraced and others resisted but that led them to begin to see themselves as a political and modern collective.

The flexibility that Chiang showed in implementing his ideals for modern China with regard to its citizens and challengers to his authority is in marked contrast to the alternative path taken by Mao. Although Mao's leadership initially looked appealing to Westerners because he created a mass organization, his later mobilization of the people in a totalitarian direction resulted in the deaths of millions.[102] It also included the torture and imprisonment of close associates and their spouses.[103] Chiang may have been authoritarian and repressive in his methods, but he rejected becoming an extreme ideologue like Mao. Instead, he accepted the haphazard manner in which citizens followed New Life directives with the hope that his values for the modern citizen would eventually be internalized. Moreover, although Chiang did put leaders who were on the same side but had challenged him (like Hu Hanmin and Zhang Xueliang) under house arrest, he did not humiliate or torture them the way that Mao did.

Furthermore, despite its shortcomings, Chiang's approach produced tangible and positive outcomes. As Fenby argues, his regime created "a time of modernisation such as China had not seen before," including "a flowering of thought, literature, art and the cinema," as well as a more militarized society.[104] By China's own measures of progress, as another biographer observes, the authority of the central government was greater than at any point since the mid-nineteenth century, and illiteracy among government troops decreased from 70 to 30 percent.[105] As mentioned already, investments in rural education and transportation networks were considerable. By not simply dismissing Chiang as the loser to Mao in the Chinese Revolution, we can better understand how he ushered China along a viable path to modernity that could be distinguished from the Western liberal, fascist, and communist paths.

Although Chiang's use of *chi* in 1934 was different from his use of it in confronting imperial powers in 1928 and 1931, this was the flip side of the same coin of his efforts to build a national identity. Yet, to adapt Rudyard Kipling's observation about England, "And what should they know of Chiang Kai-shek who only Chiang Kai-shek know?," our investigation is still incomplete. To better understand Chiang's strategized uses of *chi*, the next two chapters offer a comparative examination of his efforts with that of other Chinese and world leaders to confront imperialism and contribute to the national narrative of their countries.

PART II

Structure

CHAPTER 5

Chi *and Leaders*
of Republican China

Having examined how Chiang Kai-shek mobilized *chi* during the Nanjing era, this chapter and the next shift the focus to the political environment and how it helped or hindered Chiang in his uses of *chi* as a cultural resource. This chapter compares Chiang with two other Chinese leaders during the Republican period—Yuan Shikai, whose leadership preceded Chiang's and who ruled the early Chinese republic from 1912 to 1916, and Mao Zedong, who challenged Chiang's authority between 1935 and 1949, ultimately succeeding him as leader of China in 1949. Like Chiang, Yuan and Mao served as "national" leaders during the Republican period, invoked *chi*, and led the country during a period of domestic disunity and external threat.[1]

In studies that compare these leaders, the dichotomous framework of understanding leadership (as discussed in the introduction) appears to reassert itself. Most have been unwilling to recognize that Chiang and Mao were both leaders of a revolutionary party, viewing Chiang as simply following in the wake of Sun Yat-sen and changing the revolutionary nature of the party. The label of visionary revolutionary leader was thus reserved for Sun Yat-sen, who challenged the Qing regime and then Yuan Shikai's regime in the 1900s and 1910s, and for Mao, who opposed the Kuomintang regime in the 1920s, 1930s, and 1940s. Historians have instead categorized Chiang along with Yuan as backward-looking, a disappointment, and a sell-out. Mao's secretary, Chen Boda (1904–89), in a biography of Yuan in 1946 meant as a propaganda tool for the Chinese

Communist Party (CCP), even depicted Chiang as a worse version of the deceased Yuan Shikai.[2] Viewed not as change-makers but as maintainers of order, Chiang and Yuan have been characterized as trapped by their circumstances, seemingly unable to implement their grand reforms and ambitions.[3]

By using *chi* as a focal point for comparative analysis, this chapter encourages a rethinking of Chiang's creative agency and that of Yuan and Mao. By exploring how different political contexts provided structural opportunities or penalties for the Chinese leaders to use *chi*, this chapter examines when Chiang's adaptation of *chi* worked best, when it did not, and why. By doing so, it offers a more faithful depiction of and insight into Chiang's particular exercise of creative agency.

Yuan and Chiang

Yuan Shikai began his political career serving as a late Qing official from 1902 to 1908 and then, after the 1911 revolution, as president of the new republic from 1912 to 1916. Because he encountered external and internal threats to Chinese sovereignty similar to those that were faced by Chiang, this section investigates two seminal events during Yuan's tenure of power—the Twenty-One Demands and his bid to serve as monarch—to probe how the global, domestic, and leadership contexts during his rule were far less favorable for him to mobilize *chi* as compared with Chiang.

THE TWENTY-ONE DEMANDS AND
CONFRONTING IMPERIALISM

Often compared to the unequal treaties China had been forced to sign with Western imperial powers in the nineteenth century, the Twenty-One Demands addressed unresolved political and territorial issues between Japan and China. Presented to Yuan Shikai by Japanese Prime Minister Ōkuma Shigenobu (1838–1922) in January 1915, these demands were related to disputes in Shandong, Manchuria, the Yangtze Valley, and Fujian and to the employment of Japanese advisers in the Chinese government and among the Chinese police.[4] To understand why Yuan did not use this occasion to mobilize *chi* as Chiang did during the Jinan and Mukden Incidents, some context about nationalism and imperialism and how they informed Yuan's leadership in the new republic is needed.

In the late Qing period, it was unlikely for Chinese leaders to label an act as humiliation by an imperial power, especially by Japan, than it was a few decades later. On one hand, the Japanese victory in the First Sino-Japanese War of 1895 catalyzed Chinese nationalism. Unlike China's defeat by the British in the Opium Wars in the mid-nineteenth century, which was attributed to Commissioner Lin Zexu's (1785–1850) mistakes and could be discounted because Britain was an alien civilization, the loss to Japan—which to this point China had considered an "inferior" and a barbarian country in the Confucian order—jolted China into acknowledging its weakness.[5] On the other hand, this nationalist awakening did not yet reflect the development of mass-based nationalism of the New Culture Movement that began in the mid-1910s and therefore could not be mobilized against imperialism. Instead, in an attempt to modernize and strengthen China, the Qing regime instituted top-down reforms through proposed new policies and appointed people like Yuan to implement them.

Another factor mitigating the ability to recognize acts as humiliation was that imperialism was widely viewed as a legitimate global force. Moreover, imperial powers mutually checked one another, ameliorating the possibility of one power taking excessive advantage of China.[6] Finally, Japan, as a latecomer to the imperial game, tended to be relatively controlled and conservative in its actions toward China during the late Qing period. In the wars against China in 1895 and Russia in 1904, Japanese civilian and military officials set limited military objectives and largely avoided civilian losses. Japanese leaders also worked within the constraints of international law and commerce, emphasizing economic and trade relationships in its foreign policy.[7] Qing leaders like Yuan were thus less inclined to think of Japanese actions as humiliations because the international norms of that time were more accepting of imperialism, and Japan's limited goals tended to stay within those norms.

As the governor-general of Zhili Province (1902–8), Yuan developed an approach of pragmatic engagement toward imperial powers that avoided decrying their acts as humiliations. Described by Stephen McKinnon as "progressive," "toughminded," and "capable of fighting fiercely direct attacks on Chinese sovereignty," Yuan nevertheless operated as a realist who recognized that China was weak and financially strapped. He thus willingly made deals that indirectly compromised China's sovereignty by granting limited concessions to imperial powers, such as a new railway construction loan agreement.[8] With the exception of Britain, Yuan adeptly played one imperial power off against the others to China's benefit. With Britain, he developed a special relationship that was largely based on mutually advantageous commercial agreements and treaties that ultimately raised his international reputation.[9]

Although Sun Yat-sen and his revolutionary compatriots rejected the kinds of deals Yuan had made with imperial powers, they viewed him as a progressive and a patriot and thus offered him the presidency after the 1911 revolution in exchange for arranging the departure of the ruling family (fig. 5.1).[10] Despite the political context changing from empire to republic, Yuan continued to operate with his usual modus operandi toward imperial powers, in particular toward Japan. On August 15, 1914, when the newly begun World War I gave Japan an opportunity to make claims on China with less interference from other imperial powers, Japan demanded that Germany withdraw its vessels from Chinese and Japanese waters and give up its leasehold in Shandong. When the Germans rejected this demand, Japan placed their soldiers on Chinese territory, violating international law.[11] To respond, Yuan proceeded pragmatically to weigh his options. When informed that Chinese forces had the resources to resist the Japanese incursion for only forty-eight hours, he decided to allow the Japanese troops to pass through Shandong along a "fighting zone" to reach the Germans and observe Chinese neutrality outside of this zone.[12] By avoiding confrontation with Japanese troops, Yuan likely prevented many Chinese deaths. But in the new Republican environment, his decision to accommodate the Japanese without condemning their encroachment on Chinese soil as a humiliation or obtaining international censure would soon come to haunt him.

In January 1915, when Yuan attempted to revoke the fighting zone to get Japanese military leaders to withdraw their troops, the Japanese responded by presenting Yuan with the Twenty-One Demands, a list of "issues" they wanted resolved in return for withdrawing troops, and they insisted the list should be kept secret.[13] To ensure the best outcome for China, Yuan again used his considerable negotiating skills. He prolonged talks with Japan for as long as possible to leak contents of the

FIGURE 5.1: Yuan Shikai as president of the new republic. Photo by Rio V. De Sieux, *The World's Work*, 30 (1915): 378. Image source: Wikimedia Commons.

demands to the Chinese press and to the other powers to gain their diplomatic support (especially the Americans and the British). When the Japanese wanted to conduct meetings five days a week, the Chinese foreign minister, Lu Zhengxiang (1871–1949), under instructions from Yuan, countered that Yuan only had time to meet one day a week, and both sides eventually settled on three days. In another ploy, Lu shortened the duration of each meeting by serving tea after his opening remarks, a courtesy that the clearly irritated Japanese minister in Beijing, Hioki Eki (1861–1926), was unable to refuse.[14]

After four months, negotiators on the Japanese side ran out of patience and delivered an ultimatum to Yuan on May 7, 1915, giving him forty-eight hours to respond. By then, the original demands had been winnowed substantially, including the excision of the most odious set of demands that called for Japanese advisers to be embedded in the Chinese government. With urging from Great Britain, Yuan accepted the remaining demands on May 9. Given the country's disadvantage in material strength, Yuan felt that the Chinese side had done well in the negotiations, but nonetheless considered the result "a 'national humiliation,' a 'loss of rights,' and a 'great disaster.'"[15] It was the first time Yuan invoked humiliation—not as a political tool but as an outcome. G. E. Morrison (1862–1920) further observed that Yuan seemed obsessed with the dangers Japan continued to pose even though the acceptance of the ultimatum was supposed to settle the differences between the countries. In fact, through the summer, Beijing officials were devising ways to limit Japan's newly acquired privileges in Manchuria and Inner Mongolia.[16]

Despite Yuan demonstrating considerable skill dealing with imperial Japan, several changes in the structural context of operating in the new republic appeared to constrain his ability to legitimate a course of action. One such change was that the imperial powers, preoccupied in a world war, were unable to follow the usual rules of the game by checking Japan. Under normal circumstances, Yuan might have exercised his skill at playing one imperial power off another—in this case, Germany against Japan—and a better outcome for China would likely have resulted. A second shift was that Yuan's closest ally, Britain, had begun to alter its approach to China. Indeed, when Yuan stood his ground at the beginning of the negotiations in the hopes that the British would intervene, the British were hesitant. Yuan was consequently forced to concede progressively more as the negotiations continued, which ultimately surprised and angered even his supporters.[17]

A third shift was a rise in anti-imperialist sentiment and increased resentment toward officials who failed to guard against imperial encroachment. What was previously limited largely to the small band of Kuomintang revolutionaries had now grown among a wider swath of the population. When the negotiations were leaked to the public, many in the Chinese public suddenly formed new organizations and took part in large-scale demonstrations to protest the Twenty-One Demands. These previously unknown leaders from medium and small businesses joined overseas Chinese living in Japan and the United States in protest. On March 18, 1915, for instance, the Citizens' Association of Comrades against Japan and students who had recently returned from Japan organized a rally of 30,000 in the Shanghai International Settlement to urge Yuan to stop negotiating with Japan and start a boycott of Japanese goods.[18] As popular expectations arose that Yuan would defend China's nationalist interests, they also worked against Yuan's usual strategy of indirectly compromising sovereignty so as to get the best possible deal for China.

Although Yuan might have mitigated the public's negative reaction to his leadership by drawing on *chi* to confront the Twenty-One Demands, the changes wrought by the 1911 revolution and a world war were made clear during the Japanese negotiations, when it was too late for him to alter his approach. Furthermore, Yuan's close interactions with imperial powers and lack of credibility with the revolutionary forces made it difficult for him to change tactics and draw on a cultural story like Goujian to explain his actions. Finally, what constituted regime legitimacy in the new republic was in flux, and perhaps Yuan was simply unaware of the need to change in response to new conditions or unsure about how to do so. This uncertainty, coupled with a late Qing leadership strategy that did not work as well in the new republic, contributed to his inability to change his approach to imperial powers quickly or credibly to respond to the Twenty-One Demands.

As Zhitian Luo perceptively notes, there were unintended consequences stemming from Yuan's acceptance of the ultimatum that undermined his legitimacy as a leader. Just days after the event, business circles in Beijing and Shanghai promulgated articles in Chinese newspapers to never forget the humiliation of May 7, the day the Japanese put forward the ultimatum. On May 20, however, the Jiangsu Educational Association notified schools that they would remember the humiliation on May 9, the day Yuan accepted the terms. Shortly thereafter, the National Alliance of Provincial Educational Associations took May 9 as National Humiliation Day. Despite the disagreement between business and educational circles over the dates, a shift in public perception of blame appeared to occur. Before May 20, people took May 7 as the day of humiliation, but afterward, more people marked it as May 9, suggesting that in the beginning, people mostly blamed the Japanese, but afterward, they also blamed Yuan. Rather than appreciating that Yuan played a difficult hand well, they were now blaming him for accepting the Japanese demands. In the meantime, educators were discussing plans to revise textbooks and introduce to Chinese students the need to avenge the humiliation of the Twenty-One Demands.[19]

Compared with Yuan's acceptance of most of the Twenty-One Demands, Chiang's "acceptance" of Japan's seizure of Manchuria in 1931 was a much more egregious blow to China's sovereignty. But Chiang had more tools available to persevere in his leadership. At the end of World War I, nationalism was a stronger force, not only in China (as expressed through the 1919 May Fourth Movement) but in Asia and the world, and imperialism was on the decline. So when, despite this global change, Japan violated the 1922 Nine-Power Treaty by invading Mukden in 1931 and establishing the Manchukuo puppet state in 1932, international and domestic perceptions that Japan was humiliating China increased considerably.[20] As Japan became more militaristic and willing to violate new international norms that respected national sovereignty, Chiang was increasingly able to call its actions in this new political environment humiliations.[21] Moreover, unlike Yuan, Chiang was able to distance himself from imperial powers, having already insisted on abrogating all unequal treaties and revoking all foreign extraterritorial rights.[22] As detailed in chapter 3's analysis of the Mukden Incident, Chiang's policy of nonmilitary resistance enabled him to establish China's innocence with the international community and further highlight to the world Japan's transgressions of international norms. In addition, his policies of nondirect negotiations and nonco-

operation mitigated the blame assigned to him for conceding to imperial Japan. These factors allowed Chiang to employ Goujian's story of
enduring humiliation to politically justify his acceptance of Japanese-
occupied Manchuria while Japanese leaders managed to isolate their
own country diplomatically.

THE BID FOR THE MONARCHY AND
CONSTRUCTING A COLLECTIVE NARRATIVE

If Yuan was unable to take advantage of humiliation as a political weapon
during the Twenty-One Demands, the environment of the early republic
also appeared ill-conducive for Yuan to mobilize a nationalist narrative
based on *chi* to transform Chinese society. This constraint can be seen in
his attempt to change China's form of government from republican to
monarchical in 1915 as a way of strengthening the country to better confront imperial powers. As we shall see, without the 1919 May Fourth crys-
tallization that leaders should relate to their people as citizens and not as
subjects in a modern society, Yuan's monarchical attempt appears to be a
lone endeavor, devoid of some shared idea of the country's path forward.

Three months after accepting the Japanese ultimatums, as a likely
response to the blowback for doing so, Yuan announced his intention to
change China's form of government from a republic to a monarchy and
become its first new emperor. He was skeptical of a republican government because he believed that the revolutionaries behaved like children
and the "masses of the people . . . were intensely conservative."[23] More
important, Yuan likely pursued the emperorship to shore up his legitimacy, believing it was a weapon to confront imperial aggression and
build domestic strength by increasing order and respect for the state.[24]

In changing the government structure, Yuan was not reverting back to
the traditional past as a way to bolster his legitimacy. His method was
eclectic but consciously introduced modern elements. In switching out a
Chinese character to change "Republic of China" (Zhonghua minguo) to
"Empire of China" (Zhonghua diguo), Yuan made sure the new name differed from dynastic appellations such as "Great Qing State" (Da Qingguo).
He also eliminated the kowtow, traditional servile forms of address, and
the use of eunuchs as palace attendants. He emphasized the constitutional
nature of the monarchy—even though the process was rigged, Yuan had

himself elected as emperor.[25] His efforts toward modernizing the Chinese military, especially by emphasizing an impersonal command structure and allegiance to the center as opposed to subordinate officers, and in rejecting superstition lent credence to the "modern" aspects of the new monarchy.[26]

Although Yuan abandoned the plan in March 1916, due in part to division among his advisers and his own indecision, its failure also reflected his insularity with respect to the social and political implications of modernity. Yuan was skeptical that the people understood the ideas of republicanism, representative government, or even rights. Although he was probably correct in some of these assumptions in the new China, Yuan still had to incorporate various groups within Chinese society into his monarchical agenda. Although he paid homage to theories of popular sovereignty by getting himself elected, he ascribed to them whatever he wanted for himself rather than provide a culturally resonant story to justify the emperorship and forge a sense of shared connection with the Chinese population.[27] Yuan might have argued that he was now performing traditional rituals "as one body with the citizens."[28] He might have adapted—as a modernized version of the "mandate of Heaven"—the ideas of US political scientist Frank Goodnow of conducting a free and fair election as a method to justify launching the monarchy.[29] And if he intended the emperorship as a weapon to confront imperial aggression, he might have constructed a *chi* narrative to show how doing so would help avenge humiliation, thereby forging a connection with the people. Without justifying his decision, Yuan allowed others to step in and express their misgivings about the scheme. Scholar and philosopher Liang Qichao (1873–1929) argued that although a monarchy did have an "awe-inspiring influence" (*zunyan*) conferred by tradition, the Republican revolution had swept away this tradition, and simply reviving the monarchy could not restore it.[30]

Following the May Fourth Movement, Chiang was better able to tell a story of national injury and repair that involved both leader and followers. The push to vernacularize the Chinese language after 1919 (discussed in chapter 1) enabled Chiang to connect with the masses. Whereas Yuan followed the model of the dynastic imperial leaders by delivering hard-to-decipher edicts and memorials in print form, which only a few could understand, Chiang spoke to school children, soldiers, and policemen in the vernacular and hence could directly engage a wide range of groups.

When Chiang decided to launch the New Life Movement in 1934, he had a similar idea as Yuan in transforming China to better confront imperial powers. In contrast, however, Chiang focused on transforming the people and was more proactive in providing the movement's rationale, drawing on *chi* and other ideas in the Confucian tradition. Through shame, he attempted to motivate the Chinese to become citizens of a state freed from foreign influence, and these efforts dovetailed with his aims of identifying humiliations by foreign powers as a prelude to avenging them. Unlike Yuan, who avoided justifying his monarchical move and was disengaged from public discourse, when critics challenged Chiang's downplaying of material welfare, he immediately defended his choice—without virtues, such as *chi*, even a wealthy society would degenerate into poverty and chaos.

This comparison is not meant to suggest that Chiang's New Life Movement was an unqualified success and Yuan's monarchical movement was an abysmal failure—after all, Yuan's plan was more ambitious and revisionist—but that the lack of mass politics before 1919 would have made any formulation of a national narrative and implementation of a modern political agenda problematic. By contrast, after 1919, Chinese leaders had more tools at their disposal to mobilize the Chinese population and justify their political goals. Even though Chiang and Yuan were both authoritarian in their rule, they still needed to legitimate their regimes, just as the traditional emperors of the dynastic past had to maintain their mandate of heaven. In a political environment where mass politics had come into existence and humiliations were more self-evident, it was easier for Chiang to draw on the Confucian cultural tool of *chi* to face the problems of his day and maintain his legitimacy.

In short, this comparison between Yuan and Chiang illustrates that Yuan's problems were not simply a failure of imagination. After all, it was only after the Twenty-One Demands that the phrase "Never Forget National Humiliation" (*Wuwang guochi*) became part of popular discourse, appearing in newspapers and in textbooks, and that a day was set aside to commemorate a humiliating event.[31] Moreover, the inklings of mass nationalism in this early period were inadequate to transform the relationship between Yuan and the Chinese people. Still, it is important to note that Yuan's exercise of creative agency as a Qing official and president of the new republic did prevent disastrous confrontations with imperial powers and was far more successful than those immediately succeeding him, such as Li Yuanhong (1864–1928) and Duan Qirui (1865–1936), who were unable to hold the country together after Yuan's death in 1916.[32] Moreover, as Patrick Fuliang Shan's recent reappraisal notes, under Yuan's "dictatorship," the New Culture Movement that ushered in a notion of mass national politics ironically began under his presidency, no doubt helped by an environment in which "most newspapers published freely, civilian organizations mushroomed, and individual opinions spread."[33]

By contrast, Chiang not only inhabited a more favorable political context in which he could credibly mobilize shame and humiliation to confront external and internal threats but was able to learn from Yuan's example what he should avoid, including any kind of direct negotiations with or personal concessions to the Japanese.[34] Finally, Chiang could argue in the *shilüe* that the Japanese had taken advantage of Yuan's "overweening desire to become Emperor" and incorporate Yuan's "shameful" response into his own national narrative as another humiliation he needed to bear and overcome to move toward China's salvation.[35] Ultimately, Chiang's creative use of *chi* was enhanced by a closer relationship between leader and followers, by a change in the norms of the global and Chinese domestic environment, and by Japan's increased violations of those new norms.

Mao and Chiang

In the 1930s, as Chiang formulated the *chi* narrative to mobilize the Chinese people against a foreign invader, Mao Zedong and the CCP were developing an alternative story about China that emphasized proletarian internationalism, class struggle, and humiliation. According to Mao, Chinese workers and peasants owed no loyalty to a state that allowed China to remain in the grips of reactionary landlords and the bourgeoisie. In advancing this narrative, Mao was justifying his attempts to defeat the current government composed of Chiang and the Kuomintang to put the correct class in power.[36] In this narrative, Mao placed blame for humiliations at the hands of the Japanese on Chiang. In 1935, for instance, Japanese leaders had begun urging provincial officials in North

China to break free from Nationalist-ruled China and set up their own autonomous governments. In a manifesto, Mao avoided describing Japanese actions as humiliations even as he railed against the "viciously evil Japanese imperialist bandits," and shifted the responsibility for the Chinese humiliation onto Chiang.[37] In a later manifesto on the same issue, Mao expanded on this blame:

> The Guomindang government, however, with Chiang Kaishek as its chief culprit, casually and shamelessly acceded to these demands on Japan's part, carelessly selling out all of North China and the whole country! This is an unprecedented act of betrayal. This is truly galling and humiliating to the Chinese nation. Chiang Kaishek and the Guomindang have proven once again that he is the biggest traitor selling out the country since the beginning of Chinese history![38]

Perhaps because Mao was not the leader in charge when confronting the Japanese, there was less reason to speak of humiliations at the hands of the Japanese. Thus, CCP statements and reports in the 1920s and 1930s understandably mentioned "humiliation" and "unequal treaties" less frequently than in similar statements and reports coming from the Kuomintang.[39]

In this prewar period, Mao's alternative Marxist-Leninist story, coupled with his uses of humiliation, was not yet credible on a national level; moreover, the survival of the CCP was precarious as Chiang and the Kuomintang twice nearly annihilated it. In the first instance, under Chiang's orders, Kuomintang troops massacred 90 percent of CCP members in April 1927, and the remnants scattered to the remote provincial borderlands to establish Soviet bases.[40] This turn of events may have been a blessing in disguise because it forced the Chinese communists to develop ties with the peasantry, a receptive audience to the CCP storyline. In the second instance, Chiang conducted five extermination campaigns, and in the last one forced the CCP to embark on the Long March, which almost led to its second annihilation. By the time the arduous journey concluded in October 1935, Mao had emerged as the CCP leader but had lost 90 percent of his compatriots.[41] Far from robustly challenging the Kuomintang in the 1930s by commanding vast territories with loyal inhabitants, the CCP was a small (but resilient) band of revolutionaries. In 1937, on the eve of war, the CCP had increased its members to only 40,000 and controlled 1.5 million people out of a population of more than 500 million.[42] But as we shall see, when Japan invaded China in 1937, it changed the global and Chinese domestic dynamics in such a way as to constrain Chiang's creative agency in carrying out his template of action based on *chi* and to enable Mao to become a viable contender for national dominance.

THE SINO-JAPANESE WAR

Chiang had adapted the Goujian story to suit China in the 1920s and 1930s; however, unlike the ancient king, he continued to face internal and external threats and lacked the luxury of time to strengthen his country and fight from a position of self-reliance. Chiang thus also needed aid from other countries to avenge the humiliations imposed by the Japanese. Nonetheless, he appeared able to employ *chi* and other resources effectively enough to sustain his political agenda in the 1928 Jinan and 1931 Mukden Incidents and even in the 1934 New Life Movement.

By 1935, Japan's designs in the Far East forced Chiang to abandon a key tenet of his strategy for avenging humiliation, which was to unify the country under his authority before confronting Japan. Joseph Stalin (1878–1953), detecting a burgeoning alliance between Berlin, Rome, and Tokyo, decided to oppose fascism on all fronts in summer 1935.[43] With regard to Japan, Stalin came to believe that a Second United Front was warranted between the CCP and the Kuomintang, and through Wang Ming (1904–74), the CCP's representative in Moscow, Stalin declared that the CCP would support Chiang.[44] Because Chiang needed Soviet aid in the event of an all-out war, he not only had to abandon his goal of defeating the Chinese communists, he was now forced to "cooperate" with them.

When Japan invaded China in July 1937, yet another tenet was undermined in Chiang's approach to avenge humiliation, which was to achieve China's autonomy when imperial powers were fighting each other and through reliance on friendly imperial aid. But this plan went awry during the war. For the first four years, China was the only country fighting Japan. As a result, the humiliation story that Chiang had constructed during the Nanjing era was stretched to the breaking point by a full-scale military invasion. Indeed, Japan wiped out the preparations Chiang had made toward war within six months. Just in the war's opening in Shanghai (after the attack on the Marco Polo Bridge in Beijing) in which Chiang committed 500,000 of his best troops, 187,000 were killed or injured in action in the first three months.[45] Nanjing was the next to fall, and as chronicled by Iris Chang in *The Rape of Nanjing*, the battle was one of the most horrific of the war.[46] With Nanjing's fall, Chiang set up his wartime capital in Chongqing, and those in the east of China who could do so moved with Chiang to escape Japanese occupation. Not only did Chiang remove himself from his sources of support, he also left behind a vacuum of authority in the countryside. Chiang, it might be argued, was pushed further behind the starting line in his efforts to avenge humiliation.

By contrast, Japan's invasion helped Mao's alternative storyline gain traction with a broader audience. The communists saw no action in the disastrous Shanghai and Nanjing battles, given their location in interior North China and Yen'an, and their absence not only helped to preserve their troop strength but also exonerated Mao from being held accountable for the defeats.[47] Moreover, Japan's invasion, so much more aggressive and widespread than any of its earlier incursions, finally made imperialism a lived experience for peasants, when previously they had considered foreign affairs to be irrelevant to their daily lives. As a result, when Chiang left a power vacuum in the countryside in his retreat to interior China, the villagers naturally turned to the nearest authority figures, who happened to be the communists.[48]

Moreover, the war prompted Mao to promote Chinese communism in a national rather than international story, and this shift helped give the rural population a stake in the nation and, by extension, to the CCP cause.[49] In an interview with Helen Foster Snow (1907–97), Mao outlined "ten demands" regarding the method to resist Japan and acquire national salvation. For instance, he noted that the Chinese nation should "mobilize the whole body of the masses to join the war front against the Japanese," and at the same time, he sought "to improve and reconstruct the life of the people, including the removal of the many unjust surtaxes, decreasing the taxes, and decreasing rents."[50] Ironically, Mao also drew from his rival party's founding father Sun Yat-sen and his Three People's Principles to call the nation's attention to the importance of "arousing the popular masses" and standing against Kuomintang autocracy and suppression. He critiqued Chiang's leadership of the Second United Front for failing to involve the masses fully, stating, "The essence of the contradiction is that those who have seized the latrine pit can't shit, while people of the whole country, who suffer acutely from bloating, have no pit."[51] Resistance by the government and army alone, he further stated, could never defeat Japanese imperialism. Indeed, Mao matched rhetoric to action during the war by directing his troops to conduct "mass work" in the ways described in his ten demands to create base areas of communist support in the regions Chiang had abandoned.

Mao's alternative story of the authentic leaders of the Chinese nation received a boost of legitimacy after a battle between the Chinese communists and the Kuomintang. The New Fourth Army Incident, as the skirmish came to be known, not only enhanced the reputation of these CCP troops as national heroes, but the troops also added the title of national martyrs.[52] Chiang and CCP leader Zhou Enlai (1898–1976) had originally reached an agreement in summer 1940 that if the Chinese communists evacuated their New Fourth Army troops in central China to the north of the Huang (Yellow) River, Chiang would grant them relative autonomy from the Kuomintang government.[53] The New Fourth Army took its time to evacuate, even attacking the Nationalist Eighty-Ninth Army in October. In January 1941, the New Fourth Army was detected traveling south instead of north. The reasons for this southward move were unclear, but at his wits' end, Chiang ordered the Kuomintang troops to annihilate the remaining communists in Maolin township in a battle that lasted for ten days, wiping out 7,000 out of the 9,000 communist troops.[54]

Although both parties appeared to violate the United Front policy, the public relations outcome clearly favored Mao and the Chinese communists. Given their mass work in the areas abandoned by Chiang, CCP portrayal of themselves in these areas as vanguards in the resistance—breaching government orders for the sake of fighting Japan—appeared more credible. Although the Kuomintang was within its rights to discipline the communists, their brutal retaliation was perceived as being less committed to national salvation and resisting Japan and as committing an appalling act of humiliation against their fellow countrymen. A spokesperson of the Central Committee noted that the Kuomintang never truly wanted to incorporate the CCP into the United Front, and thereby, "incidents of humiliation, cruelty, encirclement, and attack against us have been legion."[55] In this incident, according to the spokesperson, Chiang's true intentions were revealed—what was initially called "moving north within the deadline" was actually "a trap to snare our army into encirclement to be annihilated."[56] Indeed, CCP portrayal of Chiang as conducting a civil war rather than a war of resistance and as replacing unity with splitting was also a boon to Mao's nationalist story.[57] In this new context of war, the CCP extermination campaigns and the civil wars that Chiang had conducted during the Nanjing era were now perceived by the public as unacceptable. In the end, Chiang not only lost legitimacy in his aggressive use of force against the CCP, he also failed to get the CCP to withdraw to the north of the Huang River.[58]

If there was any semblance of the United Front before the Fourth Army Incident, it clearly existed in name only afterward. The Chinese communists continued their advantageous guerrilla tactics for the remainder of the war and built support for themselves from the ground up. Because their troops were broken up into smaller units of 1,000 to 2,000 men behind enemy lines, it was difficult for the Kuomintang to keep track of the communist-controlled forces. Moreover, because the CCP was located in the vast countryside, it was impossible for the Japanese to occupy the Chinese territories fully. By the end of the war, the CCP army was able to multiply tenfold, from 50,000 to 500,000.[59]

Despite the increasing traction that Mao's alternative story was gaining among the peasants, Chiang's humiliation story appeared to reach a fruitful conclusion in 1943, when (as Kuomintang historiography later proclaimed) he successfully avenged national humiliation through the abrogation of all unequal treaties.[60] At the time, this vindication often appeared rather hollow. For one thing, because Chiang was making fewer grassroots connections with the peasantry given his more urban base, his signing new treaties with the United States and various European powers lacked meaning with peasants, who still only had a fuzzy idea about who constituted the domestic central government. Given irreconcilable differences between Chiang and Kuomintang rival leader Wang Jingwei, for instance, the latter decided to form a collaborationist Nationalist government with Japan in Nanjing.[61]

Another reason for the hollow victory was that the aid Chiang's government received from allies, especially from the United States after the bombing of Pearl Harbor in 1941, also obviated the need for him to rely on the Chinese population and failed to foster a shared sense of collective destiny. Rather, as Kathryn Edgerton-Tarpley notes, in Chiang's drive to save the nation, he sometimes appeared willing to starve his people. In the Henan famine of 1942 to 1943, one to three million of the population of thirty million died from starvation and famine-related diseases and another three million fled the province (map 3). When Chinese newspapers began to report the true conditions in the region, Chiang quickly shut down their efforts. Only when foreign journalists produced photographic evidence of the results of the famine did Chiang order the military to share grain with the peasants, making it appear that he was more concerned with losing foreign goodwill than with fostering solidarity with the peasants. Such political maneuvering when the lives of so many were at stake contributed to alienation from rather than collective connection with Chiang and his national humiliation story. The Chinese communists, by contrast, helped famine sufferers increase production, and cadres made a point of sharing their food with refugees, thereby winning over many peasants to the communist side.[62] If Yuan Shikai had exhibited no connection to the masses in the early republic, the war revealed that Chiang demonstrated only a partial urban one.

Finally, the abrogation of unequal treaties seemed hollow because it did not prevent additional humiliations. Not only did Chiang have to continue fighting the Japanese for another two years, but China's allied partners did not always treat China as an equal. In a 1943 radio address, Winston Churchill (1874–1965) stated that the aim of the war in Asia was to reclaim the lost imperial territories taken by the Japanese, which ran counter to the aims of the critics of colonialism. He made no mention of China's role in postwar plans and stated only that the country would be "rescued" from Japan, remarks the Chinese found sharply insulting.[63]

This attitude eventually translated into a new humiliation by Allied powers. In February 1945, as Germany's defeat was in sight, the Allies were able to focus on the Pacific War. When Franklin Roosevelt (1882–1945), Churchill, and Stalin met during the Yalta Conference (February 4–11, 1945) to discuss Soviet entry into the Pacific War and postwar planning, Chiang received no invitation and had to wait four months to officially learn what they had decided.[64] In return for Soviet entry into the war, Roosevelt and Churchill agreed to recognize the independence

SOVIET UNION

MANCHUKUO

OUTER MONGOLIA

Huang River

Beijing

KOREA

Yen'an

Battle of Taierzhuang

Henan Province

JAPAN

Nanjing

Chongqing

Shanghai

Yangtze River

Maolin- (Fourth Army Incident)

East China Sea

Extreme famine

Severe famine

0   200 mi
0   200 km

MAP 3. China during the Sino-Japanese War, with locations mentioned in the text. Cartographic design by Scott Walker.

of Outer Mongolia, a decision that would strike a blow to Chiang's legitimacy, much as the Twenty-One Demands had to Yuan's three decades earlier.[65] In Chinese eyes, Outer Mongolia was a part of China. Were it to be given up, Chiang's claim to be a genuine, sincere, and effective nationalist would be seriously hurt.[66] Echoing Yuan's efforts to whittle down the most onerous aspects of the demands, Chiang accomplished much while negotiating the subsequent Sino-Soviet Treaty of Friendship and Alliance, which was concluded on August 8, 1945. In particular, he resisted the Soviet Union's attempt to claim a full-blown sphere of influence in Manchuria despite conditionally accepting Stalin's demands; as he wrote in his diary, not doing so would have made reaching agreements on other issues impossible.[67] Although this treaty formalized an unequal relationship between the countries, it was remarkable that China gave up so little, given the gross disparities of power. The end result led prominent Chinese news outlets, including *Da Gong Bao* and *Dongfang Zazhi*, and many in the Chinese public to condemn Chiang's capitulation and conclude that the Nationalists were incompetent regarding domestic and foreign affairs. Although Mao could not directly exploit these sentiments without appearing to criticize his Soviet allies, he benefited from the blow to Chiang's legitimacy.[68]

Because Mao was not the incumbent leader and thus was not held accountable for wartime decisions made on China's behalf, it was easier for him to change course and sustain his legitimacy during the war. This gave him the flexibility to experiment with different stories without being penalized, such as shifting his emphasis on class conflict in the prewar period to nationalism in the war period and attacking Chiang for contributing to national humiliation while also paying homage to him when it suited his purposes, as when he wrote, "You, sir, have been leading the whole nation in fighting an unprecedented great revolutionary war, and there is no one among our countrymen who fails to look up to you."[69] With help from Stalin and fellow CCP leaders, Mao also was able to preserve Chinese communist troops while still appearing patriotic and conduct mass work to win over the peasant population, allowing him to grow CCP membership from 40,000 to 2.7 million and expanding its territory from 92,000 square kilometers to 950,000 square kilometers during the war.[70]

Chiang, who had mobilized humiliation to great effect during the Nanjing era, was unable to change his story quite so easily. As noted already, the first six months of war upended the carefully laid compromises in his humiliation narrative, and as the war neared an end, he was unable to redirect the narrative specifically tailored to Japan toward an ally who was intent on wresting Outer Mongolia away from China. Like Yuan, whose approach toward Japan that had served him well as a Qing official could not work the same way as president of a new republic, the change of circumstances was too great for Chiang to make credible adjustments in the approach and strategy that had worked in the previous decade. Even though the war undermined Chiang's humiliation story, it did not negate his creative exercise of agency during this period. It was clear to Chiang in 1937 as it was to Yuan in 1915 that Japan's superior military strength would overwhelm any direct engagement between the two sides. Yet through selective warfare, giving up land to the Japanese, and coaxing aid from Allied powers, Chiang managed to tie down Japanese troops in the Pacific theater for eight years. In addition, he appeared to negotiate the best possible outcome in the Sino-Soviet treaty, given his country's weaker position. Chiang may have failed to achieve one aspect of his Goujian story, which was to consolidate China under his authority, but he did achieve the other of helping free China from imperial exploitation and aggression.

• • •

This comparison demonstrates the multiple ways the political context shaped the three leaders' agency in their uses of *chi* and how a dramatic change in that context, as in the case of revolution or war, stretched Yuan's template for action and Chiang's humiliation narrative to breaking points. The ultimate conclusion to be drawn from these findings is not that leaders' external environment and political context matter more than their personal agency but simply that taking those factors into consideration can help us better understand the creative exercise of that agency in legitimating a course of action and creating a credible collective story. In essence, to faithfully depict a leader's creative agency, one must take into account the uneven (and sometimes changing) playing field in which leaders operate that affects their use of cultural resources and consider their achievements in terms of what worse outcomes they might have prevented. Although in 1949 Mao was finally able to declare in his opening address to the Chinese People's Political Consultative

Conference that "the Chinese people . . . have now stood up" and "ours will no longer be a nation subject to insult and humiliation," he was clearly building on the efforts of Yuan and Chiang before him.[71] In this way, rather than evaluate each leader's accomplishments based on the final outcome of consolidating China fully, which tends to diminish Chiang's and Yuan's leaderships while magnifying Mao's, we can gain a more faithful depiction of the contributions of all three men.

Given that their political contexts preempted Yuan and Mao from fully using *chi* as a cultural resource, the next chapter looks outside of China for a leader who also connected to an analogous cultural resource to confront imperialism. By turning our attention to how Mahatma Gandhi used a tool akin to *chi* to confront British imperialist expansion and exploitation, the chapter further refines our understanding of Chiang's creative uses of the *chi* narrative and the contextual factors that enabled and constrained his construction of a national identity.

CHAPTER 6

Chi *and* Satyagraha: *Chiang, Gandhi, and the Imperial Powers*

When Chiang Kai-shek met Mahatma Gandhi in Calcutta on February 18, 1942, all of Asia was under threat of being overrun by Japan. The island imperial power had already taken over Singapore on February 15 and would take Burma on March 7, the latter bringing Japanese forces to India's very doorstep.[1] In hopes of uniting against a common enemy, Chiang and Mme. Chiang Kai-shek flew to India to persuade the Indians to help China and the Allied powers fight Japan.[2] However, Gandhi was unconvinced and averse to mobilizing his compatriots to aid China and India's colonial oppressor, Britain, even if this meant that another colonizer, Japan, might take Britain's place. Nonetheless, Gandhi assured Chiang that he would not obstruct China's efforts to resist Japan, and the two men came away from their meeting with a deeper understanding of each other's problems (fig. 6.1).[3] For his part, Chiang empathized with Gandhi's position and concluded that India's terrible conditions stemmed from Britain refusing to acknowledge India's realities.[4] In a letter to Chiang, Gandhi remarked, "I can never forget the five hours' close contact I had with you and your noble wife in Calcutta. I had always felt drawn towards you in your fight for freedom, and that contact and our conversation brought China and her problem still nearer to me."[5]

Notwithstanding the leaders' mutual respect for one another's struggle against imperialism, scholars have subsequently tended to portray Gandhi as a moral, visionary leader and Chiang as a problematic, power-hungry one. Indeed, James MacGregor Burns describes Gandhi as the

FIGURE 6.1: Chiang Kai-shek and Mahatma Gandhi in Calcutta. "China Asks India Whether it Will Fight," *Life*, 12, no. 17 (April 27, 1942). Image source: World History Archive/Alamy Stock Photo.

quintessential example of transformative leadership in modern times. Gandhi, he argues, raised "the level of human conduct and ethical aspiration of both leader and led, and thus it has a transforming effect on both." By contrast, he places Chiang into the category of leaders who "all suddenly slid—or were pushed—down the 'greasy pole'" of power.[6] In another comparative assessment, Howard Gardner praises Gandhi as a creator of the modern era whose influence extended beyond national boundaries, but consigns Chiang to a group of leaders who lusted for more power, "achieved position by force," or demonstrated a "thirst for absolute power."[7]

Recent scholarship has begun to rehabilitate Chiang somewhat (as alluded to in the introduction) but has become more critical of Gandhi. Scholars have begun to see Chiang's thinking and policies as unusually similar to Mao's, arguing that Chiang envisioned himself as a revolutionary and believed in the need for revolution in China.[8] In contrast, a *Wall Street Journal* article describes Joseph Lelyveld's recent biography of Gandhi as portraying Gandhi as "a sexual weirdo, a political incompetent and a fanatical faddist."[9] Building on these recent reevaluations of the two men, a direct and more systematic comparison of these leaders is again needed to go beyond the earlier bifurcated analysis that tended to praise Gandhi and criticize Chiang.

This chapter notes that like Chiang, Gandhi was acutely sensitive to the indignities of imperialism and vigorously channeled his personal feelings of humiliation into a collective response. Just as Chiang adapted *chi* to mobilize and legitimate his political agenda, Gandhi drew on an analogous resource in his use of *satyagraha*, or truth struggle, to confront British imperial injustices. In analyzing their deployment of a similar cultural resource, this chapter enables a more faithful depiction of these men's leadership efforts and, more generally, of the common struggles leaders of weak countries face when confronting stronger foreign adversaries. Furthermore, a comparison of their political contexts demonstrates that the paths available to forge a credible story and favorable legacy tended to disadvantage Chiang.

Underdog Leaders

Gandhi and Chiang each appeared to convey outward passivity when responding to imperial powers. Over time, however, each skillfully marshaled cultural resources specific to his nation to reinterpret that passivity as building individual and collective strength. As we have seen, Chiang deliberately avoided direct military confrontations with Japan in the 1928 Jinan and 1931 Mukden Incidents, a seemingly weak-kneed response that invited sharp criticism from the Chinese public and international commentators. *Time* magazine, in reporting about the "grim, appalling spectacles of chaos and collapse" following the Japanese occupation of Manchuria in 1931, described Chiang as the "nervous, high-strung little Chinese President Chiang Kaishek, who has been squabbling for months with the other Chinese Government (the one at Canton), [and who] abruptly resigned, announcing that Canton leaders would come north and take over the Nanking, Government."[10] Even during the Sino-Japanese War, Chiang followed a similar passive strategy to preserve his army's strength, to the extreme chagrin of General Joseph Stilwell (1883–1946).[11]

Despite criticism and protest of his actions toward the Japanese, Chiang drew on *chi* to transform the perceived meaning of his apparent inaction. By drawing on the story of King Goujian, Chiang signaled to his soldiers, the public, and posterity the wisdom of refraining from lashing out at an inopportune time for the sake of survival and future liberation. After all, Goujian's show of "loyalty" to the enemy leader not only saved his life and that of his wife but allowed them to return to their homeland, begin secret preparations to strengthen their population, and eventually wage a successful war against the enemy country. Chiang communicated the imperative for patience and for uniting under his leadership to engage in a Goujian self-strengthening exercise rather than prematurely striking to achieve China's complete independence. From this cultural perspective, Chiang's response to the Japanese showed necessary restraint and self-control while gathering what was required to confront his adversaries successfully.

By drawing on the Goujian model, Chiang was suggesting that for a great task to be accomplished, great humiliations—ranging from insults to military incursions—had to be endured. As mentioned in chapter 3, Chiang advised some young men in 1931 that to become talented and help China complete the revolution required undergoing extraordinary danger and humiliation. As he constructed a national identity based on this logic, Chiang seemed to embody this advice. Indeed, two years after the embarrassing story of his Mukden retreat, *Time* put Chiang on its cover and described him as "the great soldier-statesman who gives cohesion to the most populous and strife-wracked country in the world," and in 1938, named him and Mme. Chiang as Man and Wife of the Year.[12]

A similar logic played out with Gandhi. In 1893, Gandhi was a young lawyer in South Africa when a white coachman beat him and laughed at his insistence on his rights. This encounter made him feel that British oppression of Indians in South Africa was worse than in India. Like Chiang, Gandhi channeled his feelings of deep humiliation into finding a way to overcome them for himself and his Indian compatriots. Having only spent three weeks in South Africa, at the age of twenty-four, Gandhi called a meeting of all the Indians in Pretoria to discuss the injustices, and thus began his journey of "avenging" his personal and the Indian collective humiliation.[13]

Gandhi returned to India in 1915 and continued his efforts toward resisting British imperialism. In 1930, he resolved to challenge a British ban on salt. Even though the world's best rock salts were located in India, the

British forbade the Indians to carry even a pail of seawater to their homes. Instead of allowing Indians to make superior salt locally, the British put 600,000 tons of salt into the Indian market and profited $20 million annually. At times, the salt was marked up 2,000 percent the production cost.[14] Gandhi decided to protest this monopoly by walking 240 miles from his base at the Sabarmati Ashram, near Ahmedabad, to the coastal village of Dandi, where he would break British law by making salt (map 4).

Initially Gandhi's plan provoked not support but shock and displeasure among his colleagues in the resistance movement in part because ordinary Indians were not actually agitating over the salt tax. His proposal also amused members in British and pro-British circles, leading one person to remark, "Let Gandhi soon eat his own salt."[15] According to a British-owned journal in Calcutta, "It is difficult not to laugh, and we imagine that will be the mood of most thinking Indians. There is something almost childishly theatrical in challenging in this way the salt monopoly of the Government."[16] *Time*'s initial coverage of the 1930 Salt March also questioned whether Gandhi would even be able to walk the 240 miles, reporting that when he had arrived in Nadiad, he "sank to the ground" and had "cold compresses applied to his head, his legs swabbed with ointment, before he could proceed."[17] When Gandhi declared a day of rest in Anand, "newsgatherers reported they did not believe the emaciated saint would be physically able to go much further."[18]

Despite the dismissals and doubts, Gandhi persisted in a strategy of exercising self-control and willingness to accept suffering that echoed Chiang's enduring of humiliation. Gandhi defined *satyagraha* as "the vindication of truth not by infliction of suffering on the opponent but on oneself."[19] By calling for nonconstitutional and nonviolent action that required self-control and sacrifice from himself and his followers, Gandhi used *satyagraha* to force his opponents to either enforce a policy they believed unjust or to alter it.[20] He thus sought to engage the conscience of the more powerful perpetrators of injustice and thereby persuade them to change their unjust behavior. In doing so, he provided an alternative to a dominant Western conception of courage by relying on moral sensibilities and a capacity for guilt as opposed to aggression, which was merely mastery without self-control.[21]

The power of this strategy could be seen in *Time*'s quick reversal of its assessment of Gandhi and his Salt March. A week later, noting that

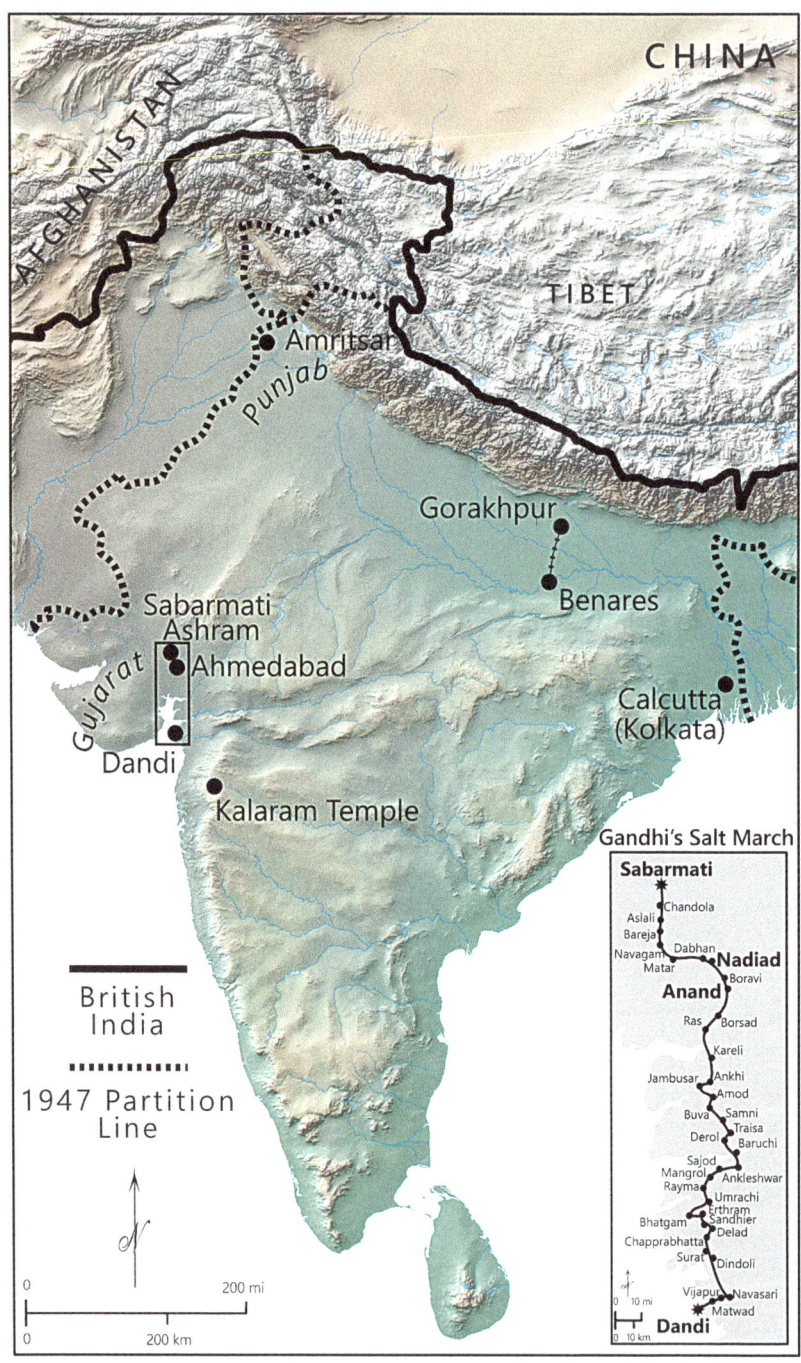

MAP 4. The Indian subcontinent, with locations mentioned in the text. Inset: route Gandhi took on his march to the sea. Cartographic design by Scott Walker.

Gandhi had kept his pace and had already walked eighty miles while ten of his accompanying disciples had become sick with fever, it declared that Gandhi's actions spoke louder than words and that his behavior was more Christian than that of the British. As it reported, the colonial government's initial amusement over Gandhi's "theatrics" had transformed into a desperate anxiety.[22]

Chiang and Gandhi thus similarly used culture-specific moral constructs of *chi* and *satyagraha*, respectively, to reinterpret actions typically deemed passive and weak as strength and self-control in response to imperial injustice. By informing their national storylines about how the collective should react to imperial powers, the two leaders lent legitimacy to their political agendas. In Chiang's case, the agenda was to consolidate his authority domestically while maintaining the country's survival in the face of Japanese encroachment; in Gandhi's, it was to serve notice to the British that their treatment of Indians was unjust, setting the stage for later demands for *Hind Swaraj* or home rule, and unite the country based on social equality. As the comparison with Gandhi suggests, Chiang's use of *chi* was by no means an unworkable resurrection of Confucian tradition but a suitable and possibly generic response to injustices committed by stronger foreign powers.

Connecting the Personal and Collective Story

Similarities can also be detected in how Chiang and Gandhi used *chi* and *satyagraha* to connect their personal stories with the collective ones and cultivate in themselves the qualities those cultural resources identified as necessary to lead the collective. As Gardner argues, a leader's personal story becomes inextricably linked to those of the polity when that leader's problems and uncertainties intersect with those of the collective, especially when the way the leader seeks to overcome his or her individual conflicts also appears to offer a solution to the collective conflict.[23] Chiang and Gandhi made these connections explicit not only in their memoirs, eulogies, and autobiographies but in their regular messages to their Chinese and Indian audiences.

Chiang and Gandhi selected stories that were personally and broadly appealing and aligned with their vision of a collective identity. Because

Chiang sought to consolidate state sovereignty under his authority and gravitated toward a pathway of enduring humiliation, he adopted King Goujian as a key model for himself and others. As alluded to in chapter 2, Goujian happened to be a popular Chinese icon in the first half of the twentieth century. The shared cultural resource in the form of the Goujian story thus served as a bridge between Chiang's personal story and the collective one he was constructing, one that spoke to both Chiang's and China's redemption. Other cultural tales were available to Chiang that would appeal to the Chinese people, legitimate his leadership, and address the concerns of militarily defending China. One such story was that of Yue Fei, who had fought valiantly against the Jins during the Southern Song dynasty before he was betrayed and executed. Although Chiang referred to the well-known military hero as an example of patriotism and loyalty in his speeches and writings, he appeared to have less personal connection: Yue Fei's story lacked a victorious ending, a hero who was a leader of a country rather than a mere general, and a process of enduring humiliation that were critical components of the Goujian story and resonated with Chiang's modus operandi.

Gandhi drew from the story of Prince Rama and his wife, Sita, heroes of a cherished Hindu epic, the *Tulasi Ramayana*, set in 1000 BCE. Although Rama was expected to become king after his father stepped down, he was instead banished for fourteen years because his stepmother wanted his brother to ascend the throne. Rama acquiesced and even refused the throne after his brother implored him to take it. Rama and Sita continued to follow their respective dharma—a Sanskrit word meaning a strict adherence to a moral code and duties that apply to an individual in a particular stage of life and station—in exile despite many tribulations that tested their adherence to dharma. In the end, Rama returned to Ayodha and became king, presiding over a kingdom where everyone followed his or her dharma.[24] In his *Autobiography*, Gandhi recalled first hearing the story from his childhood nurse and again when a Rama devotee read selections to his father when the latter was quite ill. The devotee's readings, Gandhi wrote, "laid the foundation of my deep devotion to the *Ramayana*," and he considered the work the "greatest book in all devotional literature."[25]

In his writings, Gandhi drew on themes that related to Rama's love for his devotees, his graciousness, and his care for the poor. Gandhi was also attracted to Rama's method of communicating with ordinary people through well-known symbols and the local language, which he emulated to gain the trust of local peoples during his three-week journey to the ocean. Furthermore, the Bhakti tradition of which Rama was a part also contained an undercurrent of criticism of Hindu hierarchy, which aligned with Gandhi's mission of championing the rights of the untouchables.[26] The example of Rama thus worked as a cultural bridge between Gandhi's personal admiration of the text's themes of equality and the collective aspirations of Indians to be treated as political equals, even though his embrace of this classical Hindu text made some Muslim intellectuals uncomfortable despite his championing of Hindu-Muslim unity.[27]

In addition to drawing inspiration from popular stories, both leaders selected events from their childhood to connect their individual story to the collective. When Chiang was seven, a severe blow to his family came when his father passed away and his mother, with whom he was close, had to take in sewing to make ends meet. Once Chiang was even briefly imprisoned until his mother could collect the money necessary to pay a tax collector. His mother had married into the village, and Chiang keenly felt that the family was considered outsiders after his father's death.[28] In a eulogy for his mother twenty-seven years later, he remembered that she "endured thirty-six years of hardship . . . swallowed much bitterness . . . [and] never refused any kind of toil."[29] More than four decades later, on the occasion of his fiftieth birthday, he wrote, "My family, solitary and without influence, became at once the target of . . . insults and maltreatment. . . . To our regret and sorrow none of our relatives and kinsmen was stirred from apathy."[30] By recalling these early hardships, insults, and isolation rather than the family's change of fortune by his teenage years, Chiang demonstrated that enduring humiliation had become a defining theme for him and linked his story to the collective one he was constructing regarding China's withstanding of humiliation at the hands of the Japanese.[31]

In his autobiography, which he penned in his mid-fifties, Gandhi chose to recount personal stories that stressed themes related to truth and struggle, the essential components of *satyagraha*. He recalled, for instance, that his father was incorruptible and had earned a reputation for strict impartiality. Gandhi described himself as also having a strong sense of right and wrong. Although he claimed to retain little of what he had learned in school, he vividly recalled incidents from his school years when a moral line had been crossed. In one instance, a teacher had wanted Gandhi to cheat by spelling the word *kettle* correctly to appear competent in front of the inspectors, but Gandhi refused and was the only student who misspelled the word. Gandhi also confessed to his own misbehaviors, which included a brief stint at eating meat and smoking.[32]

A more prominent theme Gandhi highlights in his autobiography is his struggle to exercise self-control. Indeed, he particularly admired Rama for his ability to sacrifice and tolerate suffering.[33] Gandhi's life-long preoccupation with self-restraint was key to ensuring that his use of *satyagraha* would be devoid of violence and hatred. He particularly admired the self-discipline of his mother, whom he considered a saint. According to her son, she chose the hardest vows and kept them without complaint. She would not eat without having performed her daily prayers or having visited the temple. Instead of taking a meal only once a day during Chaturmas, she fasted on alternate days or refused to eat until the sun shone. Gandhi recounted that on one cloudy day, when the children called her to see the sun peeping from the clouds but it disappeared before she could join them, her response was, "Oh well, god didn't mean for me to eat today."[34] Just as Chiang picked childhood stories about enduring humiliation that he thought illustrated an important collective response to imperialism, Gandhi used familial examples to build collective inner moral courage that would work as an alternative to a Western conception of courage.

Perhaps even more important, both men, determined to become the kind of leaders who could guide their countries to prevail over imperialism, used *chi* and *satyagraha* on a daily basis to motivate their leadership. Chiang concentrated on developing character and self-discipline by drawing on neo-Confucian ideas of cultivation.[35] In a chronology his secretaries compiled, *Reflections on Overcoming Difficulties (Xingkeji)*, Chiang focused on controlling his temper and recorded his shame when he failed to do so. His goal was to cultivate in himself the qualities he deemed necessary to become a leader capable of avenging humiliation.[36]

Gandhi likewise paid attention to controlling himself, and his autobiography recounted a series of experiments to realize this self-control. When he undertook a difficult fast during his time at Tolstoy Farm in South Africa that he felt was key to maintaining his *satyagraha* struggle, he again listened to readings from the *Ramayana*.[37] While imprisoned in South Africa, guards prohibited him from drinking tea or coffee and allowed him to put salt only on cooked food rather than while it was cooking, habits he decided to continue after prison, even giving up salt for a decade.[38]

Both leaders eventually came to enact Eric Erikson's insight that influential leaders come to identify their personal quest with the national quest.[39] By the Mukden Incident of 1931, as mentioned in chapter 3, Chiang was already noting that "the responsibility of the difficulties and danger of the Japanese is something that I only can take on."[40] Gandhi said at one point, "When I say that I prize my own salvation above everything else . . . it does not mean that my personal salvation requires a sacrifice of India's political . . . salvation. But it implies that the two go together."[41] Over time, self-cultivation enabled these men to envision themselves as central figures in their country's salvation.

Although some of their solutions to their countries' problems may have appeared idiosyncratic, such as Gandhi's ideas about deindustrialization, and their people may have disagreed with the details of their respective solutions, their personal embodiment of *chi* and *satyagraha* connected with the people and with the collective story. According to Lelyveld, the throngs of supporters coming to see Gandhi at each train stop between Gorakhpur and Benares in February 1921 were not there to support his program of *swaraj* in its entirety but to pay homage to him.[42] Similarly, although the Chinese may have ridiculed Chiang's New Life Movement, they still abided by its rules of hygiene and orderliness in front of authorities. Had Gandhi been a wanton meat-eating and smoking womanizer or had Chiang dressed in a disheveled fashion, their ultimate goal of standing up to imperialism would have seemed hypocritical. But their apparently sincere attempts to embody their respective philosophies also lent legitimacy to their leaderships and credence to their political agendas.

Foreign and Imperial Influences: Further Shaping the Collective Story

To inform their uses of *chi* and *satyagraha*, Chiang and Gandhi tapped into resources beyond their deep reservoir of domestic stories. By also drawing on foreign and imperial influences, the leaders demonstrated that global ideas could be integrated into these concepts to add further potency to their quest for national salvation.

Although indigenous Indian cultural resources underpinned essential elements of Gandhi's notion of *satyagraha*, the word itself was actually invented outside of India. In 1906, Gandhi sponsored a contest in the South African newspaper *Indian Opinion* to come up with a name to describe a passive resistance approach that would be devoid of connotations of violence or hatred. His uncle's grandson came up with the term *sadagraha,* which means "truth force," and Gandhi changed a letter to make the term mean "truth struggle."[43]

Despite this Indian origin, Gandhi's notion of *satyagraha* was especially informed by Leo Tolstoy's (1828–1910) *The Kingdom of God Is Within You.* This book had "overwhelmed" and "left an abiding impression" on Gandhi in its denunciations of the privileged, educated Russian upper class's hypocritical claims of Christian brotherhood while brutally exploiting the lower classes.[44] Gandhi also took to heart Tolstoy's prescription in *What Is to Be Done?* of returning to simple living and physical labor to provide for one's sustenance.[45] He reported that English writer John Ruskin's (1819–1900) *Unto this Last*—which argued that social inequalities were the outcome of industrial society's valuing of capital formation and devaluing of physical labor—similarly "captivated" and left a deep impression on him.[46]

So inspired, in 1910 Gandhi started the Tolstoy Farm southwest of Johannesburg. Tolstoy's influence on Gandhi was so strongly apparent at the time that one Indian critic accused him of being "a Russian Christian in an Indian body."[47] Yet Gandhi clearly reworked the ideas of Tolstoy, Ruskin, and even Henry David Thoreau (1817–62) to form his own practice of social equality by taking several vows, such as vegetarianism and celibacy, that reflected his personal preoccupation with exercising self-control. Lelyveld notes that Ruskin, for instance, could hardly have imagined that his ideas would result in a self-sufficient rural commune with an emphasis on physical labor as a response to colonial exploitation and rural poverty.[48] Gandhi creatively drew on foreign influences in his experiments on promoting social equality, and these adaptations were important steps toward imagining a new Indian identity.

In keeping with his goal of consolidating state power, Chiang read the biographies of foreign leaders such as Vladimir Lenin and Otto von Bismarck and histories on the French and Russian revolutions and World War I. Many of his reflections regarding those books appeared in the avenging humiliation entries in his diary, especially those that deepened his understanding of *chi*.[49]

Also shaping, or perhaps more accurately, confirming his thoughts about enduring humiliation was his conversion to Christianity in 1930. Chiang participated in Bible-reading sessions with his wife and carried a Bible while traveling. His diary includes numerous quotations from the New Testament.[50] In one entry, for instance, he mentioned characteristics he particularly admired in Jesus—his spirit of sacrifice, his ability to endure, his spirit of struggle, his purity, and his love.[51] He identified with Jesus's Job-like abilities to withstand humiliation and face suffering, and he sought to emulate those qualities alongside him: "Those who believe in Jesus must overcome one's desires and endure insults and hardships. Every day, I must also bear the cross along with Jesus, to continue the ideas of Jesus for the sake of redemption."[52] In his quest to consolidate the modern state, however, Chiang specifically repudiated one foreign influence—that of mass participation. Although nationalism, fascism, and even Christianity all contained possibilities for mobilizing the masses, this option held little attraction for Chiang, and he accordingly never considered enlisting more autonomous agency on the public's part to help shape the political agenda.

Foreign ideas provided Chiang and Gandhi with new vocabulary and ways of thinking that helped them make domestic cultural stories about ancient kings and devotional teachers relevant to twentieth-century understandings of capitalism, class structure, the modern citizen, and the nation-state. Gandhi particularly selected foreign influences that supported making liberal changes within society, the kind that would excite the May Fourth advocates in China and subsequent Western scholars. By contrast, Chiang favored foreign influences that took an authoritarian, state-centered approach to achieving sovereignty.

These leaders' uses of *chi* and *satyagraha* were also shaped by the actions and influences of the very imperialists they were resisting. Chiang, who had received two years of Japanese military education in Tokyo (1907–9) and served two years in the Imperial Japanese Army (1909–11), admired the Japanese for their frugality, cleanliness, and ability to behave in an orderly fashion in public spaces.[53] Perhaps unsurprisingly, in speeches Chiang sought to shame Chinese soldiers and the people to act more like the Japanese. He also drew from Western imperial influences, exhorting his Chinese audiences to follow German and Italian examples of obedience.[54]

Gandhi, who had studied at the University College of London for three years (1888–91), came to value the law deeply. In fact, his commitment to law did not necessarily entail ousting the British from India. If the British had abided by just rules of law, he would have willingly accepted British rule. According to the *Hind Swaraj*, which Gandhi wrote in 1909 to discuss Indian self-rule,

> If I have the power, I should resist the tyranny of Indian Princes just as much as that of the English. By patriotism I mean the welfare of the whole people, and, if I could secure it at the hands of the English, I should bow down my head to them. If any Englishman dedicated his life to securing the freedom of India, resisting and serving the land, I should welcome that Englishman as an Indian.[55]

For Gandhi, *satyagraha* meant ensuring that the law did not discriminate between colonizer and colonized, and he took this thinking a step further by arguing that the law should not distinguish between Hindus and Muslims or among members within the Hindu caste hierarchy.[56] What Gandhi therefore drew from the British aligned with his belief that the law should make no distinction among people.

Ultimately, the two men responded to imperialism with different goals in mind—Gandhi sought to transform the psychology of the oppressor and the oppressed, whereas Chiang sought to nurture a strong country and citizenry. Understandably, they drew on different influences. By borrowing liberal ideas, Gandhi's political philosophy has had more influence on and was seen as more successful by Western scholars than the more authoritarian influences borrowed by Chiang, and the latter also caused problems for him domestically, which hurt his assessment.

The Political Context and the National Story

Despite the similarities between the two men's approach to leadership, the leaders were inhabiting dissimilar political contexts, which had far-reaching influence on Chiang's and Gandhi's abilities to shape and implement their national visions. Chief among these contextual factors were (1) the degree of state centralization, (2) the degree of the leader's involvement in state power and administration, and finally (3) the degree to which an external threat suppressed domestic disunity. By examining these factors and their effect on the two leaders' abilities to legitimate a course of action and construct a viable national story, this section attempts to explain why scholars may have tended to underestimate Chiang's leadership contributions and overestimate Gandhi's.

STATE CENTRALIZATION

The degree of state centralization in India and China influenced each man's leadership and its perception. Clearly, both would have had an easier time uniting their people by means of a collective story if shared institutions already existed; however, neither the Indian nor the Chinese state had fully functional centralized political institutions with commanding authority over all localities in the time these men exercised their leaderships. Nevertheless, India was more centralized politically than China, making the construction of a unifying national story easier for Gandhi than for Chiang.

The British in India, convinced that a divided crown jewel was ill-conducive to attaining power and profit, sought to centralize the Indian subcontinent's administration after the Sepoy Mutiny in 1857.[57] The British focused on the armed services by recruiting Hindus, Muslims, and Sikhs and acculturating them into an environment of professionalism and civilian control of the military. The goal of the combined British Indian force—the officers tended to be British—was to maintain internal order and engage in imperial activities in Asia and Africa, in short functioning as a centralized imperial army. The British also centralized the state through the Indian Civil Service, whose duties included collecting taxes, maintaining order, and implementing policy on a daily basis and into remote regions of the subcontinent. Many observers considered the civil service to be the "steel frame" that held India together.[58]

Through such efforts, the British helped foster a new collective identity among Indians by incorporating them into the colonial governing system for consultation and by extending Indian representation from the lowest to the highest level. In addition, by grouping Indians into new administrative categories, such as "Landholders in the United Provinces" and the "Mohammadan Community in the Presidency of Bengal," the British further cemented this new identity by ignoring different interests and rivalries.[59]

As an unintended consequence, these Indian collaborators of the British Raj were able to build a nationalist movement on the scaffold of British centralization efforts. As Anil Seal points out, the Indian elite, schooled in British methods and enlisted to help administer the country, were now drawn together by professional ties and developed an oppositional "political structure of their own which could match the administrative and representative structure of the Raj."[60] In fact, by the time Gandhi returned to India from South Africa in 1915, the Indian National Congress (INC) had become a successful umbrella organization that even developed good relations with the Muslim League and spoke in the name of Indian nationalism.[61] Gandhi thus entered the Indian stage after others had laid a centralizing and unifying groundwork for his mobilization efforts, which allowed him to extend his strategy of *satyagraha* beyond his home province of Gujarat and speak as a national representative against British colonialism.

When Chiang entered Chinese politics in the 1920s, in contrast, most of China's centralized imperial state institutions had collapsed. As chapter 5 demonstrated, although the Qing regime belatedly started to reform its institutions in the first decade of the twentieth century—Yuan Shikai even attempted to modernize and centralize the Chinese army— by the 1910s and 1920s, the army had splintered into separate groupings led by different warlords. Moreover, Chiang's efforts to unify China during the Northern Expedition in 1928 had proven to be fleeting.

Not only was there no imperial framework (native or imposed) on which China could nurture a national opposition to foreign domination, but even Chiang's efforts at building centralizing institutions proved inadequate. Although by the beginning of the Sino-Japanese War Chiang had managed to become recognized as the leader of free China, the continuing struggle to unify the country meant that his construction of a national story vied with others (e.g., the communists') and gave opponents and later scholars an opportunity to interpret his uses of *chi* as merely a self-serving means to satisfy a personal thirst for power.

STATE POWER AND ADMINISTRATION

Another relevant contextual aspect is the degree to which state legitimacy was in dispute and the leader's relationship to that state. As Max Weber points out, charismatic authority is most often embodied by leaders who are seen as unconstrained by institutions, rather than as actively involved in the daily decision-making and administration of a discredited state power.[62] In this regard, Gandhi was arguably twice removed from the taint of state power. Although Gandhi was the INC's spiritual leader, he rarely participated in its daily affairs, and his political career, though marked by periods of intense influence, consisted mostly of relatively quiet local work.[63] He not only stood apart from an increasingly resented state imperial power but maintained a distance from the INC's routine fighting and cooperation with that state power.

A telling example of Gandhi's ability to avoid the problem of "dirty hands" was his response to Indian criticism of his support for British war efforts by forming the Ambulance Training Corps for Indians in London in 1914, which he justified by noting that the path to *ahisma* (nonviolence) was not clear-cut. Because he was being protected by British arms, he decided that as a devotee to *ahisma*, he would aid in the war effort as compassionately as possible. This stand, which Judith Brown describes as based on Gandhi's "prolonged agonizings of conscience," allowed Gandhi to maintain his moral stance on nonviolence and avoid charges of becoming a lackey of the British government (as did his refusal of Chiang's entreaties to help the British fight Japan in World War II, mentioned earlier).[64]

This outsider status provided Gandhi room to maneuver about when to enter or leave continental politics and to exercise greater control over the political actions he called his "experiments with truth."[65] Upon returning to India in 1915, Gandhi deliberately chose to distance himself from the INC and the home rule movement, which demanded that Britain give India the right to self-government.[66] Despite agreeing with the movement's goals, Gandhi was uninterested in following the tracks already laid down by its leaders, noting, "At my time of life and with views firmly formed on several matters, I could only join an organization to affect its policy and not be affected by it."[67] Instead, he chose to enter continental politics only when urged to do so by the INC after World War I, when Indians felt betrayed by the British repaying their war efforts with the Rowlatt Act and the Amritsar massacre in Punjab and were frustrated by the little headway they were making in seeking redress from the British through regular channels.

Gandhi, playing the role of Weber's charismatic savior, called on Indians to join him on his path of *satyagraha*, which he used to transform the structure of the INC and exact concessions from the British. Gandhi changed the group's creed from "attainment of self-government by constitutional and legal means" to "attainment of *Swaraj* by peaceful and legitimate means," reflecting a vision of *satyagraha* that was flexible to pursue a nonconstitutional approach, if needed.[68] He also instituted a working committee to attend to daily INC matters and opened INC's membership to the masses.[69] Moreover, he launched a nationwide *satyagraha* campaign that involved a nonviolent boycott of foreign goods, the Noncooperation Movement (1920–22), which eventually pushed the British to make positions elective in the Legislative Council via the India Act in 1921 and allow the Indian Civil Service exams to be simultaneously held in England and India.[70]

Such impressive changes gave Gandhi a larger-than-life persona that continued throughout his career. Further confirming Burns's characterization of Gandhi as a transformational leader was his astute use of *satyagraha* in intensive bursts without compromising his commitment to nonviolence. In the 1930 Salt March, Gandhi's journey encouraged tens of thousands of Indians to suspend their normal routines to join him. The march, especially the beatings of some 2,500 marchers by police, left an extraordinary impression on domestic and international audiences concerning British injustice. At the same time, as was seen in the 1920 Noncooperation Movement, Gandhi had no hesitation in ending an event when protests crossed the line into violence or when INC members, who tended to view *satyagraha* as a utilitarian strategy, became tired of the approach. As a result, his construction of this aspect of the Indian nationalist identity—courageously standing up to the oppressive British—served as an inspiration and a source of pride for the Indian people.

Yet this larger-than-life persona was made possible largely by his minimal involvement with state imperial power and administration. Although the INC ultimately turned to Gandhi when it had exhausted all constitutional means at its disposal, its members, working under a more constrained system based on constitutional and legal means, had laid an important foundation that enabled Gandhi's mobilizing of a national movement through *satyagraha*.[71] Working outside the normal avenues of politics, Gandhi could avoid disputes with competing interests over India's political and economic direction and advance a rather controversial economic plan of returning to a small-scale economy and deindustrialization that supported his moral vision of social equality. Gandhi working on the spinning wheel for an hour a day only added moral force to his goal (fig. 6.2).[72] His outsider status thus gave him latitude to implement

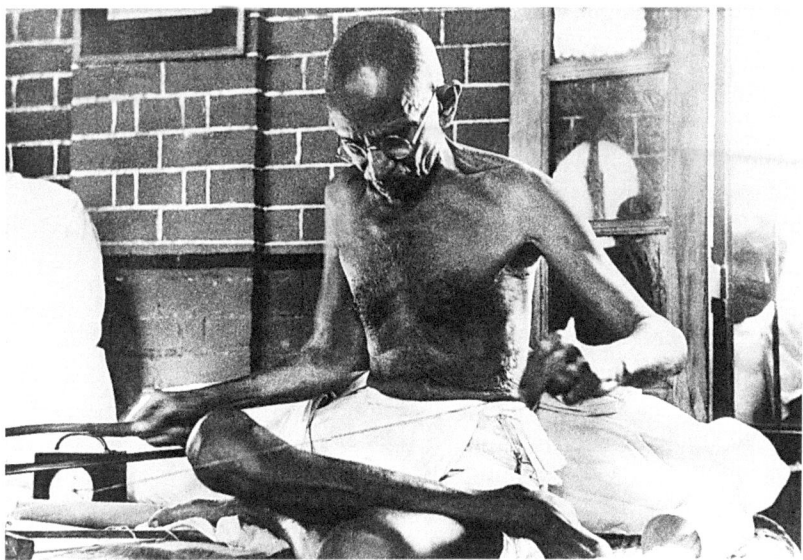

FIGURE 6.2: Mahatma Gandhi spinning yarn in the Harijan (Dalit) colony, 1940. Image source: Sueddeutsche Zeitung Photo/Alamy Stock Photo.

his moral vision, unencumbered by day-to-day compromises and ex-changes, climbing the political ladder, or taking blame for when things went badly in the INC or the British Raj.

By contrast, Chiang was the head of a weak and divided China and was thus unable to gain the same kind of moral legitimacy as an outside challenger. His monopoly on the legitimate use of force was never fully established and, coupled with China being a weak state, his exercise of state power was inadequate to ensure domestic order and well-being and protect from external incursions. Unable to successfully defend China by deploying the military and hence choosing the path of appeasement, Chiang's efforts to ensure the country's survival were often met with se-vere criticism by students and various segments of the Chinese popula-tion. Despite justifying his actions via the Goujian model of biding one's time to turn strength into weakness, his dissenters interpreted his deci-sions as just plain weakness.

When the Sino-Japanese War finally broke out, Chiang's prior re-straint appeared justified. Fighting a full war with the Japanese revealed the severely unequal military strength between the two countries and resulted in catastrophe for the Chinese. In June 1938, the Chinese mili-tary was in a "desperate state of confusion and acute anxiety," because every strategy they tried failed, and they urgently wanted to avoid an-other Nanjing massacre.[73] With the Japanese just twenty-five miles away, Chiang authorized breaching the dikes in Henan to delay and block the enemy. Although this decision may have bought the Chinese govern-ment some breathing space—giving them about five more months for combat readiness and preventing the Japanese from reaching areas west of the flooded zone for six years—the collateral damage was horrific. Although those living close to the dike had enough warning to flee, those farther away were caught unaware, and by official Nationalist esti-mates, a staggering 800,000 civilians died.[74]

However Chiang had chosen to approach the Japanese imperialists, he could not avoid dirty hands, inevitably alienating the population and affecting his use of *chi* and the Goujian story.[75] Because Chiang was still laboring to consolidate the state under his leadership, he was also unable to move from his initial strategy of enduring various humiliations to that of cultivating and strengthening the people, raising suspicions about the sincerity and validity of his use of the Goujian story. In contrast, as an outsider, Gandhi could avoid relying on an integral part of state power—violence—to achieve his political goals, which furthered his moral credibility and, by extension, his perceived agency in creating the national story through *satyagraha*.

Chiang was also directly involved in the day-to-day administration of his government, which included making strategic trade-offs and alliances to achieve his political agenda. In fact, Chiang perhaps expended too much energy in this area, once complaining that when a subordinate wrote a telegram, he would have to revise that telegram heavily.[76] As a result of having to attend to all these details, Chiang's personal attempts to model his actions after Goujian and encourage the country to do the same took on a more distinctively uncharismatic quality than Gandhi's attempt to model his ideals. Rather than draw himself and the people out of their normal routines and stage a dramatic and public Salt March–like event, such as by reenacting Goujian lying on a bed of sticks and tasting gall in Nanjing, Chiang was limited to responding to Japanese injustice by writing a daily avenging humiliation column and leading a relatively frugal life. These largely private actions, and even Chiang's public speeches on the matter, were unlikely to arouse the Chinese people out of their normal routines and persuade them to consciously bide their time and strengthen themselves to gain a final victory against the Japanese.

Ultimately, these two leaders' relation to state power and involvement in daily administration constrained Chiang but enabled Gandhi in their attempts to garner legitimacy and construct a uniting and inspirational national story. Nevertheless, as the previous chapters indicate, despite being unable to lead with undiluted moral authority, Chiang still managed to inculcate the people with an increased sensitivity to national humiliation in his pursuit of state sovereignty.

EXTERNAL THREAT OF DEATH

A final contextual factor affecting the leaders' efforts to forge a coherent national identity is the degree to which an external threat suppressed domestic conflict in the affected state. As Jeffrey Herbst has pointed out, war was critical in the formation of strong nation-states in Europe because the imminent threat of death galvanized the people to make sacrifices and unite in the face of a common enemy.[77] As Charles Tilly famously quipped, "War made the state, and the state made war."[78] But in comparison with Europe, China and India were more complex cases. In India, the subcontinent was already a British colony—despite oppressing Indian colonial subjects, the British were not posing an existential threat. In the Chinese case, while Japan posed a concrete external threat in 1928, 1931, and throughout the Sino-Japanese War (1937–45), it did not pose a life-or-death threat to the Chinese people in a sustained manner throughout this period.

When the British did use force on their Indian subjects during the founding of the colonial state and in specific years (such as 1905 and 1919), Hindus and Muslims were temporarily galvanized to unite in their efforts to resist the British. But during most of the Raj, the British, rather than attacking the Indian state from the outside, functioned internally to create civic institutions and observe certain rules of law and needed their Indian subjects to help them rule.[79] In addition, by employing a "divide and rule" tactic through separate electorate systems, the British co-opted various segments of the Indian population.

Without a persistent hostile external threat to drive disparate groups together for the sake of survival, these groups sometimes challenged Gandhi's efforts to construct an inclusive national story. Muslims not only perceived his use of *satyagraha* as biased because it drew no inspiration from Muslim tradition, they also felt they had shouldered a greater share of the costs than their Hindu counterparts. In reflecting on the Noncooperation Movement, for instance, poet Syed Mohammed Ismail Hossain Siraji (1880–1931) observed that several Hindu universities had been left open, while Muslim universities came to ruin, and that Hindus had profited enormously from selling *deshi* cloth, while Muslims were punished by having to buy coarse material at high prices.[80] By the time of the Salt March a decade later, no Muslims outside of Gandhi's native Gujarat came forward to participate.[81] The Muslim leader, Muhammad Ali Jinnah (1876–1948), may have initially advocated harmonious relations between Hindus and Muslims, at one point even occupying a position in both the INC and the Muslim League, but he eventually concluded that Muslims needed to occupy a separate homeland: "The Hindus and Muslims," he noted, "belong to two different religious philosophies. . . . To yoke together such nations under a single state, one as a numerical minority and the other as a majority, must lead to growing discontent and final destruction of any fabric that may be built up for the government of such a state."[82] He eventually conducted a successful campaign to create Pakistan and became its first governor-general.

Gandhi also faced conflicts between castes in the Hindu community. On one end of the spectrum, the Dalits, or untouchables, were highly distrustful of the Hindu elites.[83] B. R. Ambedkar (1891–1956), a prominent Indian jurist and Dalit, wanted a separate electorate for untouchables to vote in elections so that Dalits would have leaders who could voice their issues separate from the caste Hindus. Ambedkar called for this because his own *satyagraha* movement to advocate for the rights of untouchables, in which 15,000 volunteers sought to enter the Kalaram Temple, had been blocked by Brahmin authorities.[84] But Gandhi disagreed with Ambedkar, viewing the Dalits as part of the larger Hindu fold and therefore arguing for quotas for the untouchable legislators. When the British granted Ambedkar's wish for separate electorates in 1932, Gandhi protested with a fast, and although Ambedkar, fearful that Gandhi would die, yielded to the older man, his concession did little to relieve tensions within the Hindu community.

On the other end of the caste spectrum, Gandhi had trouble getting even those close to him personally and in caste to support his call for social equality for untouchables. In 1897, for instance, his wife, Kasturba (1869–1944), while living out what eventually became known as *satyagraha* principles in South Africa, rebelled against cleaning the chamber pot of a Christian whose parents were untouchables.[85] Nine months after his return to India in 1915, he faced a virtual walkout by his disciples over the presence of an untouchable in his ashram.[86] As late as 1934 he was forced to concede that "unfortunately, the higher castes have failed to identify themselves with their humbler fellows. . . . I have no excuse to offer."[87] In the end, Gandhi was unable to fully realize his vision of a united subcontinent, inclusive of different religious traditions and based on social equality. As colonizers rather than warring aggressors, the British provided insufficient motivation for Indians to suppress the differences among and within groups to face a common enemy.

In contrast, the Japanese did threaten the survival of the Chinese state during the Republican era. Prior to the Sino-Japanese War, its military incursions were limited in scope and intermittent and therefore unevenly affected Chiang in his ability to inspire and unite the Chinese. In the case of the 1928 Jinan Incident, Chiang was able to temporarily unite China via the Northern Expedition, but in the absence of a continued Japanese threat, internal disunity erupted again and delayed Chiang's implementation of the next stage of Goujian's strategy of building strength from weakness. The second Japanese imperial threat, the 1931 Mukden Incident, again enhanced Chiang's construction of a unifying national narrative by forcing the ruling elite to show internal unity against the external other. Although persevering in his policy of avoiding military engagement with Japan led Chiang to step down from power, he returned shortly thereafter in a stronger position. The absence of a direct military threat until the start of the Sino-Japanese War in 1937, however, demonstrated the superficialness of Chiang's attempt to build national unity through rules about hygiene and cleanliness, as urbanites grudgingly followed New Life rules in the presence of authority and were hardly galvanized to act as a nation.

The outbreak of the Sino-Japanese War, however, was a clear threat to China's survival and thus encouraged a Second United Front between the Nationalists and Chinese communists. But unlike the leaders during Europe's state formation, Chiang could rely on outside allied support to fight the Japanese and thus avoided the full burden of directly confronting China's external threat. As a result, he made few connections between the Chinese state and the people that would foster unity derived from a sense of shared sacrifice. Instead, the support of allies allowed both sides, and the Chinese communists in particular, to preserve their troops for the civil war that would come after the international war was over. Without providing a constant, pressing threat over the two decades of Chiang's rule, Japan did not adequately spur Chiang and his rivals to transcend or settle their disagreements. Although Chiang's Goujian story was a more broadly accessible trope to the Chinese than Gandhi's *Ramayana* was to Indians, Chiang was unable to incorporate the Chinese communists fully into the Nationalist fold or expunge them from his vision of China.

Despite the uneven external threat of war, Chiang made gains in uniting heterogeneous groups in China between 1928 and 1945, which enabled Mao to avoid starting from scratch when he took over the reins in 1949. Gandhi made gains, too. Although he was devastated by Partition, his assassination in January 1948 ironically may have taken the air out of the communal violence between Hindus and Muslims that had occurred in the preceding eighteen months. Remorse and grief took over, as did a sense that a Muslim having no place in India was an illegitimate direction to take. Although some Hindu-Muslim violence did occur after Independence, most conspicuously during the Indo-Pakistani Wars in 1965 and 1971 and pogroms against Muslims in 2002, the latter resulting in 2,000 deaths and 200,000 Muslims driven from their home, Gandhi's insistence on unity across religious lines is a view that is still important in India today.[88]

Ignoring the first two of these contextual factors—the degree of state centralization and of the leader's involvement in state power and administration—may have contributed to the aforementioned high praise of Gandhi's leadership and lukewarm assessment of Chiang's. In contrast, the third factor—the degree to which an external threat suppressed domestic disunity—may have made constructing a coherent national story difficult for both leaders, and more so for Gandhi than for Chiang. Together, however, an analysis of these factors suggests that political context did more to undermine Chiang's construction of a unifying national story and his legitimacy as a leader than it did for Gandhi and was thus likely at the root of scholars' subsequent differing evaluations of these two leaders.

• • •

Gandhi and Chiang stressed themes of self-control, sacrifice, and persistence, revealing that emphasizing building internal strength before confronting a stronger power can be an effective strategy for leaders of vulnerable states. Their joint example also suggests that people who feel deep humiliation may be particularly well suited to become leaders of such nations because their goal of avenging personal humiliation intersects with their quest for collective salvation. This comparison of the two men suggests that imperialism may have encouraged a certain kind of leader to come to the fore and inspire a people to unite to combat the strong.

At the same time, history has been kinder in evaluating Gandhi's leadership than Chiang's, and this comparison demonstrates how contextual factors made it more difficult for Chiang to construct and unify his people through a national story than it was for Gandhi. Despite the leaders sharing a goal of resisting imperialists, Chiang pursued a different path than Gandhi did, seeking to consolidate the state rather than call for equality under the law. Furthermore, the imperial relationship was different in their cases—Japan was threatening to colonize a semi-independent China, whereas Britain had already colonized the Indian subcontinent. These differences may have contributed to scholars' more negative subsequent evaluations of Chiang's leadership, as he was involved in constant power struggles, made morally compromising decisions, and, as the nominal head of a weak country, was responsible for negotiating bad outcomes for China, whereas Gandhi, as a challenger of the discredited British Raj, was able to exercise an outsider's attention and moral leverage to fight for justice and equality in India. It suggests that the paths to confronting imperialism are multiple but unequal in terms of forging a favorable legacy. The recognition that Chiang had to overcome more challenging contextual handicaps in his nation-building efforts than Gandhi should heighten, not diminish, our assessment of his real, if more partial, achievements.

Finally, a comparison of Chiang's and Gandhi's lasting legacies is also instructive. For his part, Chiang imprinted the Chinese national identity with a sensitivity to humiliation that continues to be manifest in China not resting on its laurels despite its recent economic success; the country and its leaders still demonstrate a Goujian-like motivation to improve and move forward. Gandhi's imprint on the Indian national identity was to show people a way to courage, self-respect, and political potency, and his method of *satyagraha* has inspired leaders far beyond India, including Nelson Mandela (1918–2013) and Dr. Martin Luther King Jr. (1929–68). Although Chiang may have lost China in 1949 and Gandhi may have failed to prevent the partition of the subcontinent, their efforts to forge a national story and unite heterogeneous groups in response to imperial humiliation paved the way for their successors to achieve the subsequent rise of China and India today.

CONCLUSION

The Legacy of Chiang's Chi Narrative

E ven though Taiwan emerged relatively unscathed from the ravages of World War II, my father, exposed to the Kuomintang's historiography about the war, imbibed the trauma of Japan's brutality against the Chinese on the "mainland."[1] When my parents visited me in upstate New York after the birth of my second child in 2012, I came home one day to see my father and five-year-old son sitting at the kitchen table poring over a world map. To my shock, my father proceeded to bang his fist over the outline of Japan several times, declaring it a "bad, bad" country. Never mind that my paternal grandfather had several close Japanese friends who flew to his funeral in 2003 or that my own father was highly educated and generally open-minded. His response, based on his education as a youth in Taiwan in the 1950s and 1960s, seemed to parallel Susan Shirk's observation that Chinese youth seemed more obsessed about Japan's failure to acknowledge its wartime cruelties than were their parents and grandparents, a sentiment that has no doubt been reinforced through post-Tiananmen patriotic education, propaganda, and popular media.[2] Indeed, notwithstanding my father's strong emotions, Chiang Kai-shek's use of *chi* appears to have had an even more lasting legacy in the modern-day People's Republic of China (PRC) than in the Republic of China (ROC). Through his effective mobilization of *chi* during the prewar and wartime period in mainland China, Chiang managed to imprint his adaptations of *chi* onto the Chinese collective story and identity in ways that future PRC leaders continued to find a useful cultural resource.

This aspect of Chiang's leadership has had a lasting if not always appreciated legacy on China's understanding of itself and its relation to the rest of the world. One such major aftereffect is that by the end of his tenure in power, his use of the humiliations suffered by China helped make state nationalism a more viable option for the country's future than civic nationalism. By rejecting liberal forms of government modeled after Western models, blaming the imperialist powers for China's problems, and declaring a state-led approach as the answer to those problems, Chiang narrowed the range of possible national stories that had sprung forth from the May Fourth Movement in ways that continue to be felt in China, and thus throughout the world.[3] By reacting with alarm to any perceived act of humiliation and embodying *chi* through his ascetic lifestyle, such as wearing his clothes until they were in tatters, Chiang imbued the Chinese collective story with a heightened sensitivity to humiliation that continues to this day.[4] As other commentators have noted, the lingering power of past humiliations has become tightly intertwined with China's national identity in the twenty-first century, especially with respect to its relations with Japan, Taiwan, and the United States, despite the country's current economic, political, and military might.[5] Still, Chiang's legacy was not assured; it depended on later Chinese leaders' willingness to draw on Chiang's collective story as a cultural resource to pursue their political agendas, even though the degree to which they did so varied by leader.

Chiang's Imprint on Chi *in the PRC*

When Mao took power as the leader of the PRC from 1949 to 1976, he actively suppressed memories of the Sino-Japanese War and the role his archrival Chiang had played in it to bolster his own legitimacy. Although the Chinese army's 1938 victory at Taierzhuang had been a momentous event, such as Dunkirk or Stalingrad for the Allied powers, the CCP made almost no mention of it during Mao's regime.[6] Unlike the other World War II powers, Mao's government built no memorials or museums nor commissioned any historical writings to commemorate the war against the Japanese. Official party publications portrayed Chiang as having fought against Japan only with great reluctance and as being eager to make peace, and several state-sanctioned popular movies of this era emphasized the role played by heroic peasant-led guerrillas and ignored that of Kuomintang forces.[7] The official record from the period also praised the contributions of Mao's ally, the Soviet Union, to the war effort and erased those of Chiang's allies, the United States and Great Britain. In commemorating the twentieth anniversary of the victory over Japan, CCP General Lin Biao (1907–71) went so far as to declare that it was Mao, not Chiang, who played the decisive leadership role in the War of Resistance.[8]

Mao also suppressed Chiang's legacy in pursuit of his foreign policy goals. After 1949, when countries like the United States and Japan moved to isolate Beijing diplomatically by recognizing Chiang's Nationalist government in Taiwan as the legitimate leadership of China, Mao attempted to undercut Japan's alliance with the United States by getting Japan to recognize Beijing instead. Such a strategy naturally entailed avoiding Chiang's earlier rehashing of horrific details about Japan's actions during the war.[9] Indeed, in a 1972 meeting with Japanese Prime Minister Tanaka Kakue, when Tanaka acknowledged that "by invading China Japan created a lot of trouble for China," Mao appeared not only to let bygones be bygones but to credit the Japanese for his party's success, replying, "If Japan hadn't invaded China, the Chinese Communist Party would not have been victorious."[10]

But Mao's attempt to extinguish Chiang's legacy and the memory of the Sino-Japanese War exacted a heavy human toll on China. When his Hundred Flowers Campaign (Baihua qifang) of 1956 and 1957 led to criticisms of his regime, Mao not only cracked down on those who spoke out, arresting hundreds of thousands, he also declared citizens who had served in the Kuomintang military or worked with China's Western allies "enemies of the people," stripping them of their jobs and sometimes sending them to prison. Later, during the Cultural Revolution, any evidence of collaboration with the Japanese or the Kuomintang during the war in the form of letters, diaries, or other private documents was considered proof of spying or collusion and thus considered dangerously incriminating if Red Guards invaded a home. Given such tactics, memories of the Sino-Japanese War, let alone of Chiang and the Kuomintang's role in its successful conclusion, all but disappeared from public spaces in China.[11] This forceful suppression suggests that Chiang did indeed have a powerful legacy to transmit, one that Mao and the CCP had reason to fear could undermine their own legitimacy.

Nonetheless, attempts by Mao and the CCP to quell such memories of the war proved difficult, as they were lived ones for much of the Chinese population. At one point in the war, nearly half of China's population had resided under Japanese occupation, and nearly 100 million had become refugees; civilian and military deaths from the war numbered more than 20 million.[12] Nor was Chiang alone among China's future leaders in having a personal connection to this humiliation. Mao's successor, Deng Xiaoping (1904–97), had participated in the May 4, 1919, demonstrations as a teenager, and according to his biographer, Ezra F. Vogel, his personal identity had become "inseparable from the national effort to rid China of the humiliation it had suffered at the hands of other countries."[13] Deng's successor, Jiang Zemin (b. 1926), recalled that as a student in Yangzhou in the 1920s and 1930s, each time he beheld the tombstone of Shi Kefa (1601–45), a famed Yangzhou hero who had died valiantly resisting the Qing army in 1645, he felt "strong anti-Japanese and patriotic emotions and became determined to engage in revolutionary struggle."[14]

After Mao's death, Deng Xiaoping, who led China from 1978 to 1989, did not consider Chiang a personal nemesis and pursued a different political agenda that enabled both a "new remembering" of the prewar and war period and some tentative steps toward rehabilitating Chiang and his legacy.[15] In foreign policy during the period, Deng believed that China could take a more neutral stance between the two Cold War superpowers and thus become less beholden to the West and, by extension, Japan.[16] He also hoped to woo Taiwan into a unification agreement, and after he lifted several constraints on academic research, researchers began to portray the contributions of Chiang and his generals in Taiwan in a more favorable light, if nowhere near eclipsing those of the CCP.[17] Domestically, Deng moved to partially liberalize the Chinese economy, even promoting his economic reforms with high-profile visits to Japan in 1978 and the United States in 1979. By 1980, however, these reforms had led to greater economic inequality and resistance from conservatives in the party that threatened to fragment the country.[18] Seeking new ways to unite the country, his regime turned to reinterpreting history, specifically the Chinese people's efforts in the Sino-Japanese War, as an antidote to those divisions.[19] In fact, Deng allowed three war memorials to open: the Memorial Hall of the Nanjing Massacre (1985), the Museum of Evidence of War Crimes by Japanese Army Unit 731 (1985), and the War of Resistance Museum (1987).[20] Although these museums portrayed the CCP as the primary hero of this war, they were unable to ignore Chiang's role entirely.[21]

Chiang's accomplishments and his particular imprint on the national *chi* narrative only became a potentially useful cultural resource for China's leaders after the 1989 Tiananmen Square protests, in which the government's brutal crackdown on personal liberties alienated China's youth and drew condemnation from Western countries.[22] Confronting domestic fragmentation and external opprobrium and sanctions, the CCP faced a situation reminiscent of the domestic disunity and external threats faced by Chiang. Hoping to draw on a nationalist narrative to rebuild a Chinese collective identity and regain the support of the people, Deng and his successor, Jiang Zemin, turned to Chiang's "century of humiliation" toolbox to rebuild the party's legitimacy despite concerns that doing so would in fact undercut the CCP's legitimacy. Just two months after the Tiananmen Square protests, newly installed General Secretary Jiang Zemin, who led China between 1989 and 2002, signaled a willingness to at least partially rehabilitate Chiang when the well-known film director Li Qiankuan (b. 1941) refused the order of government censors to depict Chiang as more ruthless in *Grand Ceremony of the Founding of the Country*, his saga of the communists' triumph over the Nationalist government. After a member of the Politburo Standing Committee appealed directly to the leader on Li's behalf, Jiang decided to approve the film, which went on to become recognized as one of the most important films in the genre of Chinese history.[23]

With the ice apparently broken, Jiang unhesitatingly drew on the humiliation narrative bearing Chiang's imprint to achieve his own political objectives. Sharing Chiang's belief in the importance of indoctrinating the Chinese people in right behavior, Jiang launched an "Outline for the Implementation of Patriotic Education" in 1994 intended to foster domestic cohesion and national pride by shaping the people's understanding of history, particularly remembering "the imperialist invasion and the Chinese people's heroic resistance."[24] Even seemingly objective works about the war period—such as those covering battles or reporting events behind Japanese lines—were repackaged into this nationalist frame, with chapter titles and content emphasizing the people's resistance to Japanese aggression.[25] In this reading of history, Japan, not Chiang and the Kuomintang, was China's worst enemy.

Jiang also adopted Chiang's strategy of magnifying perceived humiliations to promote patriotism.[26] In 1990, for instance, government publications shined a spotlight on claims by foreigners that Beijing's actions at Tiananmen Square should be punished by prohibiting them from hosting the 2000 Olympic Games, which predictably outraged Chinese youth, who, despite having opposed their government at Tiananmen a year earlier, now shared their government's resentment of foreign mistreatment.[27] In 1995, Jiang, in speeches in China and Japan, ignored the Maoist-era official figure that 9.32 million Chinese were killed in the Sino-Japanese War and raised the estimate to 35 million, which stands as the current official figure.[28] During a fiftieth anniversary celebration of victory speech on September 3, 1995, Jiang also raised the top-range numbers of those who died in the Nanjing massacre (to 300,000) and the amount of direct economic loss suffered by the Chinese (to US\$ 100 billion).[29]

The humiliation narrative, however, initially seemed less relevant to the political agenda of Hu Jintao (b. 1942), who led China between 2002 and 2012. Applying what he called "new thinking" toward Japan, Hu appeared to abandon the ultranationalistic stance introduced by Chiang and pursued by Jiang by emphasizing cooperation and synergy over competition between the two countries.[30] In a speech at Waseda University in Tokyo, for instance, Hu declared that he wanted to take the "strategic relationship of mutual benefit between China and Japan to a new level," hearkening back to Maoist-era interpretations of the war by laying blame on a few Japanese militarists who "inflicted untold sufferings on the Chinese nation and also brought misery to the Japanese people."[31] Yet the path Chiang had blazed over a half century earlier seems to have constrained Hu's efforts to pursue the possibilities of Sino-Japanese cooperation. Still consolidating his power and needing support from Jiang's power base, the political cost of backing down from the nationalist stance on Japan soon appeared to be too high. In Beijing in 2005, more than 10,000 students protested against Japan, still angry that the island nation had not properly acknowledged the atrocities it had inflicted on the Chinese.[32] Jiang's adaptations of Chiang's deployment of *chi* appeared to have made forgiving those humiliations more difficult for Hu politically.

Hu appears to have drawn on Chiang's *chi* narrative in other ways. In preparing for the 2008 Beijing Olympics, Hu's government echoed Chiang's orthopraxic approach to the New Life Movement by making the country and its citizens presentable to the outside world through planting thousands of trees along the route between the airport and the capital and employing the elderly to scrape off gum and remove other debris in heavily trafficked tourist areas such as Tiananmen Square.[33] During the Olympics, the government issued similar directives through public service advertisements reminding people to flush toilets, help the elderly, and not litter.[34] Similar efforts preceding the 2010 Shanghai Expo—such as building walls and fake facades to hide unattractive blocks near the exhibition site (fig. C.1)—were even more extravagant, exceeding the cost of the entire Beijing Olympics.[35] The Shanghai municipal government also sponsored programs to encourage local citizens to improve their manners, become familiar with the internet, and learn English with the goal of showing "a more amiable face and warmer arms" to the global community.[36] When I visited the expo, one driver of a brand-new cab in a fleet of cabs affiliated with the expo politely reminded me in perfect English to wear my seatbelt, even though earlier in the week I had observed a new mom leaving the hospital, climbing into the passenger seat of a car with her newborn in her arms, and departing seatbelt-less.

In contrast to Hu's reluctance to be critical of Japan, Xi Jinping, who took over as China's leader in 2012, has openly emphasized China's humiliation at the hands of the Japanese to advance a more forceful domestic and foreign agenda and in the process further rehabilitated Chiang and the Kuomintang. In 2014, Xi established two new national commemorative dates intended to criticize Japan: Martyrs' Day on September 30, and National Memorial Day for Nanjing Massacre Victims on December 13. In an inaugural speech for the latter event, Xi decried the Japanese destruction of a third of all of the buildings in the Kuomintang

FIGURE C.1. Preparations for the Shanghai Expo. Near the site of the expo, there appears to be newly erected housing (left), but turning the corner (right) reveals that it is a facade hiding an unsightly block-sized lot. Photos by author, June 2010.

capital of Nanjing in 1937, a remarkable comment given that Mao had quashed memories of this event because of the CCP's conspicuous absence during the infamous attack.[37] Xi has even pushed this narrative internationally, attempting to use a visit to Germany to contrast Germany's atonement for Nazi war crimes with Japan's refusal to apologize.[38]

Xi has gone several steps further than Jiang in portraying Chiang as something other than a capitalist-reactionary-traitor-thug. In 2013, Xi made Kuomintang veterans of World War II who had remained in China under the PRC and been persecuted during the Maoist regime eligible to collect pensions. Shortly thereafter, the Ministry of Civil Affairs released a list of 300 newly recognized martyrs, of which a third were reportedly Kuomintang soldiers. These moves were symbolically significant in their acknowledgment of the common efforts of the two parties in fighting foreign imperialism.[39] In 2017, the Chinese Ministry of Education further boosted nationalist sentiment by expanding the timeline of the War against Japanese Aggression from eight to fourteen years, and primary and secondary education textbooks now identify the Mukden Incident in 1931 as the start of the war, thereby granting new public recognition of Chiang's leadership of China during the Nanjing period.[40]

Xi has taken a page from Chiang's use of cultural resources in his ample appeals to Confucian ideas and Chinese moral stories to advance his more assertive nationalist agenda at home and internationally. Xi frequently cites Confucian texts in his speeches to legitimate the regime's policies by reminding the domestic and international community of China's brilliant cultural contributions.[41] In 2020, the *People's Daily* amplified this aspect of Xi's leadership by publishing a compilation of his storytelling, *Narrating China's Governance: Stories in Xi Jinping's Speeches*, in which they praised the leader for "conveying profound meaning" with his use of stories that "glow with 'Chinese wisdom' and 'Chinese strength.'"[42] Xi's signature ideology, encapsulated by the Chinese Dream (Zhongguo meng), aims to "rejuvenate" (*fuxing*) the Chinese nation by reviving the glories of a Confucian golden past and is reminiscent of Chiang's goals for the New Life Movement. Moreover, his reassertion of the primacy of the state and method of consolidating power in service of the Chinese Dream evokes Chiang's tendency to see dissenting views as not merely wrongheaded but intolerable.[43]

The imprint of Chiang's moralistic and top-down approach to building national identity can also be seen in the present government's implementation of a social credit system (*shehui xinyong tixi*) that shames Chinese citizens for minor infractions such as jaywalking by catching them on camera and broadcasting their misdeeds at a nearby bus stop.[44] In compliance with Xi's idea of reviving traditional Chinese culture to help women compete in the job market and prepare for domestic roles, one university, with a Chiang-like obsession to minor details, teaches its female students that "You must sit on the front two-thirds of the chair—you cannot occupy the whole chair. . . . Now, hold in your belly, relax shoulders, legs together, shoulders up."[45] But unlike Chiang, Xi has access to big data and artificial intelligence to ensure compliance through penalties and rewards and has mobilized these systems beyond keeping track of state-approved day-to-day "virtuous" behavior to monitoring conduct that might be considered harmful to the state, such as tracking the Uighur minority through mobile apps.[46]

Because the China that Chiang had ruled was weak and divided, he had focused on modernizing infrastructure, the military, and other "hard" power components of state building. Like Jiang and Hu before him, Xi appears to continue along Chiang's line of privileging wealth and power. Just as previous administrations completed the Three Gorges Dam and Shanghai's Maglev Train, Xi has continued to pursue mega infrastructural projects, such as the South–North Water Transfer Project and the Belt and Road Initiative, which try to project an image of a powerful China, even at the expense of individual well-being.[47] In the meantime, the development of a robust rule of law seems to lag behind with Xi extending his tenure of power indefinitely and with China challenging Hong Kong's Basic Law, which demarcates a "one country, two systems" until 2047.[48]

Despite uncanny similarities between Xi and Chiang, including the intolerance of dissenting views, reliance on Confucian stories, encouragement of "patriotic" behavior through social directives, and pursuit of hard power, these leaders operate in radically different environments. Chiang's imprinting of the national identity was based on a political goal of consolidating his power and unifying a weak and divided country. To do so, he was forced to delay fighting the Japanese and postpone substantively building up China, trade-offs that were often at the expense of the Chinese people and constrained the possibilities of political liberalization. In contrast, Xi has been able to deploy the humiliation narrative and appeals to Confucian values modeled by Chiang in a more selective and systematic fashion while overseeing the world's second-largest economy and military power.

Although China's leaders are still willing to mobilize shame and humiliation that bear Chiang's imprint to engender a sense of national identity and unity, some commentators have questioned whether China's current status as a rising global power still makes that accurate or effective. They have argued that China's present leadership needs to move beyond the humiliation narrative because it undermines another important goal—that of China gaining the respect in the world the Chinese elite feels it deserves.[49] Yet others believe that replacing the national narrative is difficult because the events of the Sino-Japanese War as well as those reaching back to the Opium Wars have become China's "chosen" traumas and therefore bind the Chinese individual to this collective national identity.[50] What remains to be seen is how effective these cultural tools will prove to Xi and future Chinese leaders as they attempt to legitimate their political agenda and shape the Chinese collective identity going forward.

Chiang's Imprint on Chi in Taiwan

As would be expected, Chiang also mobilized *chi* during his leadership of Taiwan. He viewed the Kuomintang's loss and retreat to Taiwan as his latest humiliation and with similar Goujian resolve set out to retake the "mainland" and eradicate the Soviet imperialism that he blamed for his loss to the communists.[51] When the beginning of the Korean War deferred the immediate threat of combat with China, Chiang used the reprieve from war to focus on the kind of reforms on the island he had been forced to postpone during his leadership of China and implement the second part of Goujian's template of success: "ten years to grow the population, and ten years to train the population."[52]

According to Brian Crozier and Eric Chou, Chiang felt that much of the blame for the Kuomintang's defeat in the Chinese civil war "lay with the Kuomintang for having done nothing to reform society or promote the people's welfare."[53] Chiang therefore promoted education on the island, and by the late 1950s, 93 percent of primary school–age children were enrolled in school.[54] He instituted agricultural reforms that boosted the Kuomintang's legitimacy and popularity among the island's rural population.[55] Moreover, Chiang's goal of eventually defeating the Chinese communists motivated him to strengthen the island's government and defense. By the end of the 1950s, Chiang had rebuilt the army into a 600,000-strong organization that was a stark contrast from the disorganized, demoralized force that had fled the mainland a decade earlier.[56] In this way, Chiang seemed to parallel the Goujian story that Paul Cohen traces through the publication of books, educational materials, and plays in Taiwan, in which the ancient king was subtly transformed from a leader obsessed with avenging humiliation to a model ruler who listened to advice, adopted enlightened social policies, and lived an ascetic life.[57]

However, Chiang's mobilization of *chi* appears to have left a less lasting legacy in Taiwan than in China. After Chiang's death in 1975, the motivation to retake the mainland seemed to have died along with its chief promoter. Despite Chiang having called the loss of Taiwan's seat in the United Nations to the "fake" PRC a humiliation, the leaders who succeeded him, including his son, Chiang Ching-kuo, who ruled Taiwan between 1978 and 1988, were disinclined to frame foreign policy in terms of national humiliation. They felt that this would further isolate Taiwan from an international order that was now recognizing the People's Republic as the real China.[58]

The waning importance of Chiang's imprint of *chi* on the collective story and identity in Taiwan also seemed to coincide with the transformation of the Kuomintang in the 1990s, when it expanded its top-level party and government leadership beyond members who had traveled with Chiang to Taiwan to include "nonmainlanders," or native Taiwanese. President Lee Teng-hui (1923–2020), who ruled Taiwan between 1988 and 2000, also allowed a shift in the teaching of Chinese history to emphasize the history of Taiwan rather than the history of Chinese dynasties and the Sino-Japanese War that had influenced Taiwanese students like my parents in the 1950s and 1960s.[59] By the 2000s, Taiwanese identity had become more multiethnic, democratic, and international, and perhaps for that reason, President Tsai Ing-wen (b. 1956), elected in 2016, made no mention of humiliation or of the Sino-Japanese War throughout her campaign and acceptance speech.[60] Nonetheless, Chiang's efforts to avenge the new humiliation of having lost the mainland instituted important reforms that set Taiwan on the path of modern economic and democratic development.

•   •   •

Leaders sometimes come to the fore not because they are the most brilliant or the best strategist but because the personal story they embody may resonate deeply with the collective story at hand. More important, what transforms such individuals into leaders is that they actively draw on the cultural resources that inform their stories to push and legitimate a collective course of action. In this process, the leader imprints a new story and identity that has lasting effects on the actions and thinking of the collective and future leaders and thus has influence beyond specific outcomes like winning or losing a war.

That Chiang specifically mobilized *chi* highlights the understudied yet important cultural tools underdog leaders can wield. The asymmetry in power between the aggressors and victims means that the use of humiliation as a cultural resource reflects a less visible exercise of agency than those more commonly studied in leadership. Although Chiang's practice of enduring humiliation appeared to do nothing outwardly in the face of imperialist aggression, his words and actions inspired those who understood the cultural references to embark on a more quiet yet demanding path to redress an injustice. Moreover, as Gandhi's use of *satyagraha* suggests, the powerful emotions triggered by shame and humiliation are hardly unique to Chinese culture; in any culture, humiliation can be a powerful motivator for action.[61] As this volume has demonstrated, using such resources to prevent a worse outcome should redound to a leader's credit, especially for leaders inhabiting challenging political contexts.

In the end, the picture of Chiang Kai-shek that emerges from the *shilüe* is that of an ordinary albeit earnest man, whose quirks and flaws demonstrate that leaders are not necessarily born. At the same time, the man who emerges expands our understanding of the range of creative strategies and contributions leaders can make. In his political uses of shame and humiliation, Chiang not only avoided the political disintegration of China, he imprinted the Chinese collective story with a sensitivity to humiliation that undergirds a template for a strong and wealthy China, albeit one with less political liberalization for its people. Chiang may have often strayed wildly from the model offered by his hero, Goujian, and his effectiveness in constructing a credible story varied depending on the political circumstances he faced, but his example illuminates how Chinese leaders can draw on *chi* and other cultural resources to articulate new understandings of what constitutes a legitimate leader, citizen, and collective and morally just treatment by one country to another, even as those definitions may be hotly contested. Far from being emotions to be avoided or dismissed, this study underscores that *chi* and its counterpart in other cultures have the power to motivate leaders of strong states to act with restraint and of weak states to build strength from weakness.

Appendix

Timelines for China, Taiwan, and India

China

Year	Events in China
1600–1900	**1642:** Ming dynasty loyalists battle Manchu invaders. Wang Xiuchu writes a riveting account of a massacre by the Manchus in Yangzhou. **1644–1912:** The Qing dynasty replaces the Ming. **1839–1860:** China is defeated by the British in the Opium Wars and signs a series of unequal treaties, beginning what in China would become known as the Hundred Years of Humiliation. **1859:** Yuan Shikai is born in Henan. **1887:** Chiang Kai-shek is born in Zhejiang. **1893:** Mao Zedong is born in Hunan. **1894–1895:** China loses to Japan in the First Sino-Japanese War. It must cede Taiwan and Liaodong Peninsula to Japan and recognize Korea's independence with the Treaty of Shimonoseki. Shortly after, in the Triple Intervention, Russia, France, and Germany pressure Japan to return Liaodong Peninsula to China in exchange for a larger indemnity, after which Russia moves in to occupy the peninsula. **1895:** Chiang's father passes away, which becomes a formative influence on Chiang's subsequent uses of *chi*. **1899:** US Secretary of State John Hay proposes the Open Door policy toward China, which stipulates that all countries must be allowed to trade with China on an equal basis.

(continued)

Year	Events in China
1901–1910	**1902–1908:** Yuan serves as governor-general of Zhili Province under Qing rule.
	1904–1905: Japan wins the Russo-Japanese War and reclaims southern Manchuria, including Liaodong Peninsula, from the Russians.
	1906: Chiang receives military training from the Baoding Military Academy.
	1907–1909: Chiang enrolls at the Tokyo Shinbu Gakkō, a Japanese military academy for Chinese students.
	1909–1911: Chiang serves in the Imperial Japanese Army.
1911–1920	**1911:** Chiang returns to China to join the Chinese Revolutionary Alliance (Tongmenghui), headed by Sun Yat-sen, and helps bring down the Qing dynasty in the Xinhai Revolution.
	1912: The Republican era of China begins. Sun steps down as the provisionary president and offers Yuan the presidency. The Chinese Revolutionary Alliance transforms into a political party, the Kuomintang or Nationalist Party.
	1914: Shortly after the outbreak of World War I, Japan demands that the Germans give up their lease in Shandong.
	January 18, 1915: When Yuan attempts to evict the Japanese military from Shandong, Japan responds by calling on China to meet the Twenty-One Demands as a condition for leaving.
	March 15, 1915: Thirty thousand Chinese protest at the Shanghai International Settlement demanding that Yuan cease negotiations and boycott Japanese goods.
	May 7, 1915: Japan gives China a forty-eight-hour ultimatum to respond to their demands.
	May 9, 1915: Yuan accepts a winnowed-down version of the demands.
	August 1915: Yuan attempts to become emperor of China.
	1915–1921: The New Culture Movement challenges traditional Confucian values and promotes Chinese nationalism, broad-based political participation, and vernacularizing classical Chinese.
	March 1916: Yuan abandons monarchical plans.
	June 1916: Yuan dies.
	1916–1928: Following Yuan's death, no government can claim legitimate authority over all of China. During this period, known as the Warlord Era, regional military leaders rule different sections of China.

Year	Events in China
	1918: Chiang joins Sun Yat-sen in Guangzhou (Canton).
	May 4, 1919: Students protest Beijing's weak response to the Treaty of Versailles, which allowed Japan to retain territories in Shandong. The resulting May Fourth Movement is a pivotal political moment within the New Culture Movement.
1921–1930	**1921:** Mao joins the Chinese Communist Party.
	1922: The Nine-Power Treaty and the Washington Naval Treaty (also known as the Five-Power Treaty) are signed at the Washington Naval Conference. The former affirms the sovereignty and territorial integrity of China and requires Japan to return territorial control of Shandong; the latter attempts to prevent an arms race by limiting naval construction.
	1924: In exchange for Soviet aid, Sun Yat-sen agrees to the First United Front, a coalition between the Kuomintang and Chinese communists. Sun appoints Chiang as commandant of Whampoa (Huangpu) Military Academy.
	May 30, 1925: Anti-imperial sentiments flare during the May 30th Incident, in which Chinese workers strike at a Japanese cotton mill in Shanghai.
	1926–1928: In carrying out a military campaign known as the Northern Expedition, Chiang, as commander-in-chief of the National Revolutionary Army, nominally unifies China under Kuomintang leadership.
	March 1927: In the Nanjing Incident, Chiang's National Revolutionary soldiers are accused of looting foreign consulates, which prompts the British and Americans to bomb the area and heightens concerns by all imperial powers about protecting their nationals during the Northern Expedition.
	April 12, 1927: In the Shanghai Massacre, also known as the April 12 Purge, Chiang and his troops massacre Chinese communists in Shanghai and areas of Nationalist control.
	December 1, 1927: Chiang marries Song Mei-ling.
	May 1928: In the Jinan Incident, a skirmish occurs between Chiang's troops and Japanese troops stationed in Jinan to protect Japanese nationals. Japan proceeds to occupy Jinan for a year.
	October 10, 1928: Chiang forms the Nanjing government and becomes its president. The Nanjing decade begins.

(continued)

Year	Events in China
	December 29, 1928: The Northern Expedition officially ends with northern warlord Zhang Xueliang declaring allegiance to the Nationalist government in Nanjing.
	1929–1930: In the Central Plains War, Chiang battles northern and southern warlords and emerges victorious.
	1930: Chiang begins the first of five encirclement campaigns to drive out the Chinese communists.
1931–1940	**July 1931:** The Wanbaoshan Incident involves a dispute between Chinese farmers and Korean workers over irrigation. The Korean Incident follows when Koreans, in response to the Wanbaoshan Incident, begin attacking Chinese merchants and residents living in Korea.
	August 1931: Japanese public sentiments are inflamed over the Japanese government's publicizing of the Nakamura Incident, in which Chinese soldiers had killed Captain Nakamura Shintara earlier in the summer.
	September 18, 1931: The Mukden Incident marks another Chinese confrontation with Japan, which results in Japan taking over all of Manchuria and violating the 1922 Nine-Power Treaty.
	December 10, 1931: The League of Nations forms the Lytton Commission to investigate the Mukden Incident.
	December 15, 1931: Chiang resigns from power due to intraparty conflict and continued protest over not resisting Japanese aggression.
	February 1932: Chiang resumes power. Sun Yat-sen's son, Sun Fo, had lacked credibility as leader of the new central government. Provinces had withheld salt tax revenues, and Whampoa generals had declared that they would only take orders from Chiang.
	March 1932: Japan establishes the Manchukuo puppet state and occupies Manchuria until its defeat in World War II.
	May 5, 1932: The Shanghai Truce concludes the military conflict in Shanghai between China's Nineteenth Route Army and Japan's Kuantung Army.
	May 31, 1932: The Tanggu Truce calls for a demilitarized zone along the Great Wall and North China.
	March 1933: Japan withdraws from the League of Nations in protest of the findings from the Lytton Report.
	February 1934: Chiang launches the New Life Movement to rejuvenate society and modernize China.

Year	Events in China
	October 1934: Chiang's fifth and last encirclement campaign fails, and Mao and the Chinese communists embark on the Long March.
	1935: The Long March concludes in Yenan, and Mao emerges as the leader of the Chinese Communist Party.
	December 1936: In the Xi'an Incident, Chiang is kidnapped by Zhang Xueliang, but, following negotiations with the Chinese communists, is released.
	1937: The Second United Front is formed between the Nationalists and Chinese communists.
	July 7, 1937: The Second Sino-Japanese War begins when Japan attacks the Marco Polo Bridge in Beijing, thus bringing the Nanjing era to an end.
	August 13–November 26, 1937: In the Battle of Shanghai, Chiang and his troops bear the brunt of heavy fighting. Chiang decides to retreat into China's interior, bypassing Nanjing.
	1937–1938: The Nanjing Massacre and rape of Chinese citizens by Japanese forces is met by only a symbolic defense due to Chiang's movement inland and Mao and the Chinese communists' location in China's northwest.
	March 24–April 7, 1938: The Battle of Taierzhuang in Shandong results in China's first major victory against Japan.
	June 1938: Chiang allows the dikes to be breached on the Huang River to delay Japanese advance, resulting in an estimated 800,000 killed by the flood.
	September 1939: World War II begins.
	1940: Chiang's secretaries begin compiling the *shilüe* chronology.
1941–1950	**January 1941:** The New Fourth Army Incident, a skirmish between the Nationalists and Chinese communists, results in Nationalist soldiers massacring communist soldiers and informally ends the Second United Front.
	December 7, 1941: Japan bombs Pearl Harbor, prompting the United States to enter the war. Joseph Stilwell is assigned to the China-Burma-India theater and must coordinate with Chiang.
	February 18, 1942: Chiang and Song Meiling meet Mahatma Gandhi in Calcutta to discuss war efforts by the two countries.

(continued)

Year	Events in China
	1942–1943: A famine in Henan causes 2–3 million deaths from starvation and approximately 4 million Chinese fleeing the province.
	1943: Most of the unequal treaties are abrogated, including US extraterritoriality, allowing Chiang to proclaim that he has successfully avenged the national humiliation.
	February 1945: At the Yalta Conference, Franklin Roosevelt, Winston Churchill, and Joseph Stalin decide in Chiang's absence to recognize the independence of Outer Mongolia in return for Soviet entry into the war.
	August 1945: Chiang signs the Sino-Soviet Treaty of Friendship Alliance, formalizing an unequal relationship between China and the Soviet Union.
	September 1945: World War II and the Second Sino-Japanese War end. China claims victory over Japan.
	1945–1949: Civil war ensues between Kuomintang and Chinese communist forces.
	1949: Chiang loses the civil war and escapes to Taiwan with remnants of his party and army.
	1949: Mao becomes leader of the People's Republic of China.
1951–1960	**1956–1957:** In the Hundred Flowers Campaign, Mao encourages people to openly express their opinions about the Chinese communist government but swiftly conducts a crackdown of those who offered criticism.
1961–1970	**1966–1976:** Mao launches the Cultural Revolution to eliminate rivals, restore Maoism, and allow Chinese youth to experience "revolution" firsthand.
1971–1980	**1976:** Mao dies.
	1977–1989: Deng Xiaoping becomes leader of China.
1981–1990	**1985:** The Memorial Hall of the Nanjing Massacre and the Museum of Evidence of War Crimes by Japanese Army Unit 731 are built.
	1987: The War of Resistance Museum is built.
	June 4, 1989: In the Tiananmen Square protests, citizens in Beijing and the nation calling for political and economic reform are met with overwhelming government force and repression.

Year	Events in China
	1989–2002: Jiang Zemin is leader of China.
1991–2000	**1994:** Jiang launches a patriotic education campaign. Construction of the Three Gorges Dam begins.
2001–2010	**2002–2012:** Hu Jintao presides over China.
	2002: Construction of the South–North Water Transfer Project and the Shanghai Maglev Train begins.
	2004: The Shanghai Maglev Train is completed.
	2005: Anti-Japanese demonstrations in China erupt over various issues, including disputes over the Senkaku Islands and an approved Japanese history textbook's portrayal of World War II, particularly of the Nanjing Massacre and Korean comfort women.
	2008: Beijing hosts the Summer Olympics.
	2010: China holds the World Expo in Shanghai, which breaks the world record for attendance with 73 million visitors.
2011–2020	**2012:** Xi Jinping is declared the leader of China.
	2012: The Three Gorges Dam becomes fully operational.
	2013: The Chinese government adopts the Belt and Road Initiative as a centerpiece of Xi's foreign policy.
	2014: The Central Route of the South–North Water Transfer Project is completed. In the process, the government resettles 330,000 people.
	2020: Beijing imposes a new National Security Law on Hong Kong that criminalizes various activities it perceives as subversive to China's authority.

Taiwan

Year	Events in Taiwan
1895–1945	Taiwan is under Japanese occupation. China had ceded the island to Japan in 1895 after losing the First Sino-Japanese War. The occupation ends after Japan's defeat in World War II in 1945, and the Kuomintang take control of Taiwan.

(continued)

Year	Events in Taiwan
1948	Chiang becomes the president of the Republic of China, continuing the name of the sovereign state of mainland China from 1912 to 1949 on the island nation.
1950–1953	Taiwan was minimally involved in the Korean War, allowing Chiang to focus on building domestic strength.
1971	The UN General Assembly declares that the People's Republic of China, not Taiwan, is the rightful representative of China.
1975	Chiang dies.
1978	Chiang's son, Chiang Ching-kuo, becomes president of Taiwan.
1988	Lee Teng-hui succeeds Chiang Ching-kuo and helps Taiwan transition to democracy.
2000	Chen Shui-bian becomes president of Taiwan, the first to emerge from the opposition party, the Democratic Progressive Party.
2008	Ma Ying-jeou of the Kuomintang becomes president of Taiwan.
2016	Tsai Ing-wen of the Democratic Progressive Party becomes the president of Taiwan.

India

Year	Events in India
1600–1873	The East India Company expands British political influence in the Indian subcontinent.
1857–1858	In the Sepoy Mutiny, Indian soldiers under British command lead a bloody uprising against British rule in India.
1858	The British government formalizes its rule over the Indian subcontinent. The era of the British Raj begins.
1869	Mohandas Gandhi is born in Porbander.
1882	Gandhi marries Kasturbai Makhanji Kapadia.
1885	The Indian National Congress party is formed.

Year	Events in India
1888–1891	Gandhi studies law at the University College of London.
1893–1914	Gandhi lives in South Africa. In his first year, a white coachman beats him for insisting on his rights.
1906	With help of a relative, Gandhi invents the term *satyagraha*. The All-Indian Muslim League is formed.
1910	Gandhi builds Tolstoy Farm near Johannesburg, which serves as headquarters of his *satyagraha* movement.
1914	Gandhi heads to London and establishes the Ambulance Training Corps of Indians to aid British efforts in World War I.
1915	Gandhi returns to India, and near the city of Ahmedabad, he builds Kochrab Ashram, where he, his family, and followers live.
1919	After World War I and despite Indians having aided Britain's war efforts, the British enact emergency power measures in March to combat subversive acts, including the Rowlatt Act, which gives police wide-ranging powers. In April, British troops kill unarmed Indian civilians in Punjab in what became known as the Amritsar Massacre and implement martial law shortly thereafter.
1920–1922	In response to the events of 1919, Gandhi organizes the Noncooperation Movement based on the principles of *satyagraha*.
1921	The British finally implement the Government of India Act of 1919, making political participation more inclusive for Indians.
1924	Gandhi becomes president of the Indian National Congress party for one year.
1930	B. R. Ambedkar, an Indian jurist, politician, and member of the untouchable (Dalit) caste, leads a protest outside of the Kalaram Temple in Maharashtra demanding that Dalits be allowed to enter.
1931	In the Salt March, Gandhi protests the British ban on salt by marching to the sea from his Sabarmati Ashram to the coastal village of Dandi.

(continued)

Year	Events in India
1932	Gandhi prevails in a debate over whether Dalits should be granted a separate electorate for representation in legislative assemblies. Ambedkar accedes to Gandhi's desire for keeping the Dalits within the Hindu fold.
1942	Gandhi meets with Chiang and Song Meiling in Calcutta but declines to mobilize his countrymen to aid China.
1947	The Indian Independence Act dissolves the British Raj and partitions the subcontinent into India and Pakistan (present-day Pakistan and Bangladesh). Afterward, India and Pakistan fight a war over the region of Kashmir.
1948	Gandhi dies, assassinated by Hindu nationalist Nathuram Godse.
1965	India and Pakistan again clash over Kashmir.
1971	India and West Pakistan fight over the liberation of East Pakistan (present-day Bangladesh).
2002	Pogroms against Muslims result in communal violence in Gujarat.

Notes

Introduction

1. Eastman, *Abortive Revolution*, 278.
2. "Man and Wife of the Year."
3. A survey of the literature produced in the 1950s through the 1980s that assesses Chiang's leadership through the lens of the 1949 defeat can be found in Alitto, "Chiang Kai-shek in Western Historiography," 719–808.
4. Eastman, *Abortive Revolution*, 278, 281–82.
5. Spence, "Enigma of Chiang Kai-shek."
6. Schoppa, *Columbia Guide*, 95.
7. Chapter 6 discusses this in more detail.
8. Sun developed the Three People's Principles (democracy, nationalism, and the people's livelihood), and Mao advocated Marxist ideology.
9. Coble, "China's 'New Remembering,'" 394–410.
10. Regarding Jonathan Fenby's 2003 biography of Chiang, Jonathan Spence ultimately concludes that it "adds nuances to our received picture, but ultimately does not alter it" ("Before the East"). Along similar lines, Charles Hayford described Jay Taylor's 2009 biography on Chiang as a "rush to revisionism," claiming that Taylor's emphasis of Chiang's strengths did not resolve contradictions about Chiang's leadership and came across as being "selective in establishing what the consensus was" ("Final Triumph").
11. Although I began reading these documents at Academia Historica, they have since been published as *JZZDSG*.
12. The other four relationships are husband to wife, father to son, elder brother to younger brother, and friend to friend. Although the last dyad appears egalitarian, practitioners often redefine the relationship hierarchically by attaching "older (*lao*)" or "younger (*xiao*)" to the surname. Nevertheless, an egalitarian tendency exists in this last dyad and thus sits uneasily in the hierarchical framework. In the form of sworn brothers and secret society members, this relationship has contributed to overturning

or severely weakening existing orders throughout Chinese history. See Kutcher, "Fifth Relationship."

13. This articulation of *chi* is derived from the twelfth-century philosopher Zhu Xi (1130–1200), who notes in the Doctrine of the Mean (*Zhongyong*): "To possess the feeling of shame/humiliation is to be near courage (*zhichi jinhu yong*)" (Kim and Hwang, *Indigenous and Cultural Psychology*, 183).

14. Selected works in this literature include Callahan, *Pessoptimist Nation*; Wang Zheng, *Never Forget National Humiliation*; and Gries, *China's New Nationalism*.

15. James MacGregor Burns described leadership as either transformational and transactional in *Leadership*; Max Weber distinguished between charismatic and routinized leadership in "Charisma and its Transformation." Although Jean Blondel's *Political Leadership* also critiques this binary framework of leadership and offers nine categories of leadership, it does not make clear how one is to compare the creative exercise of agency among leaders within or between categories.

16. Barker, *Cultural Studies*, 236, 435.

17. For example, Michael Horowitz, Allan Stam, and Cali Ellis open *Why Leaders Fight* by declaring that "History is made by people. From wars to elections to political protests, the world revolves around the way that people decide to behave. In particular, world leaders—the people that run countries big and small around the world—play a large role in shaping the destinies of their countries" (xi).

18. Lim, *Doing Comparative Politics*, 79.

19. An important example of this perspective is Theda Skocpol's examination for why revolutions occurred in China, Russia, and France. She argues that structures such as class relations, class versus state relations, and state versus state relations brought about revolutionary breakthroughs, not the "purposive" revolutionary leaders who clamored for them. Considering the third factor, she argues that countries who were militarily weak coupled with threats of invasion from a militarily stronger country provided a "space" for consolidating revolution because such efforts presented a quandary to the foreign enemy on whether to support or undermine revolutionary efforts (*States and Social Revolution*, 3–33, 236).

20. Emirbayer and Mische, "What Is Agency?," 971. Agency can also be seen in a person's ability to think in a "time-stream" of interconnected events by continually comparing the present, past, and future. See Neustadt and May, *Thinking in Time*, 247–48, 251.

21. A good example of emphasizing followers is Garry Wills, *Certain Trumpets*. Stephen Skowronek's definition of warrants can be found in *Politics Presidents Make*, 18.

22. This reconceptualization of structures as cultural and ideological builds on the work of Sewell, "Ideologies and Social Revolutions," 172–73, and Hunt, *Politics, Culture, and Class*, 21, 216, 218. It also builds on Howard Gardner's work, which argues that stories are central to leadership. Gardner, however, tends to avoid discussing how the political context might affect those stories and the perception of those leaders. Chapter 6 goes into more detail about this aspect (H. Gardner, with Laskin, *Leading Minds*, 9, 13).

23. This approach strives to avoid the potential blind spots inherent in a dichotomous framework of either focusing on a leader's personal qualities, which may filter out the structural components of action and unintentionally portray a leader as someone

larger than life, or of overemphasizing contextual factors shaping a leader's actions, which may neglect how such a leader creatively shapes his or her context.

24. Weber gave as examples of personal qualities: passion, judgment, and a sense of responsibility ("Politics as a Vocation," 113–17).

25. See, for instance, Coble, *Facing Japan*.

1. Drafting Chiang's Narrative in the Shilüe

1. These archival materials are located at Academia Historica, Taipei, Taiwan. Full citations are in the bibliography. An earlier version of this chapter was published in *Modern China* (Grace Huang, "Creating a Public Face for Posterity").

2. Recent biographies include Jay Taylor, *Generalissimo*; Jonathan Fenby, *Chiang Kai-shek*; and Yang Tianshi, *Zhaoxun zhenshi de Jiang Jieshi* and *Jiang shi midang*. A sampling of international conferences include "Reassessing Chiang Kai-shek: An International Dialogue," held at Queen's University in Kingston, Ontario, in 2009, jointly organized by Emily Hill, Jeremy Taylor, and the author; the "International Symposium on Chiang Kai-shek and Modern China," held at Zhejiang University in Hangzhou, Zhejiang, in 2010, organized by Chen Hongmin of Zhejiang University; "Chiang Kai-shek: A Reassessment in the Light of New Sources" organized by Tai-chun Kuo, Ramon Myers, and Hsiao-ting Lin of the Hoover Institution at Stanford University; the "Chiang Kai-shek and the Re-creation of the Republic of China in Taiwan" workshop, held at Oxford University in 2011; and an ongoing project and series of conferences organized by and held at Academia Sinica's Institute of Modern History, Taipei, Taiwan, headed by Huang Tzu-chin.

3. In fact, Jay Taylor's and Fenby's biographies on Chiang, written for Western audiences, fail to cite the *shilüe* entirely. Taylor bases his analysis on Chiang's diaries and on Qin Xiaoyi's 1978 official biography, *Zongtong Jianggong*. Works that do make reference to the *shilüe* have drawn on it mainly to analyze Chiang's thinking and strategies regarding such pivotal events as his kidnapping in 1936 or the battle for Manchuria between the Nationalists and Chinese communists in 1946. For example, see Tsang, "Chiang Kai-shek's 'Secret Deal,'" 9; Tanner, *The Battle for Manchuria*.

4. Zhang Yanxian, a former president of Academia Historica (2000–2003), declared that the document not only helped clarify Chiang's policies and the chronological sequence of events but also illuminated Chiang's "true" thinking (*zhenzheng xiangfa*) and internal world (*neixin shijie*) ("Qianyan," v–vi). This chapter attempts to present a more nuanced approach to the *shilüe* by considering how these various materials were consciously produced. Regarding the diary component, for instance, Keith Schoppa critiqued Jay Taylor's acceptance of the diaries as Chiang's "true thinking" in his biography of Chiang by questioning whether they reflected the leader's true feelings or what he desired posterity to know ("Diaries as a Historical Source").

5. Zhang Yanxian, "Qianyan," iv. For more on Chinese historiography and its influence, see C. Gardner, *Chinese Traditional Historiography*; Cheng, "*Ch'un ch'iu, Kung yang*"; Vogelsang, "Some Notions of Historical Judgment."

6. The Chinese character *shi* (事) in *shilüe* means "event" or "affair," and *lüe* (略) means either "neglect" or "approximate, rough, or brief" (*Hanyu dacidian*, s.v. "*shilüe*").

By using the *shilüe* format to cover the infamous Jingnan Incident of the Ming dynasty, involving a power struggle for the throne, Lu Bang could neglect the rules of, say, a year-by-year chronology (*nianpu*) of the dynasty or of a Chinese biography of an official (*zhuanji*), which might otherwise have crimped his ability to describe this pivotal event in detail. On the other hand, in the Song dynasty, Wang Cheng decided to write a *shilüe* that spanned nine generations of imperial rule (*Hanyu dacidian*, s.v. "*shilüe*").

7. As such, the components of Chiang's *shilüe* could differ from those found in the veritable records, such as adding speeches in the vernacular. It thus departed from other works of the Republican era that strictly followed the format of traditional Chinese historiography, including Mao Sicheng's compilation of Chiang's early years titled *Mr. Chiang Kai-shek and His Years before 1926* (Mao Ssu-cheng, *Minguo shiwu nian*), and that of another of Chiang's head secretary's, Chen Bulei's personal memoirs (*Hui yi lu*). These two works similarly recorded events dispassionately and conformed to the Chinese classical or *wenyanwen* style of writing. At the same time, Chiang's *shilüe* differed from Zhang Ling'ao's personal memoir about his time in Chiang's secretarial retinue, which was written in the contemporary style we are familiar with today (*Wo zai Jiang Jieshi shicongshi*).

8. The demise of the Confucian examination system in 1905 gave the initial impetus to abandon the classical Chinese system of writing in favor of the *baihua* written language. After the fall of the Qing dynasty, people like Hu Shi (1891–1962), Chen Duxiu (1879–1942), and Fu Sinian (1896–1950) believed that not only were democracy and science critical for China to habituate to modern times but that promoting *baihua* was important to support broader literacy, which would support the goals of democracy and science. See Ping Chen, *Modern Chinese*, 70–82.

9. In the summer of 1933, this office was one of three suborganizations Chiang created under the National Military Affairs Commission (along with the Bandit Suppression Headquarters [Jiaofei zongsiling bu] and the Field Headquarters [Xingying]) and was the most powerful. At the start of the war with Japan in 1937, Chiang consolidated the Office of Personal Attendants, previously located in Nanchang, Hankou, Chongqing, and Xi'an, into a single headquarters in Chongqing. See So, "Making of the Guomindang's Japan Policy," 218.

10. Ju, *Gensui Jiang Jieshi*, 16.

11. Zhang Ling'ao, *Wo zai Jiang Jieshi shicongshi*, 18.

12. Zhang Yanxian, "Qianyan," i–ii.

13. In the published version, one sees that the secretary is acknowledged as the compiler and Qin Xiaoyi as the editor. For example, see *JZZDSG*, 2003, 2/title page.

14. For instance, see Wei Li and Pye, "Ubiquitous Role of the *Mishu*," 913–36; Cheng Li, "*Mishu* Phenomenon."

15. Sun, *SG*, October 2, 1933; *JZZDSG*, 2005, 23/6–253.

16. Sun, *SG*, February 8, 1930; *JZZDSG*, 2003, 7/454.

17. This note can be found on Sun's September 1927 volume of the *shilüe*.

18. For example, Yuan, *SG*, February 5, 1934, which is indiscernible in the published edition.

19. Unlike the other two secretaries, Wang was also responsible for compiling the thematic chronologies, such as *Family and Friends* (*Aiji chugao*) and *Learning* (*Xueji*).

20. "Fenghuashi nongye xinxi wang."

21. Liu Weikai, interview.

22. For example, Wang, *SG*, June 15, 1928; *JZZDSG*, 2003, 3/520; Wang, *SG*, September 27, 1931; *JZZDSG*, 2004, 12/104–5; Wang, *SG*, May 18, 1928; *JZZDSG*, 2003, 3/376–77.

23. Wang, *SG*, July 29, 1931; *JZZDSG*, 2004, 11/454.

24. A story circulates about this move. During the Kuomintang flight, one of the planes was too heavy to fly. Rather than remove the archival materials, a passenger was bumped off the plane instead. While this anecdote remains unverified, it nevertheless attests to the premium importance Chiang placed on these materials, if only in the minds of his countrymen (author heard this anecdote from another researcher at the Academia Historica archive during her 2001–2002 stay).

25. Twitchett, *Writing of Official History*, 7–9.

26. For example, Yuan, *SG*, March 20, 1934; *JZZDSG*, 2006, 25/237–318.

27. For example, Chiang alluded to King Goujian (d. 465 BCE), who defeated the king of Wu after twenty years of preparation and Yue Fei (1103–42), a hero of the Song dynasty (960–1279) (Yuan, *SG*, February 11 and 17, 1934; *JZZDSG*, 2005, 24/387, 440–41). He also alluded to Jesus (Yuan, *SG*, May 4, 1934; *JZZDSG*, 2006, 26/24). Examples of shaping behavior can be found in Wang, *SG*, June 15, 1928; *JZZDSG*, 2003, 3/520.

28. Ray Huang, "Chiang Kai-shek and His Diary," 3.

29. See, for example, January 26 and 27, 1933, Chiang Kai-shek diaries, Box 36.

30. See, for example, Wang, *SG*, May 18, 1928; *JZZDSG*, 2003, 3/376–77; Wang, *SG*, November 10, 1931; *JZZDSG*, 2004, 12/262–63.

31. See Yuan, *SG*, May 15, 1934; *JZZDSG*, 2006, 25/79.

32. For more on Chiang's authorship, see Grace Huang, "Creating a Public Face," 630–31.

33. See, for example, Wang, *SG*, August, 6, 1931; *JZZDSG*, 2004, 11/491–514.

34. Yuan, *SG*, February 2, 1934; *JZZDSG*, 2005, 24/241.

35. Yuan, *SG*, March 26, 1934; *JZZDSG*, 2006, 25/343.

36. Liu Weikai, interview.

37. Pei-yi Wu, *Confucian's Progress*, 6.

38. For past historians, this means that compiling the veritable records of the previous ruler's reign needed to conform according to the political goals of the current reign. For instance, in 705 a group of ministers forced Empress Wu Zetian (624–705) to abdicate. In response, the empress's nephew forced those ministers out and then put great pressure on the compilers of the veritable records to present a favorable picture of the empress's reign to bolster the legitimacy of her son, Emperor Tang Zhongzong (656–710), and his own (Twitchett, *Writing of Official History*, 132–33).

39. Historians in the past tended to resolve this tension in the following way. Given that a basic norm in Chinese historiography was that twisted or unverifiable facts tarnished the credibility of the historian and thus his compilation of the veritable records, the historian often omitted those facts in the record and strategically placed the material in another section of the standard history. By putting the ill-fitting material somewhere else, such as in the annals or someone else's biography, the historian could maintain the

desired picture of individuals or events and preserve his professional integrity as an accurate recorder of the facts (Twitchett, "Problems of Chinese Biography," 30).

40. Yuan, *SG*, January 20, 1929; *JZZDSG*, 2003, 5/75.

41. Wang, *SG*, March 12, 1932; *JZZDSG*, 2004, 13/406.

42. Wang, *SG*, May 14, 1928; *JZZDSG*, 2003, 3/350.

43. The kidnapping shocked the country and threatened another large-scale civil war. Both Moscow and the Chinese communists feared that their cause would be hurt and the Japanese would gain the upper hand from this conflict. In addition to Chiang's wife and brother-in-law, CCP leader Zhou Enlai (1898–1976) arrived to mediate, and Zhang Xueliang (1901–2001) ultimately agreed to free his prisoner. This incident ironically helped Chiang shore up his credentials as a national leader and gave him a new mandate to fight Japan. See Hsü, *Rise of Modern China*, 564–65.

44. Diary entry: 上午十一時許，余正在睡中，子文忽入門，余目猶迷霧，不辨其爲子文也。少頃清醒，始識其眞爲子文。Chiang Kai-shek diaries, December 21, 1936, Box 39.

45. *Shilüe* manuscript entry: 公仍在高宅。今晨，公睡最酣。上午十一時，宋子文推門入見。公方曚瞍中幾不辨爲誰，移時清醒，乃知爲子文 (December 21, 1936).

46. An example of the editorial reverse order marks can be seen in Sun, *SG*, September 5, 1927; *JZZDSG*, 2003, 2/10, 14.

47. For example, Wang, *SG*, January 1, 2, 1929; *JZZDSG*, 2003, 5/4, 15.

48. Although Chiang had unified China in 1928 through the Northern Expedition, several regional military commanders broke off relations with him in 1929, and civil war ensued in 1930. This war pitted 300,000 of Chiang's troops against the combined 700,000 of the former northern and southern warlords. By using a divide-and-conquer strategy, Chiang emerged victorious. For more on this battle, see Worthing, *General He Yingqin*, 132; Lieberthal, *Governing China*, 35–36.

49. See, for example, Yuan, *SG*, April 28, 1929; *JZZDSG*, 2003, 5/421–34; Yuan, *SG*, June 27, 1929; *JZZDSG*, 2003, 6/79–95; Yuan, *SG*, July 6 and 9, 1929; *JZZDSG*, 2003, 6/148–73, 186–220.

50. See, for example, Wang, *SG*, January 19, 1931; *JZZDSG*, 2004, 9/461–77.

51. Yuan, *SG*, January 20, 1929; *JZZDSG*, 2003, 5/75.

52. Liu Weikai, interview.

53. For examples in the *shilüe*, see Grace Huang, "Mme. Chiang's Mission to America," 61–62.

54. Wang, April 16, 1928; *JZZDSG*, 2003, 3/133. In the 1938 Battle of Xuzhou, Chinese troops were sent to defend this city, which was strategically located at the midpoint of the north–south Tianjin-Pukou rail line. The battle was more significant than the earlier one because of its size and outcome in delaying Japanese encroachment into Wuhan, the de facto wartime capital for Chiang and the Nationalists. For more on this battle, see Mitter, *Forgotten Ally*, 150–56; MacKinnon, *Wuhan, 1928*, 31–36.

55. For the volumes of the later years, it appears that once Chiang developed his storyline, the options for changing that storyline—for example, using *chi* in a radically different way—became less feasible, especially when he became a leader on the national and international stage. Moreover, by this time the secretaries had developed their protocol for compiling the *shilüe*. Chapter 5 explores these constraints on Chiang's storyline when Chiang and Mao Zedong were vying for national power in the 1930s and 1940s.

2. Enduring Humiliation in Jinan

1. Bergère, *Sun Yat-sen*, 270–74. A preliminary version of the arguments put forward in this chapter and chapters 3 and 4 was published in *Twentieth-Century China* (Grace Huang, "Speaking to Posterity").

2. Bergère, *Sun Yat-sen*, 153–72.

3. The Canton government contributed 186,000 Chinese dollars, whereas the Soviets contributed 2.7 million Chinese dollars or 3 million rubles (Bergère, *Sun Yat-sen*, 344–45).

4. Wilbur, *Nationalist Revolution*, 5–14.

5. Iriye, *After Imperialism*, 195–96.

6. For instance, in popular and accessible introductions to modern China, John King Fairbank omits the Jinan Incident entirely in *China: A New History*, and Immanuel C. Y. Hsü gives only a one-sentence mention: "Though blocked by Japanese troops at Tsinan in Shantung Province, Chiang was able to surmount the obstacle" (*Rise of Modern China*, 530). Akira Iriye, Donald Jordan, and Shuge Wei have studied the clash in detail, but they do not convey its significance to Chiang's leadership. They note, respectively, that Sino-Japanese relations turned for the worse and foreshadowed more significant problems between the countries in the 1930s (Iriye, *After Imperialism*), that the reputation of Japanese-supported northern warlords was damaged (Jordan, *Northern Expedition*), and that the Japanese won the propaganda war over the Kuomintang government in the English-language press in portraying the Jinan Incident (Shuge Wei, "Beyond the Front Line," 188–224). Although these accounts shed light on the military, international, and media aspects of the event, what has yet to be explored is how the Jinan Incident affected Chiang, and how he developed his leadership and the trajectory of China in response to the incident.

7. For May Fourth advocates, the problem was that they were also angry about humiliations by foreigners, and hence they tended to avoid critiquing this aspect of Chiang's use of Confucianism. See Schwarcz, *Chinese Enlightenment*. Huaiyin Li traces a split in the May Fourth intellectuals between Yan Fu (1854–1921) and Liang Qichao (1873–1929), who maintained liberal values, versus Jiang Tingfu (1895–1965), Ding Wenjing, and even Hu Shi, who began discrediting these values as inadequate to ensuring the survival of the Chinese state (*Reinventing Modern China*, 33–73). Moreover, while there have been ample studies about China and humiliation, there has been little work on actual Chinese leaders deploying it, much less Chiang's specific application of *chi* outside of the New Life Movement. Some of the main works in this area include Zheng Wang, *Never Forget National Humiliation*; Callahan, *Pessoptimist Nation*; and Gries, *China's New Nationalism*.

8. Wilbur, *Nationalist Revolution*, 94–170.

9. Murdock, "Exploiting Anti-Imperialism," 72.

10. In fact, Pearl S. Buck and her family had to rely on Chinese friends to provide safety for them. See Leong, *China Mystique*, 21.

11. For a detailed account of the Nanjing Incident, see Iriye, *After Imperialism*, 125–33; Wilbur, *Nationalist Revolution*, 91–92.

12. Wilbur, *Nationalist Revolution*, 178.

13. Wilbur, *Nationalist Revolution*, 91–94.

14. That Fukuda did so without further instruction from the Japanese government supports Iriye's observation that the chain of command from the Japanese government to the field in China often broke down. In this case, Fukuda may have been trying to enhance his prestige, but in the process he committed the first serious incident of the Japanese military acting without explicit governmental consent (Iriye, *After Imperialism*, 198).

15. Wilbur, *Nationalist Revolution*, 178.

16. The Japanese version stated that about thirty of Chiang's soldiers entered the home of a Japanese resident and began looting it. The resident escaped and managed to contact the police. The police arrived but were threatened by the soldiers, and shortly thereafter, Japanese soldiers appeared on the scene and began chasing the Chinese soldiers. From there, shots were exchanged, and then fighting spread throughout the city. The Chinese version stated that some public relations officers from the army were putting up posters near the house in question when confronted by the Japanese and fighting broke out (Iriye, *After Imperialism*, 199–200).

17. Shuge Wei, "Beyond the Front Line," 189.

18. Jay Taylor, *Generalissimo*, 79.

19. Luo, "Chinese Rediscovery," 345.

20. Shuge Wei, "Beyond the Front Line," 189.

21. Wang, *SG*, May 6, 1928; *JZZDSG*, 2003, 3/281.

22. P. Cohen, *Speaking to History*, 69. Another reference to *woxin changdan* was made shortly thereafter (Wang, *SG*, May 17, 1928; *JZZDSG*, 2003, 3/423).

23. P. Cohen, *Speaking to History*, has recounted this tale in depth, portraying its variations and conveying the complexity of the Goujian character, who could be both sensitive and compassionate but also terribly cruel. Cohen unpacks how this story was understood, used, and adapted from the late Qing to the present time, even including a section on the uses of the story during Chiang's rule during the Nanjing period and during his tenure of power in Taiwan. However, Cohen's focus has been on tracking changes in the story to reflect the general changes in the political milieu as opposed to how a leader like Chiang specifically adapted and readapted aspects of the story in service of political goals.

24. P. Cohen, *Speaking to History*, 4–5.

25. P. Cohen, *Speaking to History*, 8–9.

26. P. Cohen, *Speaking to History*, 9–10; P. Cohen, *History and Popular Memory*, 92.

27. Huang Rensheng, *New Translation*, 26.

28. Huang Rensheng, *New Translation*, 26.

29. A picture of this advertisement can be seen in P. Cohen, "Remembering and Forgetting," 10.

30. *SG*, May 7, 1928; *JZZDSG*, 2003, 3/286.

31. The treaty was designed to limit the naval arms race and work through security arrangements in the Pacific. According to Iriye, its overall intention was to end imperialist diplomacy, especially toward China, although what its participants expected would take its place was unclear. See *After Imperialism*, 13–22. Treaty ports were port cities that were governed by the unequal treaties established by the imperial powers in the middle of the nineteenth century.

32. Wang included a report about the Japanese opposition parties and a section from a Chinese report about the Nanjing and Beijing governments (*SG*, May 1, 1928; *JZZ-DSG*, 2003, 3/248). Beijing had continued serving as the nominal capital of China, but by this time, the Nationalists had set up a rival capital in Nanjing.

33. Wang, *SG*, May 1, 1928; *JZZDSG*, 2003, 3/249.

34. Wang, *SG*, May 2, 1928; *JZZDSG*, 2003, 3/250. The *shilüe* offers a slightly different timeline than published accounts such as Yang, "Jinan Can'an," with the report of the clash between the Chinese and Japanese happening one day earlier.

35. Wang, *SG*, May 2, 1928; *JZZDSG*, 2003, 3/250.

36. Wang, *SG*, May 2, 1928; *JZZDSG*, 2003, 3/250; Yang, "Jinan Can'an," 679.

37. Wang, *SG*, May 3, 1928; *JZZDSG*, 2003, 3/262–63; Yang, "Jinan Can'an," 679.

38. Wang, *SG*, May 3, 1928; *JZZDSG*, 2003, 3/262.

39. After the incident began, Prime Minister Tanaka and his Cabinet authorized an additional 16,000 troop reinforcements from Manchuria and Korea to make their way to Jinan (Wilbur, *Nationalist Revolution*, 179; Jay Taylor, *Generalissimo*, 79).

40. Wang, *SG*, May 7, 1928, 301; *JZZDSG*, 2003, 3/289–90. The *SG* revealed only these three points, in contrast to Yang, who reported six points, and Iriye, who reported five (Yang, "Jinan Can'an"; Iriye, *After Imperialism*). Chiang apparently tailored a second response to the demands two days later, which was more detailed than Yang's and Iriye's reports.

41. Wang, *SG*, May 10, 1928; *JZZDSG*, 2003, 3/308. Chiang was comparing the soldiers and the regiment commander Li Yannian, whom he had left behind to guard the city, to Wen Wenshan, a prime minister during the Southern Song period (1127–1279) who had fought against the Mongol invaders and symbolized Chinese resistance to foreign invaders. Captured by the Mongols, Wen Wenshan remained their prisoner of war for four years, during which he wrote *Song of Righteousness*. Because of his unwillingness to surrender, the Mongols finally killed him (Leslie H. Dingyan Chen, *Chen Jiongming*, 14).

42. Wilbur, *Nationalist Revolution*, 180; Yang, "Jinan Can'an," 683.

43. Yang, "Jinan Can'an," 681; Wang, *SG*, May 10, 1928; *JZZDSG*, 2003, 3/307–8.

44. Wang, *SG*, May 16, 1928; *JZZDSG*, 2003, 3/361.

45. Wang, *SG*, May 15, 1928; *JZZDSG*, 2003, 3/356.

46. Iriye, *After Imperialism*, 204.

47. Wang, *SG*, May 18, 1928; *JZZDSG*, 2003, 3/371.

48. Yang, "Jinan Can'an," 684.

49. Wang, *SG*, May 4, 1928; *JZZDSG*, 2003, 3/272–73.

50. Wang, *SG*, May 9, 1931; *JZZDSG*, 2003, 3/295–302.

51. The Japanese representative was surnamed Kuroda, and the Chinese negotiator was Xiong Shihui (Wang, *SG*, May 4, 1928; *JZZDSG*, 2003, 3/264).

52. Yang, "Jinan Can'an," 680.

53. Officers from the English and US consuls made this announcement (Yang, "Jinan Can'an," 680).

54. Wang, *SG*, May 4, 1928; *JZZDSG*, 2003, 3/272–73. Iriye offers an alternative (and likely more probable) reason: Fukuda was buying time to wait for more supplies and ammunition, and, because communications between Japanese companies had been cut off, he needed time to regroup (*After Imperialism*, 201, 202).

55. Wilbur, *Nationalist Revolution*, 179; Jay Taylor, *Generalissimo*, 79.

56. Wang, *SG*, May 10, 1928; *JZZDSG*, 2003, 3/304.

57. Wang, *SG*, May 10, 1928; *JZZDSG*, 2003, 3/304.

58. Jordan, *Northern Expedition*, 160.

59. Wang, *SG*, May 22, 1928; *JZZDSG*, 2003, 3/390–91. Indeed, a resolution was delayed until the following year. On March 28, 1929, an agreement on Jinan stated that the two sides had unfortunately been unable to properly control their respective armies in Jinan, and they agreed to let bygones be bygones. The Japanese army was given two months to depart Shandong Province, which they did (Yang, "Jinan Can'an," 686). The Jinan agreement contained no statement concerning Japan's violation of China's sovereignty or demand for an apology or stipulation of reparations. These omissions were especially flagrant considering that Jinan residents had lived under a virtual reign of terror in which freedom of the press was profoundly proscribed and individuals were summarily executed if they were suspected of being a southern (i.e., Nationalist) sympathizer (Iriye, *After Imperialism*, 202).

60. Wang, *SG*, May 12, 1928; *JZZDSG*, 2003, 3/319.

61. Providing a gripping emotional dimension to this critical ten-day battle, Wang Xiuchu filled page after page with wailings and screaming as he depicted his surroundings and described how the Manchus had tortured and killed his older and younger brothers and how he was forced to hide in the cemetery with his pregnant wife and child (*Yangzhou shiri ji*).

62. These leaders included Hu Hanmin (1879–1936), Wang Jingwei, Li Shizeng (1881–1973), and Sun Yat-sen's son, Sun Ke (1891–1973).

63. Wang, *SG*, May 12, 1928; *JZZDSG*, 2003, 3/319.

64. Wang, *SG*, May 12, 1928; *JZZDSG*, 2003, 3/321.

65. Hardy, *Worlds of Bronze*, xiii.

66. Wang, *SG*, May 11, 1928; *JZZDSG*, 2003, 3/314.

67. Beasley, *Japanese Imperialism*, 186–88.

68. Yang, "Jinan Can'an," 683.

69. Wang, *SG*, May 25, 1928; *JZZDSG*, 2003, 3/422–23.

70. Wang, *SG*, May 25, 1928; *JZZDSG*, 2003, 3/422.

71. Hsü, *Rise of Modern China*, 345–46.

72. Wang, *SG*, May 9, 1928; *JZZDSG*, 2003, 3/298.

73. Wang, *SG*, May 10, 1928; *JZZDSG*, 2003, 3/308.

74. In this quotation, the Chinese verb *ji* 記 means both to "record" and to "call to mind" (Wang, *SG*, May 14, 1928; *JZZDSG*, 2003, 3/350).

75. For the diary entry cited in the previous note and as mentioned in chapter 1, Wang probably realized as he was compiling the *shilüe* in 1940 that "resist" would be the more accurate word from a historical perspective, given Japanese military superiority.

76. Wang, *SG*, May 16, 1928. These remarks were actually later crossed out by Qin Xiaoyi, who presumably did not want posterity to see shortcomings in Chiang's leadership.

77. Wang, *SG*, May 3, 1931.

78. As mentioned in chapter 1, given the regularity with which Chiang maintained this entry, it is probably unsurprising that at times several weeks went by where he just

jotted down quotations from Chinese ancient philosophers or, in later years, from the Bible.

79. Wang, *SG*, May 19, 1928; *JZZDSG*, 2003, 3/379.
80. Wang, *SG*, May 18, 1928; *JZZDSG*, 2003, 3/376–77.
81. Wang, *SG*, May 15, 1928; *JZZDSG*, 2003, 3/356.
82. Chiang drew his inspiration from the neo-Confucian philosophers Zhu Xi (1130–1200) of the Song dynasty (960–1279) and Wang Yangming (1472–1529) of the Ming dynasty (1368–1644). In general, these philosophers were more concerned with inward sageliness than with outwardly kingliness. See Liu Shu-hsin, "Neo-Confucianism," 523.
83. Wang, *SG*, June 15, 1928; *JZZDSG*, 2003, 3/520.
84. Wang, *SG*, June 15, 1928; *JZZDSG*, 2003, 3/520.
85. Four days after the above entry, he reminded himself to avoid venting his anger on others; the following day, after losing his temper again, he wondered how he could control it (*Xingkeji*, June 19 and 20, 1928).
86. *Xingkeji*, May 9, 1928.
87. Sun, *SG*, October 2, 1933; *JZZDSG*, 2005, 23/57.
88. These books are recorded throughout the *shilüe* and are also found in a separate chronology, titled *Xueji* (*Learning Chronology*).
89. Wang, *SG*, July 17, 1928; *JZZDSG*, 2003, 3/528.
90. Wang, *SG*, July 17, 1928; *JZZDSG*, 2003, 3/528.
91. *Hanyu dacidian*, s.v. "avenging humiliation (*xuechi*)."

3. Diversifying His Uses of Chi: Domestic Disunity and Foreign Conflict

1. Eastman, "Nationalist China," 12.
2. Zheng Wang's *Never Forget National Humiliation* and Dong Wang's *China's Unequal Treaties* are examples that focus mainly on humiliation and China's relations with imperial powers.
3. Eastman, "Nationalist China," 9–10.
4. Wang, *SG*, January 19, 1931; *JZZDSG*, 2004, 9/464–65.
5. Wang, *SG*, January 12, 1931; *JZZDSG*, 2004, 9/335–37.
6. P. Cohen, *Speaking to History*, 37–39.
7. Quoted in Luo, "National Humiliation," 313.
8. P. Cohen, "Remembering and Forgetting," 5.
9. P. Cohen, *Speaking to History*, 48.
10. Wang, *SG*, August 10, 1931; *JZZDSG*, 2004, 11/519–20.
11. Wang, *SG*, January 12, 1931; *JZZDSG*, 2004, 9/356.
12. Wang, *SG*, January 14, 1931; *JZZDSG*, 2004, 9/392.
13. Wang, *SG*, January 12, 1931; *JZZDSG*, 2004, 9/358–59.
14. Wang, *SG*, April 26, 1931; *JZZDSG*, 2004, 10/476.
15. Wang, *SG*, April 26, 1931; *JZZDSG*, 2004, 10/477.
16. Wang, *SG*, April 9, 1931; *JZZDSG*, 2004, 10/413–14.
17. Wang, *SG*, April 9, 1931; *JZZDSG*, 2004, 10/414–16.
18. Wang, *SG*, July 27, 1931; *JZZDSG*, 2004, 11/444.

19. Wang, *SG*, January 5, 1931; *JZZDSG*, 2004, 9/292.

20. The zeal with which Wang pursued this goal led the British foreign minister to China to jokingly refer to him in private as suffering from an "extraterritoriality complex" (Jordan, *Chinese Boycotts*, 10–11).

21. Because Chinese food and goods were subject to an export tax when entering the Kwantung territory and then subject to an import tax on reentering Chinese territory, shippers began transferring their businesses away from Japanese ports and railways to the Chinese (Jordan, *Chinese Boycotts*, 19).

22. Paine, *Japanese Empire*, 38–39, 71.

23. Lockwood, "Japanese Silk," 31.

24. Gordon, "Historiographical Essay," 141. Louise Young applies the phrase "jewel in the crown" to Manchuria, which normally references the British colonial status of the subcontinent (*Japan's Total Empire*, 21).

25. Sun, "China's International Approach," 46.

26. L. Young, *Japan's Total Empire*, 38.

27. Jordan, *Chinese Boycotts*, 21.

28. Lee, *One Year*, 18; Duara, *Sovereignty and Authenticity*, 51; Lattimore, *Manchuria*, 240–42.

29. Duara, *Sovereignty and Authenticity*, 51.

30. Wang, *SG*, August 6, 1931; *JZZDSG*, 2004, 11/509–10.

31. Jordan, *Chinese Boycotts*, 24.

32. Wang, *SG*, July 12, 1931; *JZZDSG*, 2004, 11/371.

33. Jordan, *Chinese Boycotts*, 24.

34. Wang, *SG*, August 6, 1931; *JZZDSG*, 2004, 11/508.

35. Lee, *One Year*, 21, 24.

36. Wang, *SG*, July 5, 1931; *JZZDSG*, 2004, 11/359.

37. Wang, *SG*, July 4, 1931; *JZZDSG*, 2004, 11/354.

38. Lee, *One Year*, 23.

39. Wang, *SG*, July 4, 1931; *JZZDSG*, 2004, 11/354.

40. Jordan, *Chinese Boycotts*, 37–46.

41. Wang, *SG*, July 18, 1931; *JZZDSG*, 2004, 11/395–96.

42. Lee, *One Year*, 22.

43. Wang, *SG*, August 12, 1931; *JZZDSG*, 2004, 11/525–26.

44. Wang, *SG*, August 16, 1931; *JZZDSG*, 2004, 11/550.

45. Ramsdell, "Nakamura Incident," 53, 54.

46. Wilson, *Manchurian Crisis*, 19.

47. Ramsdell, "Nakamura Incident," 65.

48. Ramsdell, "Nakamura Incident," 62.

49. Wang, *SG*, September 1, 1931; *JZZDSG*, 2004, 12/29.

50. Wang, *SG*, September 4 and 7, 1931; *JZZDSG*, 2004, 12/37, 54.

51. Wang, *SG*, September 13, 1931; *JZZDSG*, 2004, 12/65.

52. Ray Huang, "Chiang Kai-shek," 67.

53. See Lee, *One Year*, 42.

54. Coble, *Facing Japan*, 33.

55. Wang, *SG*, September 26, 1931; *JZZDSG*, 2004, 12/101.
56. Sun, "China's International Approach," 48–49.
57. Clubb, *20th Century China*, 175.
58. Bianco, *Origins of the Chinese Revolution*, 148; Eastman, *Abortive Revolution*, 246.
59. Coble, *Facing Japan*, 377–79.
60. Wang, *SG*, September 20, 1931; *JZZDSG*, 2004, 12/80.
61. Wang, *SG*, September 20, 1931; *JZZDSG*, 2004, 12/80–81.
62. Wang, *SG*, September 19, 1931; *JZZDSG*, 2004, 12/78.
63. Wang, *SG*, September 22, 1931; *JZZDSG*, 2004, 12/85.
64. Wang, *SG*, September 21, 1931; *JZZDSG*, 2004, 12/83.
65. Wang, *SG*, September 27, 1931; *JZZDSG*, 2004, 12/104–5.
66. Wang, *SG*, September 22, 1931; *JZZDSG*, 2004, 12/88–89.
67. Wang, *SG*, September 22, 1931; *JZZDSG*, 2004, 12/89.
68. Wang, *SG*, September 22, 1931; *JZZDSG*, 2004, 12/89.
69. Wang, *SG*, September 22, 1931; *JZZDSG*, 2004, 12/89.
70. Wang, *SG*, September 28, 1931; *JZZDSG*, 2004, 12/105.
71. Wang, *SG*, October 7, 1931; *JZZDSG*, 2004, 12/140–41.
72. Wang, *SG*, December 14, 1931; *JZZDSG*, 2004, 12/459.
73. In terms of public opinion, I draw on Coble, who makes the tentative assessment that popular sentiment among the 5 to 10 percent of Chinese who could read newspapers and journals were inclined to favor resistance to Japan (*Facing Japan*, 76).
74. Wang, *SG*, September 28, 1931; *JZZDSG*, 2004, 12/105.
75. So, "Making of the Guomindang's Japan Policy," 215.
76. Wang, *SG*, September 21, 1931; *JZZDSG*, 2004, 12/83.
77. Wang, *SG*, September 23, 1931; *JZZDSG*, 2004, 12/92.
78. Wang, *SG*, September 23, 1931; *JZZDSG*, 2004, 12/92.
79. Jordan, "Place of Chinese Disunity," 43.
80. Nish, *Japan's Struggle*, 241.
81. A. Kuhn, "Lytton Report," 96.
82. Wang, *SG*, October 25, 1931; *JZZDSG*, 2004, 12/199.
83. A. Kuhn, "Lytton Report," 96.
84. "Lytton Commission."
85. Nish, *Japan's Struggle*, 238.
86. Nish, *Japan's Struggle*, 240.
87. Nish, *Japan's Struggle*, 240.
88. Wang, *SG*, September 25, 1931; *JZZDSG*, 2004, 12/98.
89. Wang, *SG*, November 5, 1931; *JZZDSG*, 2004, 12/246–47.
90. So, "Making of Guomindang's Japan Policy," 222–24.
91. So, "Making of Guomindang's Japan Policy," 226–27.
92. Eastman, "Nationalist China," 13–14.
93. Jordan, "Place of Chinese Disunity," 44–54.
94. Wang, *SG*, April 2, 1931; *JZZDSG*, 2004, 10/379–80.
95. Wang, *SG*, October 10, 1931; *JZZDSG*, 2004, 12/149.
96. Wang, *SG*, November 10, 1931; *JZZDSG*, 2004, 12/263.

97. Pakula, *Last Empress*, 247; Jay Taylor, *Generalissimo*, 95–96.
98. Wang, *SG*, December 27, 1931; *JZZDSG*, 2004, 12/505–6.
99. Fenby, *Chiang Kai-shek*, 205; Wang, *SG*, December 22, 1931; *JZZDSG*, 2004, 12/478.
100. Wang, *SG*, December 31, 1931; *JZZDSG*, 2004, 12/523.
101. Sun, "China's International Approach," 51.
102. Li Huaiyin, *Reinventing Modern China*, 35, 62, 66.
103. Jay Taylor, *Generalissimo*, 97–98.
104. See Trampedach, "Chiang Kaishek," 132; Eastman, "Nationalist China," 23.

4. The New Life Movement in Context: Deploying Shame to Modernize China

1. Oldstone-Moore, "New Life Movement," 17, 77–79.
2. Dirlik, "Ideological Foundations," 949–50.
3. Between 1936 and 1949, Song Meiling took over the movement, and church and missionary organizations played more important roles (Dirlik, "Ideological Foundations," 948). I focus on the initial three years because Chiang was more personally involved and because the movement was most active and visible. By 1936, newspaper articles about the New Life Movement had virtually vanished (Oldstone-Moore, "New Life Movement," 12).
4. For instance, one commentator described the May Fourth intellectuals as launching China "onto the path of genuine modernity" (Schwarcz, *Chinese Enlightenment*, 5). Another commentator called Chiang's New Life a modern counterrevolution, the implication being that Chiang's approach was arresting the true revolution (Dirlik, "Ideological Foundations," 968).
5. William Kirby and Arif Dirlik both argue that the movement was unable to bring about willing mass participation (Kirby, *Germany and Republican China*, 184; Dirlik, "Ideological Foundations," 975). Stephen C. Averill argues that its fundamental failure lay in the "persistent and intractable local elite determined to retain and even extend its powers" ("New Life in Action," 596). Mary Clabaugh Wright argues that the movement was a "dismal failure" in that it attempted to revive a sorely outdated Confucian ideology (*Last Stand of Chinese Conservatism*, 312). Finally, Wennan Liu notes that by seeking to discipline the population to become qualified citizens through its deployment of its old political framework, the Nationalist regime failed to institutionalize the New Life directives with a systematic disciplinary mechanism ("Redefining the Moral and Legal Roles," 338).
6. Rudolph and Rudolph, *Modernity of Tradition*, 9–10.
7. Yuan, *SG*, March 18, 1934; *JZZDSG*, 2006, 25/180.
8. Yuan, *SG*, March 18, 1934; *JZZDSG*, 2006, 25/179; Asada, "From Washington to London," 147, 148, 184.
9. Yuan, *SG*, March 18, 1934; *JZZDSG*, 2006, 25/179–80.
10. Paine, *Wars for Asia*, 173.
11. In the 1920s, the United States excluded the Soviet Union from being a signatory because it refused to recognize the Bolshevik government (Miller and Wich, *Becoming Asia*, 12–13; Grenville, *History of the World*, 185).

12. Miller and Wich, *Becoming Asia*, 13.

13. Yuan, *SG*, February 12, 1934; *JZZDSG*, 2005, 24/404.

14. Yuan, *SG*, March 18, 1934; *JZZDSG*, 2006, 25/180.

15. Leys, *Analects of Confucius*, 56, as noted in Schoppa, "From Empire to People's Republic," 42.

16. See, for instance, Yuan, *SG*, January 6, 1934; *JZZDSG*, 2004, 24/167. Leaders of the Nineteenth Route Army wanted to overthrow the Nanjing government because they were dissatisfied with Chiang's appeasement policies toward Japan and the army's deployment to a poor province after its heroic stand to defend Shanghai against the Japanese in 1932. By the end of January 1934, however, the leaders of the rebellion either fled the country or went back to Chiang (Litten, "CCP and the Fujian Rebellion," 57–58).

17. For more on the exterminating campaigns, see Hsü, *Rise of Modern China*, 558–59. For more on labeling communists as bandits, see Bertram, *First Act in China*, 272.

18. Billingsley, *Bandits in Republican China*, 10.

19. "Nine Powers Treaty."

20. Miller and Wich, *Becoming Asia*, 10.

21. Yuan, *SG*, May 11, 1934; *JZZDSG*, 2006, 26/67.

22. Yuan, *SG*, May 21, 1934; *JZZDSG*, 2006, 26/162–63.

23. Yuan, *SG*, March 27, 1934; *JZZDSG*, 2006, 25/361.

24. Yuan, *SG*, March 27, 1934; *JZZDSG*, 2006, 25/361–63.

25. Yuan, *SG*, March 28, 1934; *JZZDSG*, 2006, 25/370.

26. Yuan, *SG*, February 11, 1934; *JZZDSG*, 2005, 24/387–88.

27. Yuan, *SG*, February 17, 1934; *JZZDSG*, 2005, 24/450.

28. Cochran and Hsieh, with Cochran, *One Day in China*, xi–xiii.

29. Wu Jun, "My Diary for Today," 252.

30. Wu Jun, "My Diary for Today," 253.

31. Hao Baicun, interview. Hao also mentioned later that he met the Generalissimo in Nanjing for the first time and recalled that Chiang, in his signature cloak, possessed a sparkle in his eyes and was awe-inspiring.

32. Yu, "1911 Revolution," 896. Of relevance was that a political battle occurred in the transition between the Qing imperial regime and the Republican period over whether China should become a constitutional monarchy, as advocated by Kang Youwei (1858–1927) and Liang Qichao, or a republic, as represented by Sun Yat-sen, Huang Xing (1874–1916), and Song Jiaoren (1882–1913). The latter group won, and the goals represented by Sun's Three People's Principles were meant to guide the Kuomintang and the new republic in the areas of nationalism, democracy, and the people's livelihood.

33. According to Sun's formulation, democracy would be realized after passing through three stages: military rule, in which a republican foundation would be laid; tutelage rule, in which people would be trained in administration and governance; and finally, constitutional rule, which represented the successful conclusion of the revolution. According to Nationalist historiography, China entered the period of Nationalist tutelage rule after the Northern Expedition in 1928, and so the New Life Movement was part of this second stage of training citizens and preparing them for democracy. The Republic of China would enter the final stage, constitutional rule, in 1946 (Yu, "1911 Revolution," 896–904).

34. Yuan, *SG*, April 16, 1934; *JZZDSG*, 2006, 25/490.

35. Guan, *Guanzi*, 3.

36. Guan, *Guanzi*, 53–54.

37. On a first reading, Chiang underlined passages in black ink. Margin notes tended to repeat key words from the text. On a second reading, he underlined passages in red ink, often next to passages already underlined in black. Infrequent blue and red pencil markings imply that he read certain passages a third or fourth time. The author perused Chiang's personal copy of the *Guanzi* at the Archives of President Chiang Kai-shek.

38. *Xueji*, March 6, 1934.

39. Yuan, *SG*, February 17, 1934; *JZZDSG*, 2005, 24/441.

40. Yuan, *SG*, March 22, 1934; *JZZDSG*, 2006, 25/321.

41. Chiang, "Essentials of the New Life," 801.

42. Chiang, "Essentials of the New Life," 801.

43. Yuan, *SG*, February 17, 1934; *JZZDSG*, 2005, 24/446. In comparing the speech excerpt referring to *Guanzi* in the *shilüe* to Li Mian's Chinese edition, Chiang quoted the text verbatim (*Guanzi Jinzhu Jinyi*, 41–42). I used Rickett's translation (Guan, *Guanzi*, 97).

44. Yuan, *SG*, February 17, 1934; *JZZDSG*, 2005, 24/446.

45. As a local leader, Chen Ping was extremely fair in distributing meat to his townspeople. In response to his praiseworthy action, Chen Ping replied, "If I can manage the world, I'll manage it in the same manner as I distribute meat, so that all people in the world will not need to be poor or hungry." See Ban, "Biography of Chen Ping."

46. Yuan, *SG*, February 2, 1934; *JZZDSG*, 2005, 24/234–35.

47. Yuan, *SG*, February 19, 1934; *JZZDSG*, 2005, 24/465.

48. Yuan, *SG*, May 9, 1934; *JZZDSG*, 2006, 26/58–59.

49. Yuan, *SG*, May 9, 1934; *JZZDSG*, 2006, 26/58.

50. Yuan, *SG*, May 9, 1934; *JZZDSG*, 2006, 26/60.

51. Yuan, *SG*, May 9, 1934; *JZZDSG*, 2006, 26/58–59.

52. Spence, *Search for Modern China*, 340. A contemporary women's magazine, *Linlong*, gave voice to the "modern girl" (Yen, "Body Politics," 166). Underlying these competing notions of the modern woman in China lay the question of policing the boundaries of national governance. Reformist intellectuals, among which Chiang and the New Life Movement could be included, wanted to ensure that modern China included "virtue and education" and a warning to avoid following feminist ideas blindly in the face of the commercial sector's rising influence (Edwards, "Policing the Modern Woman," 123).

53. Yuan, *SG*, February 19, 1934; *JZZDSG*, 2005, 24/470, 472–74.

54. Yuan, *SG*, March 5, 1934; *JZZDSG*, 2006, 25/46.

55. Yuan, *SG*, February 2, 1934; *JZZDSG*, 2005, 24/233.

56. Fitzgerald, *Awakening China*, 9, 104.

57. Lloyd Eastman puts forward this view in *Abortive Revolution*, 68–69.

58. Payne, *History of Fascism*, 337–38.

59. Oldstone-Moore, "New Life Movement," 15.

60. Yuan, *SG*, February 11, 1934; *JZZDSG*, 2005, 24/388; Jay Taylor, *Generalissimo*, 91.

61. Copy of "China Mail File No. 146," January 8, 1935, YMCA, WS 27a, China 1935, quoted in Ferlanti, "New Life Movement," 974.

62. Yuan, *SG*, March 20, 1934; *JZZDSG*, 2006, 25/294–95.

63. The *shilüe* includes this pamphlet (Yuan, *SG*, May 15, 1934; *JZZDSG*, 2006, 25/79). Although Chiang was presented as the author, Yang Yongtai (1880–1936) in fact drafted it. A Guangdong native, Yang was an important contributor to the New Life Movement, along with Xiong Shihui, Yan Baohang, and Deng Wenyi (Ferlanti, "New Life Movement," 968).

64. Yuan, *SG*, May 15, 1934; *JZZDSG*, 2006, 26/87.

65. Yuan, *SG*, May 15, 1934; *JZZDSG*, 2006, 26/87.

66. For more on orthopraxy and orthodoxy, see Watson and Rawski, *Death Ritual*; Lieberthal, *Governing China*, 8. Also, further discussion of Watson's ideas regarding orthopraxy can be found in a special edition of *Modern China*, in which five authors discuss his notion of orthopraxy and in which Watson responds to them (*Modern China*).

67. Watson, "Structure of Chinese Funerary Rites," 3–19.

68. Although Lieberthal notes this as weakness in the orthopraxic approach (*Governing China*, 8), Chiang appeared to believe that this was the most practical approach.

69. Wu Jun, "My Diary for Today," 252.

70. Chiang initially relied on groups of one policeman leading three inspectors to examine almost every household in Nanchang. Wang Jingwei criticized this method because he felt that the movement was in essence about morality, and therefore bringing the police into people's houses was an excessive use of state power, threatening people's freedom to do as they pleased in their own homes (Wennan Liu, "Redefining the Moral and Legal Roles," 34, 38).

71. Yuan, *SG*, February 27, 1934; *JZZDSG*, 2005, 24/518.

72. Yuan, *SG*, March 4, 1934; *JZZDSG*, 2006, 25/39.

73. Fenby, *Chiang Kai-shek*, 248.

74. Benson, "Consumers Are also Soldiers," 100–105, 117–18.

75. See, for instance, W. Wei, *Counterrevolution in China*; Averill, "New Life in Action."

76. Bian, *Making of the State Enterprise System*, 118.

77. James Thomson identified three obstacles in China's rural reconstruction: the land tenure problem and the oppressive conditions in which tenants worked; the land tax problem, which allowed the abusive continuation of local authorities to collect taxes with no central government involvement or ability to receive taxes; and the rural credit problem, in which one half of the rural population was always in debt (*While China Faced West*, 198–203). For more on rural reconstruction in Taiwan, see Studwell, *How Asia Works*, 29–34.

78. Lieberthal, *Governing China*, 91.

79. Oldstone-Moore, "New Life Movement," 134.

80. Ferlanti, "New Life Movement," 978–79.

81. Harrison, *Making of the Republican Citizen*, 60–63.

82. Ferlanti, "New Life Movement," 983, 989–90.

83. Ferlanti, "New Life Movement," 982.

84. Shapiro, *Mao's War against Nature*, 86–89.

85. As a Qing official, Yuan Shikai made strides toward modernizing the Qing army—in this case by cementing allegiance to the center rather than locality through interchanging subcommanders (see MacKinnon, *Power and Politics*, 91–103, 215–16)— but those gains in national cohesion were generally erased after his death in 1916 when China was plunged into the warlord period.

86. Yuan, *SG*, March 4, 1934; *JZZDSG*, 2006, 25/39.

87. Yuan, *SG*, March 11, 1934; *JZZDSG*, 2006, 25/121.

88. Yuan, *SG*, March 11, 1934; *JZZDSG*, 2006, 25/122.

89. Yuan, *SG*, March 11, 1934; *JZZDSG*, 2006, 25/122.

90. Yuan, *SG*, May 22, 1934; *JZZDSG*, 2006, 26/185.

91. Fenby, *Chiang Kai-shek*, 218–19.

92. Yuan, *SG*, March 5, 1934; *JZZDSG*, 2006, 25/48.

93. Yuan, *SG*, March 5, 1934; *JZZDSG*, 2006, 25/50.

94. Jay Taylor, *Generalissimo*, 21–22, 51–52, 89–90, as cited in Kaplan, *Asia's Cauldron*, 159.

95. See Diamant, *Embattled Glory*.

96. Yuan, *SG*, February 27, 1934; *JZZDSG*, 2005, 24/517–18.

97. Yuan, *SG*, March 4, 1934; *JZZDSG*, 2006, 25/38–39.

98. Yuan, *SG*, March 4, 1934; *JZZDSG*, 2006, 25/40.

99. Eastman, *Abortive Revolution*, 209–12; for anecdotes about the conscription and working on road repairs, see Shen, "Fourth Day," 98–100; Kang, "Sketch of Road," 100–104.

100. Hsü, *Rise of Modern China*, 567–68.

101. Shen, "Fourth Day," 99.

102. Kaplan, *Asia's Cauldron*, 161.

103. One notable example was Liu Xiaoqi (1898–1969) and his wife, Wang Guang-mei (1921–2006).

104. Fenby, *Chiang Kai-shek*, 501.

105. See F. F. Liu, *Military History*, 143, as cited in Jay Taylor, *Generalissimo*, 121.

5. Chi *and Leaders of Republican China*

1. I omit Sun Yat-sen from this comparative analysis because his time in the national spotlight was short—two months in 1912 before he handed over the presidency to Yuan and then a brief vying for national power in the mid-1920s before his death in 1925. Moreover, the context of his political leadership was similar to Mao's in that just as Sun challenged Yuan in the early period, Mao challenged Chiang in the later period.

2. Chen Boda, *Jieshao qieguo*, 3, 89, 108, quoted in Shan, *Yuan Shikai*, 237.

3. E. Young, *Presidency of Yuan Shikai*, 249. Just as there has been revisionist scholarship on Chiang post–Cold War, there has been a revisionist trend to understanding Yuan Shikai. For example, see Shan, *Yuan Shikai*.

4. Koo, *Wellington Koo Memoir*, 86.

5. Lieberthal, *Governing China*, 24; Paine, *Sino-Japanese War*, 5.

6. Hence, when Japan imposed a harsh settlement on China after 1895, the Three Powers moved in to adjust the settlement. When Russian troops refused to withdraw

from Manchuria, Japan allied with the English to push the Russians out. See Nish, "Overview of Relations," 601–2.

7. Paine, *Japanese Empire*, 178–85.

8. These concessions nevertheless did cause controversy. Regarding the Suzhou-Hangzhou-Ningbo line, for instance, Yuan was accused of agreeing to unfavorable terms with the British (MacKinnon, *Power and Politics*, 184, 217).

9. Yuan facilitated the Beijing-Shenyang railway agreement in 1902 and a number of commercial treaties in 1903. In return, the British helped him stay in power by intervening on his behalf at the Imperial Court in 1902 and 1903. Yuan befriended Sir John Jordan (1852–1925), the British minister in Beijing, and G. E. Morrison (1862–1920) of the London *Times* who broadcasted Yuan's accomplishment to the outside world. There was no question, as the Qing dynasty was falling, that the British enabled Yuan's comeback in 1911 (MacKinnon, *Power and Politics*, 218).

10. Rankin, "State and Society," 278. For accounts of the Xinhai revolution and Sun offering the presidency to Yuan, see Hsü, *Rise of Modern China*, 452–75; Spence, *Search for Modern China*, 249–54.

11. Koo, *Wellington Koo Memoir*, 80–84.

12. There was precedent to this strategy. The Qing government had marked a "fighting zone" for the Japanese troops in the Russo-Japanese War (Koo, *Wellington Koo Memoir*, 80–84).

13. Friesen, "Republic to Monarchy," 126.

14. Koo, *Wellington Koo Memoir*, 88.

15. Lowe, *Great Britain and Japan*, 251; E. Young, *Presidency of Yuan Shikai*, 191.

16. E. Young, *Presidency of Yuan Shikai*, 191–92.

17. Friesen, "Republic to Monarchy," 244 50.

18. Luo, "National Humiliation," 301–2.

19. Luo, "National Humiliation," 309–12.

20. For more on these events, see S. Brown, "Japan Stuns World."

21. Japanese military insubordination that had begun during the Jinan Incident in 1928 and had unmistakably occurred in the 1931 Mukden Incident finally freed Japan's armed forces from civilian rule in 1932. When the Japanese prime minister tried to rein in the military, naval officers assassinated him. Now dominating East Asia, the Japanese military rulers shifted from being a maritime power interested in promoting mutual prosperity and economic growth to being a continental power bent on supporting security goals that included confiscating territory and wealth. A contest of powers was occurring between rising Japan and a rising United States, but early in this contest, Theodore Roosevelt decided that US economic interest in East Asia would be a low priority, and he preferred that Japan expand its power continentally as opposed to expanding in the direction of the Philippines, Hawaii, or even the West Coast of the United States. But Japan lacked the necessary resource endowment to conduct land wars. It began to overextend itself in wars with no clear end or exit strategy. In later war engagements—the 1937 Sino-Japanese War and World War I—the military brooked no hesitation to involve noncombatants. See W. Cohen, "Foreign Impact," 9–10; Paine, *Japanese Empire*, 178.

22. Dong Wang, *China's Unequal Treaties*, 88–89.

23. E. Young, *Presidency of Yuan Shikai*, 220.

24. This view, advanced by Ernest Young, seems most plausible given Yuan's pragmatic approach to politics (*Presidency of Yuan Shikai*, 220). However, some have portrayed his pursuit of the monarchy as driven by purely selfish gains. Hsü, for instance, describes Yuan's quest as "personal ambitions" that "knew no limits" (*Rise of Modern China*, 478). Yuan's political adviser, G. E. Morrison, observed that "In his mad ambition to wear the purple, Yuan Shih-kai has wrecked his own career and gravely involved his country" (*Correspondence*, 515). The question remains, however, as to why Yuan's ambitions took this particular form. According to Young, the pursuit of "yellow robes and dynastic splendor was at most a minor factor in his decision," but public power was very much at issue (*Presidency of Yuan Shikai*, 212). Jerome Ch'en also notes that Yuan wanted more than just power, he wanted a strong China (*Yuan Shih-k'ai*, 164).

25. E. Young, *Presidency of Yuan Shikai*, 215–16.

26. In reorganizing and modernizing the Beiyang Army as a Qing official, Yuan had modeled after the Japanese (MacKinnon, *Power and Politics*, 91–103). When a report surfaced that a fossilized dragon had been discovered in Hubei Province in 1915 and that it was a good omen for the new monarchical era, Yuan dismissed this interpretation, noting that "Science is steadily advancing and everything must be thoroughly probed for its truth value" (E. Young, *Presidency of Yuan Shikai*, 205).

27. "Position of Yuan Shih-Kai," 225; E. Young, *Presidency of Yuan Shikai*, 214, 222–25.

28. Kuo, "Redeploying Confucius," 84.

29. Pugach, "Embarrassed Monarchist," 513–17.

30. E. Young, *Presidency of Yuan Shikai*, 231.

31. Callahan, "National Insecurities," 210; Luo, "National Humiliation," 312.

32. I thank Lin Minde, research fellow at the Institute of Modern History, Academia Sinica, Taiwan, for pointing out this comparison.

33. Shan, *Yuan Shikai*, 234.

34. As chapter 2 noted, Chiang let Huang Fu take the blame for the apology to the Japanese.

35. Yuan, *SG*, May 11, 1934; *JZZDSG*, 2006, 26/67; Chiang, *China's Destiny*, 71.

36. Sheng, *Battling Western Imperialism*, 5, 6.

37. Mao Zedong, "Declaration Opposing Japan's Annexation," 12.

38. Mao Zedong, "Manifesto of the Central Committee," 40.

39. Mao Zedong, "Manifesto of the Central Committee," 40.

40. The Soviet Union had chosen to train Sun Yat-sen's Kuomintang in the quest to unite China and affirmed that the two parties should work together. As mentioned in chapter 2, this cooperation was known as the First United Front. Upon Sun's death in 1925, Chiang continued the mission, but he betrayed the CCP in the April 1927 coup.

41. Out of the 80,000 men and 2,000 women who started the march, only 8,000 survived (Mitter, *A Bitter Revolution*, 161).

42. T'ien-wei Wu, "Chinese Communist Movement," 79; "China: Historical Demographical Data."

43. Italy's Benito Mussolini, for instance, was invading Ethiopia, and Germany's Adolf Hitler was defying a provision regarding rearmament in the 1919 Treaty of Versailles (Mitter, *China's War with Japan*, 63).

44. Had the warlord Zhang Xueliang known about this verbal agreement for a Second United Front, he might not have kidnapped Chiang in December 1936 to force cooperation with the communists. Known as the Xi'an Incident, Zhang kidnapped Chiang to force a change in policies toward Japan and to stop the civil war with the Chinese communists in order to resist Japan jointly. See Mitter, *China's War with Japan*, 66; Short, *Mao*, 322. The CCP Red Army was reorganized into the New Fourth Army and the Eighth Route Army under the command of Chiang's National Revolutionary Army (Paine, *Wars for Asia*, 104).

45. Mitter, *China's War with Japan*, 101.

46. Chang, *Rape of Nanjing*.

47. Zheng Wang, *Never Forget National Humiliation*, 86–88.

48. Johnson, *Peasant Nationalism*, 45, 47–48.

49. Li Lifeng, "Rural Mobilization," 98.

50. Mao Zedong, "Interview with Nym Wales," 18. Helen Foster Snow was a US journalist who wrote under the name Nym Wales.

51. Mao Zedong, "Urgent Tasks," 69.

52. Johnson, *Peasant Nationalism*, 139–40.

53. The area the Chinese communist troops occupied was strategic to Chiang because, once the Japanese were beaten, he planned to reestablish Nanjing as the capital and Shanghai as the financial center of China. He wanted to eject the communists from this region and send a message to any semi-autonomous groups who might entertain thoughts about challenging his authority (Fenby, *Chiang Kai-shek*, 363).

54. Mao may have intended to provoke an incident, thinking that this group was expendable, or its commander may have intended to return to his old communist base in Anhui and continue guerrilla warfare independently of CCP leadership (Jay Taylor, *Generalissimo*, 175–77). See also Schram, *Mao Tse-tung*, 200–201.

55. "Talk Given by the Spokesman," 639.

56. "Talk Given by the Spokesman," 641.

57. "Talk Given by the Spokesman," 641.

58. Jay Taylor, *Generalissimo*, 177.

59. Schram, *Mao Tse-tung*, 188.

60. China signed new treaties with the United States and the United Kingdom in January 1943. These treaties started a chain reaction in which the remaining powers, including France, Belgium, and Portugal, followed suit in normalizing relations by 1947 (Ku, "Abolition of China's Unequal Treaties," 83). Of course, credit for avenging humiliation was vigorously challenged by the Chinese communists (Dong Wang, *China's Unequal Treaties*, 93–95).

61. Johnson, *Peasant Nationalism*, 11.

62. Edgerton-Tarpley, "Saving the Nation," 324–25, 341, 357–59.

63. Laura Tyson Li, *Madame Chiang Kai-shek*, 222.

64. Fenby, *Chiang Kai-shek*, 450.

65. "League of Nations Archive."

66. Garver, *Chinese-Soviet Relations*, 229.

67. These other issues included securing the territorial and administrative integrity of Manchuria and Xinjiang and clarifying the problem of the Chinese communists (Garver, *Chinese-Soviet Relations*, 218).

68. Garver, *Chinese-Soviet Relations*, 229–30.

69. Mao Zedong, "Letter to Chiang," 452–53.

70. T'ien-wei Wu, "Chinese Communist Movement," 79.

71. Mao Zedong, "Chinese People Have Stood Up."

6. Chi *and* Satyagraha*: Chiang, Gandhi, and the Imperial Powers*

1. With the fall of Burma, China could rely only on India to provide an alternate supply route to the vital Burma Road. See Ghose, *Jawaharlal Nehru*, 112; Chan, "Britain's Reaction," 52.

2. In a speech to the Indian people just prior to his visit with Gandhi, Chiang stated that "In these horrible times of savagery and brute force . . . the people of India, should . . . give their united support to the principles embodied in the [1941] Atlantic charter [between the United States and Great Britain] and in the joint declaration of twenty-six nations and ally themselves with the anti-aggression front." See Sitaramayya, *History of the Indian National Congress*, 306.

3. Although K. C. Chan views this outcome as a failure for Chiang, since his stated goal of the visit was to gain India's active participation in the war ("Britain's Reaction," 60), Jay Taylor sees India's pledge not to interfere as a successful diplomatic contribution to the Allied cause (*Generalissimo*, 195–96).

4. Chan, "Britain's Reaction," 60–61.

5. Jack, *Gandhi Reader*, 352.

6. Burns, *Leadership*, 20, 424.

7. H. Gardner, *Creating Minds*; H. Gardner with Laskin, *Leading Minds*, 13, 251–68.

8. Julia Strauss and Morris Bian have posited this revisionist view in contrast to the earlier views by Mary Wright and Harold Isaac (Taylor and Huang, "Deep Changes," 114).

9. Lelyveld, *Great Soul*. Given that Gandhi is still revered in India, this biography (which its critics claimed presented Gandhi as bisexual, although the author denies the claim) would understandably have a difficult reception in India. The book was actually banned in the state of Gujarat (Roberts, "Among the Hagiographers").

10. "Strong Policy."

11. Stilwell, *Stilwell Papers*.

12. "China: Generalissimo's Last Straw"; "Man and Wife of the Year."

13. Rudolph and Rudolph, *Gandhi*, 27–28.

14. "March to the Sea."

15. R. Gandhi, *Gandhi*, 305.

16. R. Gandhi, *Gandhi*, 305.

17. "March to the Sea."

18. "March to the Sea."

19. This statement was part of Gandhi's definition of *satyagraha* submitted on January 9, 1920, to the Disorders Inquiry Committee to explain the turmoil in Punjab and Gujarat (M. Gandhi, "Written Statement").

20. Rudolph and Rudolph, *Gandhi*, 29–30.

21. Rudolph and Rudolph, *Gandhi*, 30–31.

22. "Pinch of Salt." This article is also discussed in Guha, "Gandhi, India, and the World," 27.

23. Howard Gardner draws on Erik Erikson's work to argue this thesis (with Laskin, *Leading Minds*, 239–40).

24. Koller, "Dharma," 131.

25. M. Gandhi, *Autobiography*, 31–32.

26. Rudolph and Rudolph, *Gandhi*, 3, 18.

27. See Guha, "Gandhi, India, and the World," 29.

28. Fenby, *Chiang Kai-shek*, 20–21.

29. Loh, *Early Chiang Kai-shek*, 7.

30. Fenby, *Chiang Kai-shek*, 21.

31. After the father's death, the family moved from their quarters at the family-owned salt store to a three-room house farther down the street by the river. Their situation appeared to improve, as their residence eventually expanded to include an ancestral hall, a rock garden, and a large reception room, and there was even money to educate Chiang in Japan (Fenby, *Chiang Kai-shek*, 20).

32. M. Gandhi, *Autobiography*, 6–8, 19–26.

33. Bhosale, "Indian Nationalism," 421.

34. M. Gandhi, *Autobiography*, 4–5.

35. Jay Taylor, *Generalissimo*, 14.

36. See for example, Wang, *Xingkeji*, June 15, 1928.

37. M. Gandhi, *Autobiography*, 344.

38. M. Gandhi, *Autobiography*, 325–26.

39. H. Gardner with Laskin, *Leading Minds*, 240.

40. Wang, *SG*, September 27, 1931; *JZZDSG*, 2004, 12/104–5.

41. Rudolph and Rudolph, *Gandhi*, 4, 5.

42. Lelyveld, *Great Soul*, 142–43.

43. M. Gandhi, *Autobiography*, 318–19.

44. M. Gandhi, *Autobiography*, 137; Lelyveld, *Great Soul*, 36–37.

45. Lelyveld, *Great Soul*, 37.

46. Lelyveld, *Great Soul*, 86; M. Gandhi, *Autobiography*, 90.

47. Lelyveld, *Great Soul*, 37.

48. Lelyveld, *Great Soul*, 86.

49. For example, see Wang, *SG*, July 17, 1928; *JZZDSG*, 2005, 3/528.

50. Jay Taylor, *Generalissimo*, 91.

51. Yuan, *SG*, February 11, 1934; *JZZDSG*, 2005, 24/388.

52. Yuan, *SG*, May 4, 1934; *JZZDSG*, 2006, 26/24.

53. Yuan, *SG*, February 19, 1934; *JZZDSG*, 2005, 24/470.

54. Yuan, *SG*, March 5, 1934; *JZZDSG*, 2006, 25/46–47.

55. M. Gandhi, *Hind Swaraj*, 76–77. For more on the origins of Indian Anglophilia, see Kenney, "Strikes against the Crown."

56. Lelyveld, *Great Soul*, 39.

57. Seal, "Imperialism and Nationalism," 326.

58. Kohli, *State-Directed Development*, 235–40.

59. Seal, "Imperialism and Nationalism," 334.

60. Seal, "Imperialism and Nationalism," 326.

61. J. Brown, "Gandhi as Nationalist Leader," 59.

62. Weber, "Charisma and Its Transformation."

63. J. Brown, "Gandhi as Nationalist Leader," 53.

64. J. Brown, *Gandhi*, 96.

65. Judith Brown notes that during Gandhi's early days in India, it was more questionable as to who initiated and was in control of protests (*Gandhi*, 108). Regarding Gandhi's lack of political ambition, see *Gandhi*, 105.

66. Chandra, *India's Struggle*, 166–68.

67. J. Brown, *Gandhi*, 124; Chandra, *India's Struggle*, 177.

68. Chandra, *India's Struggle*, 186.

69. Chandra, *India's Struggle*, 184–87.

70. Walsh, *Brief History*, 200.

71. Lokomanya Tilak, for instance, had originally proposed the idea of a working committee to handle the day-to-day affairs of Congress, only to face rejection. Tilak and Anne Besant's earlier efforts with home rule also helped create a generation of nationalists and network of organizational links between the center and the localities (Chandra, *India's Struggle*, 169).

72. Cosgrove, "Gandhi and His Spinning Wheel."

73. Lary, "Drowned Earth," 196–97.

74. Lary, "Drowned Earth," 201–4; Jay Taylor, *Generalissimo*, 155.

75. Weber highlights this dilemma in "Politics as a Vocation," 121.

76. Wang, *SG*, December 8, 1931; *JZZDSG*, 2004, 12/448.

77. Herbst, "War and the State," 117–39.

78. Tilly, *Formation of National States*, 42.

79. Chandra, *India's Struggle*, 506.

80. Grossman, *Riots and Victims*, 64.

81. Guha, "Gandhi, India, and the World," 29.

82. Guha, *Makers of Modern India*, 216.

83. Guha, "Gandhi, India, and the World," 30–31.

84. Keer, *Dr. Ambedkar*, 136–40.

85. Lelyveld, *Great Soul*, 43.

86. Lelyveld, *Great Soul*, 150.

87. Lelyveld, *Great Soul*, 276.

88. Lelyveld, *Great Soul*, 345–46.

Conclusion

1. The Kuomintang historiography also suppressed the fact that under Japanese occupation, 200,000 Taiwanese served in the Japanese army and that the Americans had conducted a deadly air raid in 1945 on Taipei, which killed 3,000 people. See Ramzy, "Gap Lingers."

2. Shirk, *China: Fragile Superpower*, 155–56.

3. A number of authors allude to the narrowing of possibilities for a national Chinese identity, but they have not explicitly discussed Chiang's contribution. See, for example, Kaufman, "'Century of Humiliation,'" 3; Suisheng Zhao, *Nation-State by Construction*, 23–29.

4. Qin Xiaoyi, interview. Qin recalled his surprise when Chiang asked him to hold his signature cloak at a public event, and he saw how threadbare it was on the inside.

5. See for instance, Shirk, *China: Fragile Superpower*.

6. Mitter, "'Old Ghosts,'" 123.

7. These movies included *Guerillas Sweep the Plains*, *Railroad Guerrillas*, and *Landmine Warfare*. I thank Sinan Chu, research fellow at the German Institute of Global and Area Studies, for bringing these films to my attention.

8. "The basic reasons" for the victory, according to Lin Biao, "were that the War of Resistance against Japan was a genuine people's war led by the Communist Party of China and Comrade Mao Tse-tung" (Coble, "China's 'New Remembering,'" 395–96).

9. Mitter, "'Old Ghosts,'" 118; He, "Remembering and Forgetting," 47.

10. Zheng Wang, *Never Forget National Humiliation*, 89. In a joint communiqué following the summit, Japan acknowledged the "serious damage that [it] caused in the past to the Chinese people through war, and deeply reproaches itself" ("Communiqué of the Government"). Believing this expression of remorse was adequate, Mao concluded it was unnecessary for Japan to continue apologizing for its actions, and instead he tended to demonize only a few Japanese militarists (Shirk, *China: Fragile Superpower*, 158–59).

11. Coble, "China's 'New Remembering,'" 396–97.

12. Coble, "China's 'New Remembering,'" 396–97.

13. Vogel, *Deng Xiaoping*, 17.

14. Gilley, *Tiger on the Brink*, 14.

15. Parks Coble notes that the phrase "new remembering" of the Second Sino-Japanese War was coined by Arthur Waldron ("China's New Remembering of World War II"), and he elaborates on it in "China's 'New Remembering.'"

16. He, "Remembering and Forgetting," 54–55.

17. Coble, "China's 'New Remembering,'" 397–402.

18. Vogel, *Deng Xiaoping*, 294–348; Zheng Wang, *Never Forget National Humiliation*, 92; He, "Remembering and Forgetting," 52.

19. Mitter, "'Old Ghosts,'" 120.

20. Shin and Sneider, *Divergent Memories*, 15.

21. This tension was observed by one visitor to the War of Resistance Museum: "I did notice a few things that left more questions than answers such as this photograph of Chiang Kai-shek with his wife and the American Joseph Stilwell. The commentary I

had heard up to this point had stressed how the fight against the Japanese had been led by the Communist party and then, here was the a [*sic*] photo of the Americans who were assisting the fight against the Japanese, but they seemed closer with the other side in the Chinese Civil War, the republicans led by Chiang Kai-shek. Why were the Americans siding with them if they were the junior partner?" (Aitchison, "Museum of the War").

22. Vogel, *Deng Xiaoping*, 661.

23. Li was aware that his refusal would likely mean the film would never be released, and he later expressed his gratitude toward Jiang: "Given the political situation and Jiang's recent appointment as Party general secretary, that he would allocate three and a half hours to watch and discuss the film, and then support my nontraditional portrayal of Chiang Kai-shek was unprecedented" (R. Kuhn, *Man Who Changed China*, 182–86).

24. He, "Remembering and Forgetting," 56–57.

25. Coble, "China's 'New Remembering,'" 404.

26. Zhao, *Nation-State by Construction*, 232–33.

27. Vogel, *Deng Xiaoping*, 662–63.

28. Kristof, "Burying the Past."

29. Coble, "China's 'New Remembering,'" 404–5.

30. Lam, *Chinese Politics in the Hu Jintao Era*, 202; Jiang, "China's 'New Thinking.'"

31. "Speech by Chinese President." He did not tailor this interpretation to his Japanese audience. A year later at the Fortune Global Forum in Beijing, Hu again avoided mentioning the Japanese role in the war by simply referring to the "brutal foreign aggressions and corrupt and incompetent feudal rulers" ("Full Text").

32. He, "Remembering and Forgetting," 64; Shirk, *China: Fragile Superpower*, 140.

33. Author's observation on a trip to Beijing, June 2008.

34. On public service advertisements, see Stockmann, "Greasing the Reels," 851–69.

35. "China-Shanghai-Expo."

36. Jiao, "World Expo Preparation."

37. Cathcart, "Xi Jinping's Tripod."

38. German Chancellor Angela Merkel declined to take sides in the East Asian propaganda war by abstaining from accompanying Xi to the Memorial to the Victims of Fascism and Militarism ("Xi Jinping's Germany Trip"); Lam, *Chinese Politics in the Era of Xi Jinping*, 240.

39. Kaufman, "Xi Jinping as Historian."

40. Lo, "Textbooks Change."

41. One might further note that Confucian quotations also served as centerpieces of China's official exhibition at the Shanghai Expo. See Hubbert, "Back to the Future."

42. *People's Daily, Narrating China's Governance*, v.

43. Economy, *Third Revolution*, 10. For more on Xi's concerted attempts to eliminate his rivals, see Economy, *Third Revolution*, 20–35; McGregor, "Party Man."

44. Jaywalking example found in Tracy, "China's Social Credit System."

45. Rauhala, "'Hold in Your Belly.'"

46. Backer, "China's Social Credit System," 213. A low social credit score could prevent a citizen from buying plane tickets, getting a loan, or even renting a house. Fifteen

million citizens, as of 2018, have been prevented from flying; according to Ben Tracy, some suspect that the government plans to "use the social credit scoring system to punish people who are not sufficiently loyal to the communist party, and trying to clear your name or fight your score is nearly impossible since there is no real due process" (Tracy, "China's Social Credit System").

47. The Belt and Road Initiative is a massive infrastructural project involving the building of railways and ports that connect China to Southeast Asia, Central Asia, Europe, and Africa. The South–North Water Project aims to divert water from the Yangtze River to the Huang River Basin in arid northern China.

48. Buckley and Bradsher, "China Moves to Let Xi Stay." After China had ceded Hong Kong to the British in the aftermath of the Opium Wars in the mid-nineteenth century, this relinquishment became the start of the Hundred Years Humiliation Narrative. Although the British returned Hong Kong to China in 1997, the Basic Law was put in place (to expire in 2047) stipulating that Hong Kong could continue to operate autonomously from China. In 2020, however, Beijing accelerated its reclamation of Hong Kong by passing new security laws that would undermine Hong Kong's status of maintaining a separate legal system from China. See Bradsher, Ramzy, and May, "China Moves to Tighten."

49. Schell and Delury, "Rising China." See also by the same authors, *Wealth and Power*, 398–400. Criticisms about Xi's Belt and Road Initiative, for instance, might be construed as Xi turning the humiliation narrative on its head by advancing policies that are insensitive to host countries' culture, environment, and ethnicity, and may potentially further destabilize vulnerable economies (Economy, *Third Revolution*, 195). According to one observer, "Chinese policy has shifted from fear of being bullied into unequal treaties into becoming a bully itself and forcing unequal agreements on weaker nations (Rappeport, "19th Century 'Humiliation'").

50. Zheng Wang, "Chinese Dream," 3. In Sino–US trade talks, for instance, an impasse occurred between Xi and Donald Trump because the United States had insisted on being able to impose tariffs if China did not adhere to the trade agreement. Moreover, China would be unable to retaliate with tariffs in kind. Given China's history of having to accept unequal treaties, the Chinese were reluctant to accept this kind of enforcement mechanism (Rappeport, "19th-Century 'Humiliation'").

51. P. Cohen, *History and Popular Memory*, 94.

52. Tucker, *Patterns in the Dust*, 198, 205–6; Copper, *Taiwan*, 46.

53. Cozier, with Chou, *Man Who Lost China*, 375.

54. P. Cohen, *History and Popular Memory*, 95.

55. Hickey, *Foreign Policy Making in Taiwan*, 81–82.

56. P. Cohen, *History and Popular Memory*, 95.

57. P. Cohen, *History and Popular Memory*, 96–104.

58. Callahan, "National Insecurities," 209–10. Taiwan nevertheless began to lose recognition as a sovereign country separate from China. Today, only around twenty countries, all of which have little economic power, recognize Taiwan as the Republic of China, and although the United States is Taiwan's ally, it does not recognize Taiwan's independence.

59. This opened opportunities to create a more complete history of Taiwan that incorporated events that had previously been suppressed and enemies that include not

only the Japanese and Chinese communists but also the Kuomintang during the White Terror (Baishe kongbu) period in the 1950s and 1960s when Chiang installed martial law to crush perceived communist sympathizers, those who wanted Taiwan to have an independent path from China, and any Taiwanese or mainlander who sought to undermine the regime (Rigger, *Why Taiwan Matters*, 64–65).

60. Resar, "Beyond National Humiliation."

61. For example, the French and US cultures experience these emotions, too. Barbara Tuchman, in her study of the origins of World War I, noted that the themes of revenge and humiliation were present in the French army in the early 1910s as it recalled the loss of Alsace-Lorraine to Germany in the early 1870s and were a likely but rarely acknowledged cause of World War I (Tuchman, *Guns of August*, 47; Scheff, *Bloody Revenge*, 87). Both authors are cited in Harkavy, "Defeat, National Humiliation," 348–49. Chris Hayes, an observer of US race relations, also noted that "humiliation may be the most powerful and most underappreciated force in human affairs" (*Colony in a Nation*, 69).

Glossary of Chinese Characters

The entries are alphabetized letter by letter of the romanization. Major cities and provinces are excluded. Traditional characters are used for references prior to the establishment of the PRC and in Taiwan. With events and personages whose main contributions have been in the PRC, simplified characters are used.

aihu guojia	愛護國家
Aiji chugao	愛記初稿
annei rangwai	安內攘外
Bai Chongxi	白崇禧
baihua	白話
Baihua qifang	百花齐放
Baise kongbu	白色恐怖
bao	報
Beiyang	北洋
Cai Gongshi	蔡公時
Chen Boda	陳伯達
Chen Bulei	陳布雷
Chen Duxiu	陳獨秀
chi	恥
Chiang Ching-kuo	
(Jiang Jingguo)	蔣經國
Chiang Kai-shek	
(Jiang Jieshi)	蔣介石
cun	寸

Da Gong Bao	大公報
Dai Jitao	戴季陶
Dangjiazhuang	黨家莊
dao	盜
Da Qingguo	大清國
Da Xue	大學
Deng Xiaoping	邓小平
didian	地點
Dongfang zazhi	東方雜誌
Duan Qirui	段祺瑞
fanxing	反省
fei	匪
Fengtian	奉天
Feng Yuxiang	馮玉祥
Fuchai	夫差
Funü xin shenghuo	
laodong fuwutuan	婦女新生活勞動服務團
Fu Sinian	傅斯年
fuxing	復興
Fuxing zhuibi	復興贅筆
gaoben	稿本
gong	公
Goujian	勾踐
Guan Zhong	管仲
Guanzi	管子
guoti	國體
Hao Baicun (Hau Pei-tsun)	郝柏村
Huang Fu	黃郛
Huangpu	黃埔
Huang Xing	黃興
Hu Hanmin	胡漢民
Hu Jintao	胡锦涛
Hu Shi	胡適
ji	記
Jiang Dingwen	蔣鼎文
Jiang Tingfu	蔣廷黻
Jiang Zemin	江泽民
jiao	剿
jiaofei	剿匪
Jiaofei zongsiling bu	剿匪總司令部
jiaoxun	教訓
Jiaozhou–Jinan	膠州–濟南

Kang Youwei	康有爲
kou	寇
Kunmianji	困勉記
Kuomintang (Guomindang)	國民黨
lao	老
Lee Teng-hui	李登輝
li (one-third of an English mile)	里
li (propriety)	禮
Liang Qichao	梁啓超
Liji	禮記
Lin Biao	林彪
Lin Zexu	林則徐
Li Qiankuan	李前寬
Li Shizeng	李石曾
Lixingshe	力行社
liyilianchi	禮義廉恥
Li Yuanhong	黎元洪
lizhi yangqi	立志養氣
Li Zongren	李宗仁
luan	亂
lüe	略
Lu Xun	魯迅
Lu Zhengxiang	陸徵祥
Manzhouguo	滿洲國
Mao Dun	矛盾
Mao Sicheng	毛思誠
Mao Zedong	毛澤東
Minjindang	民進黨
mishu	秘書
neixin shijie	内心世界
ni	逆
nianpu	年譜
qianyan	前言
qihou	氣候
Qi Huan Gong	齊桓公
qijuzhu	起居注
Qin Xiaoyi	秦孝儀
rending shengtian	人定勝天
Sanminzhuyi	三民主義
shehui xinyong tixi	社会信用体系

shi	事
Shicongshi	侍從室
Shiji	史記
Shi Kefa	史可法
shilu	史錄
shilüe	事略
Shilüe gaoben	事略稿本
shinian shengju, shinian jiaoxun	十年生聚、十年教訓
Sima Qian	司馬遷
Song Jiaoren	宋教仁
Song Meiling (Soong Mei-ling)	宋美齡
Song Ziwen (T. V. Soong)	宋子文
Sun Ke (Sun Fo)	孫科
Sun Yat-sen	孫中山
Sun Yi	孫詒
Sunzi	孫子
Tang Enbo	湯恩伯
Tanggu xieding	塘沽協定
Tang Zhongzong	唐中宗
Tao Xisheng	陶希聖
Tianjin–Pukou	天津–浦口
tiyao	提要
Tongmenghui	同盟會
Tsai Ing-wen	蔡英文
tufei	土匪
Wanbaoshan	萬寶山
Wang Jiang	汪蔣
Wang Jingwei	王精微
Wang Ming	王明
Wang Yangming	王陽明
Wang Yugao	王宇高
Wang Zhengting	王正廷
wendu	溫度
Wen Wenshan (Wen Tianxiang)	文文山 (文天祥)
Wenxue she	文學社
wenyanwen	文言文
wokou	倭寇
woxin changdan	臥薪嘗膽
Wu	吳
wuhu	嗚呼
Wumu (Yue Fei)	武穆
Wuwang guochi	勿忘國恥
Wu Yue Chunqiu	吳越春秋
Wu Zetian	武則天

xian	縣
xian annei, hou rangwai	先安內後攘外
xiansheng	先生
xiao	小
Xi Jinping	习近平
Xikou	溪口
Xingkeji	省克記
Xingying	行營
Xinhai	辛亥
Xin shenghuo yundong	新生活運動
Xiong Shihui	熊式輝
xuechi	雪恥
xuechi zhidao	雪恥之道
xue guochi	雪國恥
Xueji	學記
xunlian	訓練
Xunzi	荀子
Yan Fu	嚴復
Yan Xishan	閻錫山
yeman minzu	野蠻民族
yemanren	野蠻人
Youji	游記
Yuan Huichang	袁惠常
Yuan Shikai	袁世凱
yubang xiangzheng,	
yuren deli	鷸蚌相爭，漁人得利
yuding	預定
Yue	越
Yue Fei (Wumu)	岳飛（武穆）
yuqi	語氣
Zang Shiyi	臧式毅
zei	賊
Zeng Guofan	曾國藩
Zhan Guo Ce	戰國策
Zhang Xuecheng	章學誠
Zhang Xueliang	張學良
Zhang Zuolin	張作霖
Zhengqi ge	正氣歌
zhengshi	正史
zhenzheng xiangfa	眞正想法
zhichi	知恥
zhichi jinhu yong	知恥進乎勇
Zhili	直隸
Zhongguo meng	中国梦

Zhonghua diguo	中華帝國
Zhonghua minguo	中華民國
Zhongyang junxiao	中央軍校
Zhongyong	中庸
Zhongyuan dazhan	中原大戰
Zhongzheng (another name for Chiang Kai-shek)	中正
Zhou Enlai	周恩來
Zhou Hongtao	周宏濤
zhuanji	傳記
Zhu Xi	朱熹
zhuyi	注意
zisi zili	自私自利
zouzipai	走資派
zunyan	尊嚴

Bibliography

Archival Sources

Archives of President Chiang Kai-shek [蔣中正總統檔案], Academia Historica [國史館], Taipei, Taiwan.
Aiji chugao 愛記初稿 [Family and friends draft chronology]
Fuxing zhuibi 復興贅筆 [Supplementary writings on reviving the country]
Guanzi 管子 (Chiang's personal four-volume copy of *Guanzi* with notes in the margins)
Jianggong shilüe gaoben (*SG*) 蔣公事略稿本 [Mr. Chiang's draft manuscript]. Compiled by Sun Yi, Wang Yugao, and Yuan Huichang, 1927–49.
Kunmianji 困勉記 [Difficulties and self-encouragement chronology]
Xingkeji 省克記 [Reflections on overcoming difficulties chronology]
Xueji 學記 [Learning chronology]
Youji 遊記 [Holidays chronology]

Chiang Kai-shek Diaries. 1917–23; 1925–72. Hoover Institution Archives, Stanford, CA.

Interviews

Hao Baicun. Interview by author and Alicia Wen-ting Chen. Taipei, Taiwan, May 2003.

Liu Weikai. Interview by author. Taipei, Taiwan, January 2003.

Qin Xiaoyi. Interview by author and Jay Taylor. Taipei, Taiwan, May 2003.

Printed Sources

Aitchison, Bill. "The Museum of the War of Chinese People's Resistance Against Japanese Aggression Tour." Tour of All Tours, January 11, 2015. http://tourofalltours .blogspot.com/2015/01/the-museum-of-war-of-chinese-peoples.html.

Alitto, Guy. "Chiang Kai-shek in Western Historiography." In *Proceedings of Conference on Chiang Kai-shek and Modern China*, 1:719–808. Taipei: China Culture Service, 1986.

Asada, Sadao. "From Washington to London: The Imperial Japanese Navy and the Politics of Naval Limitation, 1921–30." In *The Washington Conference, 1921–22: Naval Rivalry, East Asian Stability and the Road to Pearl Harbor*, edited by Erik Goldstein and John Maurer, 147–91. Portland, OR: Frank Cass, 1994.

Averill, Stephen C. "The New Life in Action: The Nationalist Government in South Jiangxi, 1934–1937." *China Quarterly* 88 (December 1981): 594–628.

Backer, Larry Catá. "China's Social Credit System: Data-Driven Governance for a 'New Era.'" *Current History* 118, no. 809 (January 2019): 209–14.

Ban Gu. "Biography of Chen Ping." In *Book of Han* 40. https://zh.wikisource.org/wiki /漢書/卷040.

Barker, Chris. *Cultural Studies: Theory and Practice.* Thousand Oaks, CA: Sage, 2005.

Beasley, W. G. *Japanese Imperialism 1894–1945.* New York: Oxford University Press, 1987.

Benson, Carlton. "Consumers Are also Soldiers: Subversive Songs from Nanjing Road during the New Life Movement." In *Inventing Nanjing Road: Commercial Culture in Shanghai, 1900–1945*, edited by Sherman Cochran, 91–132. Ithaca, NY: Cornell University East Asia Program, 1999.

Bergère, Mary-Claire. *Sun Yat-sen.* Translated by Janet Lloyd. Stanford, CA: Stanford University Press, 1998 (1994).

Bertram, James M. *First Act in China: The Story of the Sian Mutiny.* New York: Viking Press, 1938.

Bhosale, B. G. "Indian Nationalism: Gandhi vis-à-vis Tilak and Savarkar." *Indian Journal of Political Science* 70, no. 2 (April–June 2009): 419–27.

Bian, Morris. *The Making of the State Enterprise System in Modern China.* Cambridge, MA: Harvard University Press, 2009.

Bianco, Lucien. *Origins of the Chinese Revolution, 1915–1949.* Stanford, CA: Stanford University Press, 1967.

Billingsley, Phil. *Bandits in Republican China.* Stanford, CA: Stanford University Press, 1988.

Blondel, Jean. *Political Leadership: Towards a General Analysis.* Beverly Hills, CA: Sage, 1987.

Bradsher, Keith, Austin Ramzy, and Tiffany May. "China Moves to Tighten Its Control of Hong Kong." *New York Times*, May 21, 2020.

Brown, Judith M. "Gandhi as Nationalist Leader, 1915–1948." In *Cambridge Companion to Gandhi*, edited by Judith M. Brown and Anthony Parel, 51–70. New York: Cambridge University Press, 2011.

———. *Gandhi: Prisoner of Hope.* New Haven, CT: Yale University Press, 1989.

Brown, Steward. "Japan Stuns World, Withdraws from League." United Press International, February 24, 1933. https://www.upi.com/Archives/1933/02/24/Japan-stuns -world-withdraws-from-league/2231840119817/.

Buckley, Chris, and Keith Bradsher. "China Moves to Let Xi Stay in Power by Abolishing Term Limit." *New York Times,* February 25, 2018.

Burns, James MacGregor. *Leadership.* New York: Harper and Row, 1978.

Callahan, William A. "National Insecurities: Humiliation, Salvation, and Chinese Nationalism." *Alternatives* 29 (March 2004): 199–218.

———. *Pessoptimist Nation.* New York: Oxford University Press, 2012.

Cathcart, Adam. "Xi Jinping's Tripod: Updating the National Humiliation Narrative in Nanjing." *SinoMondiale,* December 22, 2014. https://adamcathcart.com/2014/12 /22/xi-jinpings-tripod-updating-the-national-humiliation-narrative-in-nanjing/.

Chan, K. C. "Britain's Reaction to Chiang Kai-shek's Visit to India, February 1942." *Australian Journal of Politics and History* 21, no. 2 (August 1975): 52–61.

Chandra, Bipan. *India's Struggle for Independence 1857–1947.* New York: Penguin Books, 1989.

Chang, Iris. *The Rape of Nanjing: The Forgotten Holocaust of World War II.* New York: Basic Books, 2012.

Chen Boda. *Jieshao qieguo dadao Yuan Shikai* [An introduction to the national usurper: Yuan Shikai]. Zhangjiakou: Jincha jiri baoshe, 1946.

Chen Bulei. *Chen Bulei huiyi lu* [Chen Bulei's memoirs]. Taipei: Zhuanji wenxue chubanshe, 1967.

Ch'en, Jerome. *Yuan Shih-k'ai.* Stanford, CA: Stanford University Press, 1972.

Chen, Leslie H. Dingyan. *Chen Jiongming and the Federalist Movement: Regional Leadership and Nation Building in Early Republican China.* Ann Arbor: Center for Chinese Studies, University of Michigan, 1999.

Chen, Ping. *Modern Chinese: History and Sociolinguistics.* New York: Cambridge University Press, 1999.

Cheng, Anne. "*Ch'un ch'iu, Kung yang, Ku liang,* and *Tso chuan.*" In *Early Chinese Texts: A Bibliographical Guide,* edited by Michael Loewe, 67–76. Berkeley: Society for the Study of Early China, Institute of East Asian Studies, University of California, 1993.

Chiang Kai-shek. *China's Destiny and Chinese Economic Theory.* New York: Roy, 1947.

———. "Essentials of the New Life Movement." In *Sources of Chinese Tradition,* edited by Wm. De Bary, with Wing-tsit Chan, Burton Watson, 800–806. New York: Columbia University Press, 1960.

"China: Generalissimo's Last Straw." *Time,* December 11, 1933.

"China: Historical Demographical Data of the Whole Country." Populstat, 2003. http://www.populstat.info/Asia/chinac.htm.

"China-Shanghai-Expo 2010-Preparations." Getty Images, April 8, 2010. https://www .gettyimages.com/detail/news-photo/shanghai-world-expo-2010-sign-in-front-of -jingan-sports-news-photo/536221692#/shanghai-world-expo-2010-sign-in-front-of -jingan-sports-center-in-picture-id536221692.

Clubb, O. Edmund. *20th Century China*. New York: Columbia University Press, 1964.

Coble, Parks M. "China's 'New Remembering' of the Anti-Japanese War of Resistance, 1937–1945." *China Quarterly* 190 (July 2007): 394–410.

———. *Facing Japan: Chinese Politics and Japanese Imperialism, 1931–1937*. Cambridge, MA: Harvard University Asia Center, 1991.

Cochran, Sherman, and Andrew C. K. Hsieh with Janis Cochran. *One Day in China: May 21, 1936*. New Haven, CT: Yale University Press, 1983.

Cohen, Paul A. *History and Popular Memory: The Power of Story in Moments of Crisis*. New York: Columbia University Press, 2014.

———. "Remembering and Forgetting National Humiliation in Twentieth-Century China." *Twentieth-Century China* 27, no. 2 (April 2002): 1–39.

———. *Speaking to History: The Story of King Goujian in Twentieth-Century China*. Berkeley: University of California Press, 2009.

Cohen, Warren I. "The Foreign Impact on East Asia." In *Historical Perspectives on Contemporary East Asia*, edited by Merle Goldman and Andrew Gordon, 1–41. Cambridge, MA: Harvard University Press, 2000.

"Communiqué of the Government of Japan and the Government of the People's Republic of China." *Ministry of Foreign Affairs of Japan*, September 29, 1972. http://www.mofa.go.jp/region/asia-paci/china/joint72.html.

Copper, John F. *Taiwan: Nation-State or Province*. Boulder, CO: Westview, 2009.

Cosgrove, Ben. "Gandhi and His Spinning Wheel: The Story behind an Iconic Photo." *Life*, September 10, 2014.

Crozier, Brian, with Eric Chou. *The Man Who Lost China: The First Full Biography of Chiang Kai-shek*. New York: Scribner's, 1976.

De Sieux, Rio V. *The World's Work 30*. New York: Doubleday, 1915.

Diamant, Neil J. *Embattled Glory: Veterans, Military Families, and the Politics of Patriotism in China, 1949–2007*. Lanham, MD: Rowman and Littlefield, 2009.

Dirlik, Arif. "The Ideological Foundations of the New Life Movement: A Study in Counterrevolution." *Journal of Asian Studies* 34, no. 4 (August 1975): 945–80.

Duara, Prasenjit. *Sovereignty and Authenticity: Manchukuo and the East Asian Modern*. New York: Rowman and Littlefield, 2003.

Eastman, Lloyd E. *The Abortive Revolution: China under Nationalist Rule, 1927–1937*. Cambridge, MA: Harvard East Asian Series, 1974.

———. "Nationalist China during the Nanking Decade, 1927–1937." In Lloyd E. Eastman, Jerome Ch'en, Suzanne Pepper, and Lyman P. Van Slyke, *The Nationalist Era in China 1927–1949*, 1–52. New York: Cambridge University Press, 1991.

Economy, Elizabeth C. *The Third Revolution: Xi Jinping and the New Chinese State*. New York: Oxford University Press, 2018.

Edgerton-Tarpley, Kathryn. "Saving the Nation, Starving the People? The Henan Famine of 1942–1943." In *1943: China at the Crossroads*, edited by Joseph W. Esherick and Matthew T. Combs, 323–64. Ithaca, NY: Cornell University East Asia Program, 2015.

Edwards, Louise. "Policing the Modern Woman in Republican China." *Modern China* 26, no. 2 (April 2000): 115–47.

Emirbayer, Mustafa, and Anne Mische. "What Is Agency?" *American Journal of Sociology* 103, no. 4 (January 1998): 962–1023.

Fairbank, John King. *China: A New History.* Cambridge, MA: Harvard University Press, 1992.

Fenby, Jonathan. *Chiang Kai-shek: China's Generalissimo and the Nation He Lost.* New York: Carroll and Graf, 2003.

"Fenghuashi nongye xinxi wang: Gujin mingren" [Fenghua farmer's association online news: famous people past and present]. N.d. http://www.fhagri.com.cn/XUXIA /character/wyg.htm (accessed May 11, 2010).

Ferlanti, Federica. "The New Life Movement in Jiangxi Province, 1934–1938." *Modern Asian Studies* 44, no. 5 (September 2010): 961–1000.

Fitzgerald, John. *Awakening China: Politics, Culture, and Class in the Nationalist Revolution.* Stanford, CA: Stanford University Press, 1996.

Friesen, Oris D. "Republic to Monarchy: The Impact of the Twenty-One Demands Crisis on the Yüan Shih-k'ai Presidency, 1914–1915." PhD diss., Arizona State University, 1982.

"Full Text of Hu Jintao's Address." CNN, May 17, 2005. http://www.cnn.com/2005 /WORLD/asiapcf/05/16/eyeonchina.hujintao.fulltext/index.html.

Gandhi, Mohandas K. *An Autobiography: The Story of My Experiments with Truth.* Boston: Beacon Press, 1957.

———. *Hind Swaraj and Other Writings.* Edited by Anthony J. Parel. New York: Cambridge University Press, 1997.

———. "Written Statement" Evidence submitted to the Disorders Inquiry Committee regarding events in Punjab and Gujarat, January 9, 1920. http://sfr21.org/sources /satyagraha.html.

Gandhi, Rajmohan. *Gandhi: The Man, His People, and the Empire.* Berkeley: University of California Press, 2008.

Gardner, Charles S. *Chinese Traditional Historiography.* Cambridge, MA: Harvard University Press, 1970.

Gardner, Howard, *Creating Minds.* New York: Basic Books, 1993.

Gardner, Howard, with Emma Laskin. *Leading Minds: An Anatomy of Leadership.* New York: Basic Books, 2011.

Garver, John W. *Chinese-Soviet Relations 1937–1945: The Diplomacy of Chinese Nationalism.* New York: Oxford University Press, 1988.

Ghose, Sankar. *Jawaharlal Nehru: A Biography.* New Delhi: Allied Publishers, 1993.

Gilley, Bruce. *Tiger on the Brink: Jiang Zemin and China's New Elite.* Berkeley: University of California Press, 1998.

Gordon, David M. "Historiographical Essay: The China-Japan War, 1931–1945." *Journal of Military History* 70, no. 2 (January 2006): 137–82.

Grenville, J. A. S. *A History of the World in the Twentieth Century.* Cambridge, MA: Belknap Press, 1994.

Gries, Peter Hays. *China's New Nationalism: Pride, Politics, and Diplomacy.* Berkeley: University of California Press, 2004.

Grossman, Patricia A. *Riots and Victims: Violence and the Construction of Communal Identity Among Bengali Muslims, 1905–1947.* Boulder, CO: Westview Press, 1999.

Guan Zhong. *Guanzi: Political, Economic, and Philosophical Essays from Early China,* vol. 1. Translated by W. Allyn Rickett. Princeton, NJ: Princeton University Press, 1985.

Guerillas Sweep the Plains. Directed by Su Li and Wu Zhaodi. Changchun: Changchun Film Studio, 1955.

Guha, Ramachandra. "Gandhi, India, and the World." In *Makers of Modern Asia,* edited by Ramachandra Guha, 16–39. Cambridge, MA: Belknap Press, 2014.

———. *Makers of Modern India.* Cambridge, MA: Belknap Press, 2011.

Hanyu dacidian [Comprehensive Han language dictionary]. Shanghai: Hanyu dacidian chubanshe, 1993.

Hardy, Grant. *Worlds of Bronze and Bamboo: Sima Qian's Conquest of History.* New York: Columbia University Press, 1999.

Harkavy, Robert E. "Defeat, National Humiliation, and the Revenge Motif in International Politics." *International Politics* 37, no. 3 (September 2000): 345–68.

Harrison, Henrietta. *The Making of the Republican Citizen: Political Ceremonies and Symbols in China, 1911–1929.* New York: Oxford University Press, 2000.

Hayes, Chris. *A Colony in a Nation.* New York: W. W. Norton, 2017.

Hayford, Charles. "The Final Triumph of Chiang Kai-shek? The Rush to Revisionism." Review of *The Generalissimo: Chiang Kai-shek and the Struggle for Modern China,* by Jay Taylor. H-Diplo Review Forum, December 21, 2011.

He, Yinan. "Remembering and Forgetting the War: Elite Mythmaking, Mass Reaction, and Sino-Japanese Relations, 1950–2006." *History and Memory* 19, no. 2 (October 2007): 43–74.

Herbst, Jeffrey. "War and the State in Africa." *International Security* 14, no. 4 (1990): 117–39.

Hickey, Dennis Van Vranken. *Foreign Policy Making in Taiwan: From Principle to Pragmatism.* New York: Routledge, 2006.

Horowitz, Michael C., Allan C. Stam, and Cali M. Ellis. *Why Leaders Fight.* New York: Cambridge University Press, 2015.

Hsü, Immanuel C. Y. *The Rise of Modern China.* New York: Oxford University Press, 2000.

Huang, Grace C. "Creating a Public Face for Posterity: The Making of Chiang Kai-shek's *Shilüe* Manuscripts." *Modern China* 36, no. 6 (November 2010): 617–43.

———. "Mme. Chiang's Mission to America." In *1943: China at the Crossroads,* edited by Joseph W. Esherick and Matthew Combs, 41–74. Ithaca, NY: Cornell University East Asia Program, 2015.

———. "Speaking to Posterity: Shame, Humiliation, and the Creation of Chiang Kai-shek's Nanjing Era Legacy. *Twentieth-Century China* 36, no. 2 (July 2011): 148–68.

Huang, Ray. "Chiang Kai-shek and His Diary as a Historical Source: Proposals for the Revision of Modern Chinese History." *Chinese Studies in History* 29, nos. 1 and 2 (Fall–Winter 1995–96).

Huang Rensheng, annot. and trans., Li Zhenxin, rev. *Xinyi Wuyue Chunqiu* [A new translation of Wu and Yue during the Spring and Autumn Period]. Taipei: Sanmin shuju, 1996.

Hubbert, Jennifer. "Back to the Future: The Politics of Culture at the Shanghai Expo." *International Journal of Cultural Studies* 20, no. 1 (2017): 48–64.

Hunt, Lynn. *Politics, Culture, and Class in the French Revolution.* Berkeley: University of California Press, 1984.

Iriye, Akira. *After Imperialism: The Search for a New Order in the Far East 1921–1931.* Cambridge, MA: Harvard University Press, 1965.

Jack, Homer A. *The Gandhi Reader: A Sourcebook of His Life and Writings.* New York: Grove Press, 1956.

Jiang, Wenran. "China's 'New Thinking' on Japan." *China Brief* 5, no. 3 (February 2005). https://jamestown.org/program/chinas-new-thinking-on-japan/.

Jiang Zhongzheng zongtong dang'an: shilüe gaoben (*JZZDSG*) [President Chiang Kai-shek's archives: The *shilüe* manuscripts]. 81 vols. Taiwan: Guoshiguan, 2003–2013.

Jiao Xiaoyang. "World Expo Preparation Going on Smoothly." *China Daily,* August 6, 2007.

Johnson, Chalmers A. *Peasant Nationalism and Communist Power: The Emergence of Revolutionary China, 1937–1945.* Stanford, CA: Stanford University Press, 1962.

Jordan, Donald A. *Chinese Boycotts versus Japanese Bombs: The Failure of China's "Revolutionary Diplomacy," 1931–32.* Ann Arbor: University of Michigan Press, 1991.

———. *The Northern Expedition: China's National Revolution of 1926–1928.* Honolulu: University Press of Hawaii, 1976.

———. "The Place of Chinese Disunity in Japanese Army Strategy during 1931." *China Quarterly* 109 (March 1987): 43–63.

Ju Yiqiao. *Gensui Jiang Jieshi ershi nian* [Following Chiang Kai-shek for twenty years]. Changsha: Hunan renmin chubanshe, 1988.

Kang Yimin. "A Sketch of Road Construction." In *One Day in China: May 21, 1936,* edited by Sherman Cochran and Andrew C. K. Hsieh with Janis Cochran, 100–104. New Haven, CT: Yale University Press, 1983.

Kaplan, Robert D. *Asia's Cauldron: The South China Sea and the End of a Stable Pacific.* New York: Random House, 2014.

Kaufman, Alison A. "The 'Century of Humiliation' and China's National Narratives." Testimony before the U.S.-China Economic and Security Review Commission Hearing on "China's Narratives Regarding National Security Policy," March 10, 2011. https://www.uscc.gov/sites/default/files/3.10.11Kaufman.pdf.

———. "Xi Jinping as Historian: Marxist, Chinese, Nationalist, Global." Asan Forum, October 15, 2015. http://www.theasanforum.org/xi-jinping-as-historian-marxist-chinese-nationalist-global/.

Keer, Dhananjay. *Dr. Ambedkar: Life and Mission.* Mumbai: Popular Prakashan, 1990.

Kenney, Nicholas. "Strikes against the Crown: The Ideological Origins of the Irish and Indian Nationalist Movements." PhD diss., Tufts University, 2015.

Kim, Uichol, and Kwang-kuo Hwang. *Indigenous and Cultural Psychology: Understanding People in Context.* New York: Springer, 2006.

Kirby, William C. *Germany and Republican China.* Stanford, CA: Stanford University Press, 1984.

Kohli, Atul. *State-Directed Development: Political Power and Industrialization in the Global Periphery.* New York: Cambridge University Press, 2004.

Koller, John M. "Dharma: An Expression of Universal Order." *Philosophy East and West* 22, no. 2 (April 1972): 131–44.

Koo, Wellington. *The Wellington Koo Memoir.* Chinese Oral History Project. New York: Columbia University, East Asian Institute, 1975.

Kristof, Nicholas D. "Burying the Past: War Guilt Haunts Japan." *New York Times,* November 30, 1998.

Ku, Charlotte. "Abolition of China's Unequal Treaties and the Search for Regional Stability in Asia, 1919–1943." *Chinese (Taiwan) Yearbook of International Law and Affairs* 12 (1994): 67–86.

Kuhn, Arthur K. "The Lytton Report on the Manchurian Crisis." *American Journal of International Law* 27, no. 1 (January 1933): 96–100.

Kuhn, Robert Lawrence. *The Man Who Changed China.* New York: Crown, 2004.

Kuo, Ya-pei. "Redeploying Confucius: The Imperial State Dreams of the Nation, 1902–1911." In *Chinese Religiosities: Afflictions of Modernity and State Formation,* edited by Mayfair Mei-hui Yang, 65–84. Berkeley: University of California Press, 2008.

Kutcher, Norman. "The Fifth Relationship: Dangerous Friendships in the Confucian Context." *American Historical Review* 105, no. 5 (December 2000): 1615–29.

Lam, Willy Wo-Lap. *Chinese Politics in the Era of Xi Jinping: Renaissance, Reform, or Retrogression?* New York: Routledge, 2012.

———. *Chinese Politics in the Hu Jintao Era: New Leaders, New Challenges.* Armonk, NY: M. E. Sharpe, 2006.

Landmine Warfare. Directed by Wu Jianhai, Tang Yingqi, and Xu Da. Beijing: Zhongyang dianshi tai, 1962.

Lary, Diana. "Drowned Earth: The Strategic Breaching of the Yellow River Dyke, 1938." *War in History* 8, no. 2 (April 2001): 191–207.

Lattimore, Owen. *Manchuria: Cradle of Conflict.* New York: Macmillan, 1932.

"League of Nations Archive: Chronology." Yalta Conference, February 7–12, 1945. http://www.indiana.edu/~league/1945.htm.

Lee, Edward Bing-Shuey. *One Year of the Japan-China Undeclared War and the Attitude of the Powers.* Shanghai: Mercury Press, 1933.

Lelyveld, Joseph. *Great Soul: Mahatma Gandhi and His Struggle with India.* New York: Knopf, 2011.

Leong, Karen J. *The China Mystique: Pearl S. Buck, Anna May Wong, Mayling Soong, and the Transformation of American Orientalism.* Berkeley: University of California Press, 2005.

Leys, Simon, trans. *The Analects of Confucius.* New York: W. W. Norton, 1997.

Li, Cheng. "The *Mishu* Phenomenon: Patron-Client Ties and Coalition-Building Tactics." *Chinese Leadership Monitor* 4 (Fall 2002).

Li, Huaiyin. *Reinventing Modern China: Imagination and Authenticity in Chinese Historical Writing.* Honolulu: University of Hawaii Press, 2012.

Li, Laura Tyson. *Madame Chiang Kai-shek: China's Eternal First Lady.* New York: Grove Press, 2006.

Li Lifeng. "Rural Mobilization in the Chinese Communist Revolution: From the Anti-Japanese War to the Chinese Civil War." *Journal of Modern Chinese History* 9, no. 1 (June 2015): 95–116.

Li Mian, comm. and trans. *Guanzi jinzhu jinyi* [Guanzi, commentary and translation]. 2 vols. Taipei: Taiwan shangwu yinshuguan, 1988.

Li, Pichon. *The Kuomintang Debacle of 1949: Conquest or Collapse?* Lexington, MA: D. C. Heath, 1966.

Li, Wei, and Lucian W. Pye. "The Ubiquitous Role of the *Mishu* in Chinese Politics." *China Quarterly* 132 (December 1992): 913–36.

Lieberthal, Kenneth. *Governing China: From Revolution through Reform.* New York: W. W. Norton, 2004.

Lim, Timothy C. *Doing Comparative Politics: An Introduction to Approaches and Issues.* Boulder, CO: Lynne Rienner, 2016.

Litten, Frederick S. "The CCP and the Fujian Rebellion." *Republican China* 14, no. 1 (November 1988): 57–74.

Liu, F. F. *A Military History of Modern China, 1924–1949.* Princeton, NJ: Princeton University Press, 1956.

Liu, Shu-hsin. "Neo-Confucianism." In *The Cambridge Dictionary of Philosophy*, edited by Robert Audi, 523. New York: Cambridge University Press, 1995.

Liu, Wennan. "Redefining the Moral and Legal Roles of the State in Everyday Life: The New Life Movement in China in the Mid 1930s." *Cross-Currents: East Asian History and Culture Review* 2, no. 2 (November 2013): 335–65.

Lo Kinling. "Textbooks Change: China's War against Japanese Aggression Lasted 14 Years Instead of Eight." *South China Morning Post* (Hong Kong), January 10, 2017.

Lockwood, William W., Jr. "Japanese Silk and the American Market." *Far Eastern Survey* 5, no. 4 (February 1936): 31–36.

Loh, Pichon P. Y. *The Early Chiang Kai-shek: A Study of His Personality and Politics, 1887–1924.* New York: Columbia University Press, 1971.

Lowe, Peter. *Great Britain and Japan 1911–15: A Study of British Far Eastern Policy.* London: Macmillan, 1969.

Luo, Zhitian. "The Chinese Rediscovery of the Special Relationship: The Jinan Incident as a Turning Point in Sino-American Relations." *Journal of American–East Asian Relations* 3, no. 4 (1994): 345–72.

———. "National Humiliation and National Assertion: The Chinese Response to the Twenty-One Demands." *Modern Asian Studies* 1, no. 2 (May 1993): 279–319.

"Lytton Commission." *Encyclopedia Britannica*, 1998. https://www.britannica.com/event/Lytton-Commission.

MacKinnon, Stephen R. *Power and Politics in Late Imperial China: Yuan Shi-kai in Beijing and Tianjin, 1901–1908.* Berkeley: University of California Press, 1980.

————. *Wuhan, 1928: War, Refugees, and the Making of Modern China.* Berkeley: University of California Press, 2008.

"Man and Wife of the Year." *Time,* January 3, 1938.

Mao Ssu-cheng, ed. *Minguo shiwu nian yiqiande Jiang Jieshi xiansheng* [Mr. Chiang Kai-shek and his years before 1926]. Hong Kong: Longmen chubanshe, 1965 (1937).

Mao Zedong. "The Chinese People Have Stood Up." In *Selected Works of Mao Tse-tung,* September 21, 1949. https://www.marxists.org/reference/archive/mao/selected-works /volume-5/mswv5_01.htm.

————. "Declaration Opposing Japan's Annexation of North China and Chiang Kaishek's Treason (June 15, 1935)." In *Mao's Road to Power: Revolutionary Writings, 1912–1949,* edited by Stuart R. Schram with Nancy J. Hodes, 5:12–15. Armonk, NY: M. E. Sharpe, 1999.

————. "Interview with Nym Wales on Negotiations with the Guomindang and the War with Japan (August 13, 1937)." In *Mao's Road to Power: Revolutionary Writings, 1912–1949,* edited by Stuart R. Schram with Nancy J. Hodes, 6:16–19. Armonk, NY: M. E. Sharpe, 2004.

————. "A Letter to Chiang Kaishek (September 9, 1938)." In *Mao's Road to Power: Revolutionary Writings, 1912–1949,* edited by Stuart R. Schram with Nancy J. Hodes, 6:452–53. Armonk, NY: M. E. Sharpe, 2004.

————. "Manifesto of the Central Committee of the Chinese Communist Party on the Annexation of North China by Japanese Imperialism, and Chiang Kaishek's Sellout of North China and of the Whole Country (November 13, 1935)." In *Mao's Road to Power: Revolutionary Writings, 1912–1949,* edited by Stuart R. Schram with Nancy J. Hodes, 5:39–42. Armonk, NY: M. E. Sharpe, 1999.

————. "Urgent Tasks of the Chinese Revolution Following the Establishment of Guomindang-Communist Cooperation (September 29, 1937)." In *Mao's Road to Power: Revolutionary Writings, 1912–1949,* edited by Stuart R. Schram with Nancy J. Hodes, 6:66–77. Armonk, NY: M. E. Sharpe, 2004.

"March to the Sea." *Time,* March 24, 1930.

McGregor, Richard. "Party Man: Xi Jinping's Quest to Dominate China." *Foreign Affairs* 98, no. 5 (September/October 2019): 18–25.

Miller, Alice Lyman, and Richard Wich. *Becoming Asia: Change and Continuity in Asian International Relations since World War II.* Stanford, CA: Stanford University Press, 2011.

Mitter, Rana. *A Bitter Revolution: China's Struggle with the Modern World.* Oxford: Oxford University Press, 2004.

————. *China's War with Japan, 1937–1945: The Struggle for Survival.* London: Allen Lane, 2013.

————. *Forgotten Ally: China's World War II 1937–1945.* Boston: Houghton Mifflin Harcourt, 2013.

————. "'Old Ghosts, New Memories': China's Changing War History in the Era of Post-Mao Politics." *Journal of Contemporary History* 38, no. 1 (January 2003): 117–31.

Modern China 33, no. 1 (January 2007).

Morrison, G. E. *The Correspondence of G. E. Morrison, 1912–1920,* vol. 2, edited by Lo Hui-Min. New York: Cambridge University Press, 1978.

Murdock, Michael G. "Exploiting Anti-Imperialism: Popular Forces and Nation-State-Building during China's Northern Expedition, 1926–1927." *Modern China* 35, no. 1 (January 2009): 65–95.

Neustadt, Richard E., and Ernest R. May. *Thinking in Time: The Uses of History for Decision-Makers.* New York: Free Press, 1986.
"Nine Powers Treaty." *Papers Relating to the Foreign Relations of the United States 1922,* vol. 1. Department of State Publication 2033. Washington, DC: Government Printing Office, 1938.
Nish, Ian. *Japan's Struggle with Internationalism.* New York: Kegan Paul, 2000.
———. "An Overview of Relations between China and Japan, 1895–1945." *China Quarterly* 124 (December 1990): 601–23.

Oldstone-Moore, Jennifer Lee. "The New Life Movement of Nationalist China: Confucianism, State Authority and Moral Formation." PhD diss., University of Chicago, 2000.

Paine, S. C. M. *The Japanese Empire: Grand Strategy from the Meiji Restoration to the Pacific War.* New York: Cambridge University Press, 2017.
———. *The Sino-Japanese War of 1894–1895: Perceptions, Power, and Primacy.* New York: Cambridge University Press, 2003.
———. *The Wars for Asia, 1911–1949.* New York: Cambridge University Press, 2012.
Pakula, Hannah. *The Last Empress: Madame Chiang Kai-shek and the Birth of Modern China.* New York: Simon and Schuster, 2009.
Payne, Stanley G. *A History of Fascism, 1914–1945.* Madison. University of Wisconsin Press, 1995.
People's Daily, Department of Commentary. *Narrating China's Governance: Stories in Xi Jinping's Speeches.* Translated by Jing Luo. Singapore: Springer, 2020.
"Pinch of Salt." *Time,* March 31, 1930.
"The Position of Yuan Shih-Kai." *North-China Herald,* January 26, 1916.
Pugach, Noel. "Embarrassed Monarchist: Frank J. Goodnow and Constitutional Development in China, 1913–1915." *Pacific Historical Review* 42, no. 4 (November 1973): 499–517.

Qin Xiaoyi, ed. *Zongtong Jianggong dashi changbian chugao* [A lengthy first draft of the major events of President Mr. Chiang]. 8 vols. Taipei: Kuomintang Party Historical Archives Publishers, 1978.

Railroad Guerrillas. Directed by Ming Zhao. Shanghai: Shanghai Film Studios, 1956.
Ramsdell, Daniel B. "The Nakamura Incident and the Japanese Foreign Office." *Journal of Asian Studies* 25, no. 1 (November 1965): 51–67.
Ramzy, Austin. "A Gap Lingers in Taiwan's Wartime Memory." *New York Times,* July 15, 2015.
Rankin, Mary Backus. "State and Society in Early Republican Politics, 1912–1918." *China Quarterly* 150 (June 1997): 260–81.

Rappeport, Alan. "19th-Century 'Humiliation' Haunts China-U.S. Trade Talks." *New York Times*, March 27, 2019.

Rauhala, Emily. "'Hold in Your Belly . . . Legs Together': Chinese College Teaches Female Students to Be 'Perfect.'" *Washington Post*, June 25, 2018.

Resar, Alyssa. "Beyond National Humiliation: Taiwanese Identity Transformed." *Harvard Political Review*, April 19, 2016.

Rigger, Shelley. *Why Taiwan Matters: Small Island, Global Powerhouse*. New York: Rowman and Littlefield, 2011.

Roberts, Andrew. "Among the Hagiographers: Early on Gandhi Was Dubbed a 'Mortal Demi-God'—and He Has Been Regarded that Way Ever Since." *Wall Street Journal*, March 26, 2011.

Rudolph, Susanne Hoeber, and Lloyd I. Rudolph. *Gandhi: The Traditional Roots of Charisma*. Chicago: University of Chicago Press, 1983.

———. *The Modernity of Tradition: Political Development in India*. Chicago: University of Chicago Press, 1967.

Scheff, Thomas. *Bloody Revenge*. Boulder, CO: Westview, 1994.

Schell, Orville and John Delury. "A Rising China Needs a New National Story: To Move Forward, the Country Must Move on from its Emphasis on a Century of 'National Humiliation.'" *Wall Street Journal*, July 12, 2013.

———. *Wealth and Power: China's Long March to the Twenty-First Century*. New York: Random House, 2013.

Schoppa, R. Keith. *The Columbia Guide to Modern Chinese History*. New York: Columbia University Press, 2000.

———. "Diaries as a Historical Source: Goldmines and/or Slippery Slopes." *Chinese Historical Review* 17, no. 1 (Spring 2010): 31–36.

———. "From Empire to People's Republic." In *Politics in China: An Introduction*, edited by William A. Joseph, 41–71. New York: Oxford University Press, 2014.

Schram, Stuart R. *Mao Tse-Tung*. New York: Simon and Schuster, 1966.

Schwarcz, Vera. *The Chinese Enlightenment: Intellectuals and the Legacy of the May Fourth Movement of 1919*. Berkeley: University of California Press, 1986.

Seal, Anil. "Imperialism and Nationalism in India." *Modern Asian Studies* 7, no. 3 (May 1973): 321–47.

Sewell, William H., Jr. "Ideologies and Social Revolutions: Reflections on the French Case." In *Social Revolutions in the Modern World*, edited by Theda Skocpol, 169–98. New York: Cambridge University Press, 1994.

Shan, Patrick Fuliang. *Yuan Shikai: A Reappraisal*. Vancouver: University of British Columbia Press, 2018.

Shapiro, Judith. *Mao's War against Nature: Politics and the Environment in Revolutionary China*. New York: Cambridge University Press, 2001.

Shen Tianyu. "The Fourth Day of Drafting Workers for Road Construction." In *One Day in China: May 21, 1936*, edited by Sherman Cochran and Andrew C. K. Hsieh with Janis Cochran, 98–100. New Haven, CT: Yale University Press, 1983.

Sheng, Michael M. *Battling Western Imperialism: Mao, Stalin, and the United States*. Princeton, NJ: Princeton University Press, 1997.

Shin, Gi-Wook, and Daniel Sneider. *Divergent Memories: Opinion Leaders and the Asia-Pacific War*. Stanford, CA: Stanford University Press, 2016.

Shirk, Susan L. *China: Fragile Superpower: How China's Internal Politics Could Derail Its Peaceful Rise*. New York: Oxford University Press, 2007.

Short, Philip. *Mao: The Man Who Made China*. New York: I. B. Tauris, 2017.

Sitaramayya, B. Pattabhi. *History of the Indian National Congress 1935–1947*, vol. 2. Delhi: S. Chand, 1969.

Skocpol, Theda. *States and Social Revolutions: A Comparative Analysis of France, Russia, and China*. New York: Cambridge University Press, 1979.

Skowronek, Stephen. *The Politics Presidents Make: Leadership from John Adams to George Bush*. Cambridge, MA: Belknap Press, 1993.

So, Wai-Chor. "The Making of the Guomindang's Japan Policy, 1932–1937: The Roles of Chiang Kai-shek and Wang Jingwei." *Modern China* 28, no. 2 (April 2002): 213–52.

"Speech by Chinese President Hu Jintao at Waseda University." Ministry of Foreign Affairs of the People's Republic of China, June 8, 2008. http://www.fmprc.gov.cn/mfa_eng/wjdt_665385/zyjh_665391/t464200.shtml.

Spence, Jonathan. "Before the East Was Red." Review of *Chiang Kai-shek: China's Generalissimo and the Nation He Lost*, by Jonathan Fenby. *New York Review of Books*, February 29, 2004.

———. "The Enigma of Chiang Kai-shek." Review of *The Generalissimo: Chiang Kai-shek and the Struggle for Modern China*, by Jay Taylor. *New York Review of Books*, October 22, 2009.

———. *The Search for Modern China*. New York: W. W. Norton, 2013.

Stilwell, Joseph W. *The Stilwell Papers*. Edited by Theodore H. White. New York: Da Capo Press, 1948.

Stockmann, Daniela. "Greasing the Reels: Advertising as a Means of Campaigning on Chinese Television." *China Quarterly* 208 (December 2011): 851–69.

"Strong Policy." *Time*, December 28, 1931.

Studwell, Joe. *How Asia Works: Success and Failure in the World's Most Dynamic Region*. New York: Grove Press, 2013.

Sun, Youli. "China's International Approach to the Manchurian Crisis, 1931–1933." *Journal of Asian History* 26, no. 1 (1992): 42–77.

"Talk Given by the Spokesman of the Central Committee of the Chinese Communist Party Regarding the Southern Anhui Incident (January 18, 1941)." In *Mao's Road to Power: Revolutionary Writings, 1912–1949*, edited by Stuart R. Schram with Nancy J. Hodes, 7:639–43. Armonk, NY: M. E. Sharpe, 2005.

Tanner, Harold M. *The Battle for Manchuria and the Fate of China: Siping, 1946*. Bloomington: Indiana University Press, 2013.

Taylor, Jay. *The Generalissimo: Chiang Kai-shek and the Struggle for Modern China*. Cambridge, MA: Belknap Press, 2009.

Taylor, Jeremy E., and Grace C. Huang. "'Deep Changes in Interpretive Currents'? Chiang Kai-shek Studies in the Post–Cold War Era." *International Journal of Asian Studies* 9, no. 1 (January 2012): 99–121.

Thomson, James C., Jr. *While China Faced West: American Reformers in Nationalist China, 1928–1937.* Cambridge, MA: Harvard East Asian Series, 1969.

Tilly, Charles. *The Formation of National States in Western Europe.* Princeton, NJ: Princeton University Press, 1975.

Tracy, Ben. "China's Social Credit System Keeps a Critical Eye on Everyday Behavior." CBS News, April 24, 2018. https://www.cbsnews.com/news/chinas-social -credit-system-keeps-a-critical-eye-on-everyday-behavior-even-jaywalking-2018 -04-24/.

Trampedach, Tim. "Chiang Kaishek between Revolution and Militarism, 1926/27." In *The Chinese Revolution in the 1920s: Between Triumph and Disaster,* edited by Mechthild Leutner, Roland Felber, M. L. Titarenko, and A. M. Grigoriev, 125–38. New York: Routledge, 2002.

Tsang, Steve. "Chiang Kai-shek's 'Secret Deal' at Xian and the Start of the Sino-Japanese War." *Palgrave Communications* 1 (January 2015): 1–12.

Tuchman, Barbara. *The Guns of August.* New York: Dell, 1962.

Tucker, Nancy Bernkopf. *Patterns in the Dust: Chinese-American Relations and the Recognition Controversy, 1949–1950.* New York: Columbia University Press, 1983.

Twitchett, Denis. "Problems of Chinese Biography." In *Confucian Personalities,* edited by Arthur F. Wright and Denis Twitchett, 24–42. Stanford, CA: Stanford University Press, 1962.

———. *The Writing of Official History under the T'ang.* New York: Cambridge University Press, 1992.

Vogel, Ezra. *Deng Xiaoping and the Transformation of China.* Cambridge, MA: Belknap Press, 2011.

Vogelsang, Kai. "Some Notions of Historical Judgment in China and the West." In *Historical Truth, Historical Criticism, and Ideology: Chinese Historiography and Historical Culture from a New Comparative Perspective,* edited by Helwig Schmidt-Glintzer, Achim Mittag, and Jörn Rüsen, 143–75. Leiden: Koninklijke Brill, 2005.

Waldron, Arthur. "China's New Remembering of World War II: The Case of Zhang Zizhong." *Modern Asian Studies* 30, no. 4 (October 1996): 945–78.

Walsh, Judith E. *A Brief History of India.* New York: Facts on File, 2011.

Wang, Dong. *China's Unequal Treaties: Narrating National History.* Lanham, MD: Lexington Books, 2005.

Wang Xiuchu. *Yangzhou shiri ji* [Record of the ten days in Yangzhou]. Shanghai: Shanghai shudian, 1982.

Wang, Zheng. "The Chinese Dream: Concept and Context." *Journal of Chinese Political Science* 19, no. 1 (December 2013): 1–13.

———. *Never Forget National Humiliation: Historical Memory in Chinese Politics and Foreign Relations.* New York: Columbia University Press, 2012.

Watson, James L. "The Structure of Chinese Funerary Rites: Elementary Forms, Ritual Sequence, and the Primacy of Performance." In *Death Ritual in Late Imperial and Modern China,* edited by James L. Watson and Evelyn S. Rawski, 3–19. Berkeley: University of California Press, 1988.

Watson, James L., and Evelyn S. Rawski, eds. *Death Ritual in Late Imperial and Modern China*. Berkeley: University of California Press, 1988.

Weber, Max. "Charisma and its Transformation." In *Economy and Society: An Outline of Interpretive Sociology*, edited by Guenther Roth and Claus Wittich, 1111–58. Berkeley: University of California Press, 1978.

———. "Politics as a Vocation." In *From Max Weber: Essays in Sociology*, translated and edited by H. H. Gerth and C. Wright Mills, 77–128. New York: Oxford University Press, 1958.

Wei, Shuge. "Beyond the Front Line: China's Rivalry with Japan in the English-Language Press over the Jinan Incident, 1928." *Modern Asian Studies* 48, no. 1 (January 2014): 188–224.

Wei, William. *Counterrevolution in China: The Nationalists in Jiangxi during the Soviet Period*. Ann Arbor: University of Michigan Press, 1985.

Wen Xie. *Huoguo yangmin de Jiang Jieshi* [Chiang Kai-shek: The man who brought calamities on the nation]. Beijing: Zhongguo qingnian chubanshe, 1962.

Wilbur, Martin C. *The Nationalist Revolution in China, 1923–1928*. New York: Cambridge University Press, 1983.

Wills, Garry. *Certain Trumpets: The Call of Leaders*. New York: Simon and Schuster, 1994.

Wilson, Sandra. *The Manchurian Crisis and Japanese Society, 1931–33*. New York: Routledge, 2002.

Worthing, Peter. *General He Yingqin: The Rise and Fall of Nationalist China*. Cambridge: Cambridge University Press, 2016.

Wright, Mary Clabaugh. *The Last Stand of Chinese Conservatism: The T'ung-Chih Restoration, 1862–1874*. Stanford, CA: Stanford University Press, 1957.

Wu Jun. "My Diary for Today." In *One Day In China: May 21, 1936*, edited by Sherman Cochran and Andrew C. K. Hsieh with Janis Cochran, 251–53. New Haven, CT: Yale University Press, 1983.

Wu, Pei-yi. *The Confucian's Progress, Autobiographical Writings in Traditional China*. Princeton, NJ: Princeton University Press, 1990.

Wu, T'ien-wei. "The Chinese Communist Movement." In *China's Bitter Victory: The War with Japan, 1937–1945*, edited by James C. Hsiung and Steven I. Levine, 79–106. Armonk, NY: M. E. Sharpe, 1992.

"Xi Jinping's Germany Trip: Berlin Nixes Holocaust Memorial Request." *Der Spiegel*, March 3, 2014.

Yang Tianshi. *Jiang shi midang yu Jiang Jieshi zhenxiang* [The secret files of Mr. Chiang and the truth about Chiang Kai-shek]. Beijing: Shehui kexue wenxian, 2002.

———. "Jinan Can'an" [The tragedy of Jinan]. In *Zhonghua Minguoshi, Beifa zhanzheng yu Beiyang junfade fuzai* [The history of Republican China, the Northern Expedition and the defeat of the northern warlord armies], edited by Yang Tianshi, vol. 5. Beijing: Zhonghua shuju, 1996.

———. *Zhaoxun zhenshi de Jiang Jieshi: Jiang Jieshi riji jiedu* [In search of the real Chiang Kai-shek: reading the Chiang Kai-shek diaries]. Taiyuan: Shanxi Renmin Chubanshe, 2008.

Yen Hsiao-Pei. "Body Politics, Modernity and National Salvation: The Modern Girl and the New Life Movement." *Asian Studies Review* 29, no. 2 (June 2005): 165–86.

Young, Ernest P. *The Presidency of Yuan Shikai: Liberalism and Dictatorship in Early Republican China.* Ann Arbor: University of Michigan Press, 1977.

Young, Louise. *Japan's Total Empire: Manchuria and the Culture of Wartime Imperialism.* Berkeley: University of California Press, 1998.

Yu, George T. "The 1911 Revolution: Past, Present, and Future." *Asian Survey* 31, no. 10 (October 1991): 895–904.

Zhang Ling'ao. *Wo zai Jiang Jieshi shicongshi de rizi* [The days I spent in Jiang Jieshi's personal retinue]. Taipei: Zhouzhi wenhua chubanshe, 1995.

Zhang Yanxian. "Qianyan" [Preface]. In *JZZDSG*, 3: i–ix. Taiwan: Guoshiguan, 2003.

Zhao Longzhi. *Goujian.* Taipei: Huaguo chubanshe, 1953.

Zhao, Suisheng. *A Nation-State by Construction: Dynamics of Modern Chinese Nationalism.* Stanford, CA: Stanford University Press, 2004.

Index

Page numbers for maps and figures are in italics.

Harvard East Asian Monographs
(most recent titles)

Harvard East Asian Monographs